STUFF
Good Players Should Know

Intelligent Basketball from A to Z

Dick DeVenzio

Foreword by Dena Evans

www.pgcbasketball.com

Fourth E

D1087595

STUFF Good Players Should Know: Intelligent Basketball from A to Z
Published by PGC Basketball
P.O. Box 4301
Victoria, TX 77903

For more information about our books, please write to us, call 866.338.2308, or visit our website at www.pcgbasketball.com.

Library of Congress Control Number: 2006925008

ISBN-13: 978-0-9839380-2-6

Original publication date: January 15, 1983

For information, purchases or permissions, go to:
http://www.pgcbasketball.com

Cover Design by Priyanka Kodikal

10 9 8 7 6 5 4

Credits

Special thanks for editorial assistance to Deborough Blalock, Huck DeVenzio and Mr. John Wooden.

To My Dad

who retired from coaching in 1990 (for the last time?!) with nearly 1000 victories in two sports

A Great Coach

Contents

GAME STUFF:
THE FINE POINTS OF BASKETBALL
FROM A to Z

A. 1—Help **across,** not up 2—**Ahead** near the end of the game…on defense 3—**Ahead** near the end of the game…on offense 4—**Alibis** 5—**Alternating** current 6—**Anticipation** 7—**Approaching** the ball 8—Go **at** defenders to get free 9—**Attitude** 10—**Availability**

B. 11—**Backdoor** cuts 12—**Bad**-fake fakes 13—**Bad** shots 14—**Ball** defense 15—**Beg** for the ball 16—**Behind** near the end of the game…on defense 17—**Behind** near the end of the game…on offense 18—The **bent-**elbow pass 19—**Blocking** out 20—**Blocking** shots 21—**Block** out details 22—**Bounce** passes go slowly 23—**B-U-B** 24—**Bullet** passes

1829

C. 25—Taking a **charge** 26—**Click,** click, click 27—When the **clock** is stopped 28—Against good teams, **complete** passes 29—**Consistency** 30—**Countering** changing defenses 31—**Criticism**

D⁴

D. 32—**Dance** 33—**Defending** a stronger player 34—**Desperation** shots 35—**Double**-teaming on defense 36—Beating **double** teams 37—**Drag** a foot 38—The use of one **dribble** 39—**Dribbling** too much 40—**Ducking** out of sight

"Sorry, Folks"

M. 85—A **magnificent** move for a quick guard 86—Three kinds of **man-to-man** defense 87—**Mental** toughness 88—**Mistake** response: Hustle-CAT 89—**Momentum** 90—**Move** your man 91—**"My** fault!"

N. 92—**Nervousness** 93—Always know the **next** man 94—**Nod** to the coach 95—**Noisy** screens 96—**Nostril** time

The Little Layup Shooter

O. 97—Nothing **off**-balance counts 98—**One-on-one** 99—Going for **one** shot 100—Defending a team that is playing for **one** shot 101—**Opportunistic** on offense... and defense 102—**Out**-of-bounds stuff 103—**Overplaying** on defense

P. 104—**Passes** that should've been caught 105—**Patience** 106—P-dribble 107—**Picking** up a dribbler in the midcourt area 108—**Pickup** games 109—**Point** 110—**POOP** 111—**Positive** thinking garbage 112—**PREP** 113—Applying **pressure** 114—Beating **pressure** 115—**Pulling** out a defense 116—**Putting** the ball into play

Q. 117—**Question** yourself 118—Looking **quick** 119—Improving your **quickness** 120—**Quick**-release groove shots 121—"Never **quit**"

R. 122—The **race** track 123—**Reaching** 124—**Read** the defense 125—Stripping a **rebound** 126—"**Handling**" **referees** 127—**Releasing** early for an unmolested layup 128—**Releasing** to guard a strong, low post man 129—**Run** through the ball

Ready, Aim...

S. 130—**Saving** the ball 131—**SCOT** 132—**Secret** plans 133—**Seeing** the ball, 31:52 134—**Seek**-hide-n-go 135—**Setting** screens 136—**Setting** someone up (with space) 137—**Shooting** practice 138—**SNORT** 139—**Spirit** 140—**Stalling** and the "sooner" concept 141—**Statue** charges 142—**Stealing**... from the air 143—**Stop** on

Stupid

Someday…

FOREWORD
by Dena Evans

When I was growing up, my mom, a high school English teacher, was always bringing home books for me to read. Usually, they were basketball-related books since those were the only kind she could be sure her basketball-obsessed girl would read. When I was twelve years old, she bought me a book called *STUFF Good Players Should Know* by a man named Dick DeVenzio.

Even though I was the daughter of a college coach and had been around the game my whole life, even though I had already read everything about basketball I could get my hands on, *STUFF* immediately struck me as different. It wasn't a book about proper shooting form, how to shoot a layup, or how to throw seven different types of passes. I already knew *that* stuff. And it wasn't a book by a famous player or coach that just sought to entertain the reader with story after story of his already well-publicized career. Those books were interesting to me, but they didn't offer me what I was *really* after, which was information and ideas on how I could actually get *better*.

But when I read *STUFF*, I felt as if I had been given some secrets to the game—invaluable secrets that every player who wanted to excel *should* know, but was never told. It became my basketball bible. There was information in its pages that I'd never heard anyplace else—commonsense instructions about the game that weren't common at all. It was a book for players like me who already knew how to play, but who wanted to improve.

I read *STUFF* cover to cover, and then never really put it away. It ended up by my bedside, in my locker at school, in my gym bag, always close at hand. It went with me through high school, college, and even when I traveled overseas to play pro ball in Switzerland and New Zealand. I read it so much that I memorized certain passages like a childhood song.

But no matter how many times I read it, *STUFF* always seemed to have just the words I needed to solve a problem I was facing on the court or to give me some inspiration for the next time I went to play. It always felt like having a great teacher of the game right next to me, whispering tips and inspiration in my ear to make me a better player.

In all those years of carrying around his book, it never occurred to me to seek out this Dick DeVenzio until I came across his name in a different context the summer after I graduated from college. At that time, I was sharing an apartment with a college teammate, and she had just attended a new basketball camp especially for point guards. One day, I happened to notice a brochure for the camp lying on our coffee table that read, "Dick DeVenzio's Point Guard Basketball College." *Dick DeVenzio*?! The name was as unforgettable as the lessons in his book. And so, ten years after picking up *STUFF* for the first time and convinced that seeing his name on that brochure was no coincidence, I decided to seek him out and say thanks.

Taking his address off the back of the brochure, I wrote him a letter thanking him for writing *STUFF* and letting him know how much it had meant to me and to my basketball career. I never expected to hear anything back from him, but less than a week later, I was elated to receive a box in the mail with some of his *other* books and a handwritten note from Dick. In his note, he said that he had followed our teams at the University of Virginia for the four years that I played there, and he had even seen me play in person in one of the biggest games of my career—a triple-overtime win over Maryland in the championship game of the ACC tournament my senior year.

Touched by the realness and friendliness of his note and amazed that he actually knew who I was and had seen me play, I didn't hesitate at all to contact him again. And that was the beginning of not only a great friendship, but of the next phase in Dick's mentorship of me as a basketball player. Just out of college at that point, I was still trying to play the game that I loved and was getting opportunities to try out for US national teams and to play on professional teams in the US and abroad. Over the course of the next three or four years, I spent as much time with Dick as I could to soak up some of his basketball genius and apply it to my game.

In the days and weeks that I got to spend with Dick before my playing days were over, I learned more about basketball than I had learned in my previous sixteen years of playing the game. He put me through shooting workouts, talked to me for hours about the game, and pointed things out to me during games that we'd watch together on video. He even watched me play pickup games with pen and pad (and sometimes even video camera) in hand, and then broke it all down with me afterwards.

At 5'4", I'd always been a small player, usually the smallest on the court. Dick was also a small (5'9") guard during his playing days as a high school All-American and star at Duke University, and he taught me ways to play bigger than my size. He explained clever ways to get my shot off against bigger defenders, subtle techniques to gain advantages against quicker players, and so much more. It was as if *STUFF* had come to life.

But with Dick, it wasn't just *what* he taught, but *how* he taught it. The very first "workout" he gave me was of the mental kind—a two-hour essay-writing assignment on eleven aspects of the game that he had identified for me to focus on, just to be sure I had thoroughly thought them through. And there were his many "made-up" words and creative terminology that made me laugh and that to this day I couldn't forget if I tried.

And then there was the time I was feeling particularly stressed and uptight about an upcoming tryout, and he abruptly canceled the day's workout and instead drove me to a big lake. As if on a mission, he pulled a tiny, inflatable, yellow raft from the trunk of his car, told me to get in, and paddled us to the middle of the lake. At first, I was thoroughly confused over why we were in the middle of a lake instead of working in the gym, but as we floated peacefully on the water beneath the warm sunshine, his lesson became as clear to me as the crystal blue sky on that beautiful spring day: *Relax. Enjoy this opportunity. Enjoy life. Don't be so serious about what you're doing that you forget to have fun and enjoy yourself.*

It was a lesson I never forgot, and it was typical Dick DeVenzio. He could have just *told* me to relax, but instead he went to the trouble to take me out to the middle of a lake in a raft on a beautiful spring day. He didn't just teach lessons, he taught them to you in ways that made sure you never forgot them—always with passion, enthusiasm, and, best of all, humor.

While the basketball knowledge I learned from Dick was significant, it was what he taught me about life that mattered most. His creative ideas and sense of humor encouraged me to think outside the box and opened my eyes and my heart to the possibilities of who I could be in the world. His uplifting attitude and his unique perspectives on life made me want to think bigger and be better. "Do your best at everything where your efforts can make a difference, ignore everything you have no control over, drop pettiness, drop worry, plan intelligently," he would say. He made me not only a better player, but a better person.

Dick DeVenzio died of colon cancer at the age of 52 in the spring of 2001. There will never be another author, coach, camp director, motivational speaker, activist (just ask the NCAA!) like him. He was utterly unique. Brilliant. Creative. Passionate. Witty. Often outspoken. Always direct. Even irreverent at times. A genius in the way he saw basketball and in the way he saw the world.

Now, almost twenty years after reading *Stuff* for the first time as a kid dreaming of basketball greatness, it seems that everything has come full circle. I've had the honor and privilege of owning and directing the Point Guard College programs that he started in 1993 and of helping to keep his legacy alive by passing along his words, ideas, and spirit to the next generation of players and coaches.

Part of continuing the Dick DeVenzio legacy is this update of the now classic *STUFF Good Players Should Know*. Not much has changed. There's an updated cover and a few grammatical and punctuation changes to reflect a more current style. And a few names in the book have been changed to make references more familiar to today's readers. But, in every other way, this is still the same unmistakable DeVenzio wisdom that has inspired and influenced countless coaches and athletes over the years.

I still have that copy of *STUFF* that my mom bought for me when I was twelve. Its pages are dog-eared; its cover is tattered and torn. But, now twenty years later, I still believe it's the best book ever written for basketball players who are committed to becoming the best they can be.

And that old copy of *STUFF* serves as a constant reminder of how lucky I am that *STUFF* and Dick DeVenzio became part of my game and part of my life. Now, you have this copy of *STUFF* in your hands. And with it, you too will have one of the greatest teachers of the game right next to you, whispering tips and inspiration in your ear to make you a better player.

—Dena Evans, 2006

PRE-GAME STUFF

BASKETBALL PROGRESS

You're no good.
You're not bad.
You're fair. You're okay.
You're pretty good.
You're good.
You're real good.
You're terrific!
You're fantastic!!
You're great!!!
You're amazing!!!!
You're sooooper!!!!!
You can play.

A FEW WORDS TO PLAYERS

"**Y**ou're no good."

No one likes to be told that he's no good, but most players, even ones who people say are good, fail to do many, many important things game after game.

You probably don't even know all the things you aren't good at. On a night you score 16 or 20 points, you probably go home thinking you played well, even though very few coaches may have been impressed. So you put in a few jumpers, got a couple of layups, picked off some rebounds and your man only scored eight. Does that mean you were good? Maybe. Maybe not.

There are a thousand "little things" that actually decide whether or not you can play. Even on nights you shoot one for nine, you can still play well if you do the little things.

A good player is good regardless of how he shoots on a given night and even regardless of how many points his man scores. A good player makes it tough for the other team to score. If they score, okay; they are good, too. But they score with difficulty because a good player makes it tough to get easy baskets. A good player helps his teammates stop their men, and he helps his teammates score more. A good player contributes in many ways that the average fan and even the average player never notices or thinks about. But coaches and winning teams know what a good player is, and if *you* want to be a good player, you'd better know, too.

This book is a sort of giant checklist, a discussion of the little things that a good player does and is aware of. You can't just read through it once and expect suddenly to be a good player. You have to concentrate and make point after point part of your *habit of play*, gradually, consistently.

Habit of play is a crucial phrase. The world is full of players who can properly perform some task when they are told to concentrate on just that or when they are asked to do it in a drill. But do they do it in games? Do they do it consistently?

For example, take offensive rebounding. Without even considering technique, ask yourself one question: Do you go after—I mean *actively seek*—every rebound after your team shoots? I don't mean make a casual effort to go toward the ball. I mean, assume someone said, "If you get the next offensive rebound, I will give you $1,000." You know what kind of effort you would give. You might not get the rebound, but it certainly would be obvious that you were after it.

And yet, during the course of most games, it is rarely obvious that anyone is making that kind of effort, rarely obvious that *you* are making that kind of effort, even though you tell your coach and your friends and yourself that you want to be a good basketball player.

What excuse do you give yourself for not doing your best every time? Have you ever considered that a coach could watch you play, even on a night you score 20 points, and he could tell you dozens of things you never bothered doing? Undoubtedly, there are many things that you should do that you don't.

But if you really want to be a good player, if you really care about constant improvement, this book can help you. If you are willing to read it and really try to make these fine points a part of your game...if you strive to do the little things consistently, there won't be any doubt in anyone's mind what kind of player you are. People may not say that you are great or wonderful or fantastic, but coaches will do better than that. They will say *you can play*.

There is no higher compliment in the game.

A FEW WORDS TO FEMALE PLAYERS

I wrote this book with phrases like "Get your *man*" or "If *he* goes back-door, you can pick *him* up" and so forth, always referring to male players. I did this out of habit and to be at ease in the writing.

In doing so, I had no intention of slighting female players. Indeed, I hope that you will enjoy this book despite my failure to speak directly to you.

DON'T BE STUPID

The concepts in this book are generally acceptable to coaches, and they will serve you well on any court, anywhere. However, if your coach disagrees on some particular point, don't be stupid and argue with him. *Do it his way*.

There are many ways to skin a cat, as the saying goes, and many ways to score a basket or stop an opponent. None of the concepts in this book are stupid, but there *are* other ways of doing them. Any coach will be delighted if you can master these ideas and use them in games. So try to learn to do all of them *while* being prepared to alter some of them if your coach feels you can get a slight edge by doing them differently.

Take, for example, individual defense. Some of the top coaches in the nation teach that you should have your weight on your front foot, so you can push off it when your man goes and you need to retreat. But I teach that you should have your weight back, so you get in your man's face but are thinking "retreat." Whatever you lose in push-off, I feel you gain in readiness.

Who is right? Your coach is right. Do it his way. *He* is the one who puts you into and out of games. *He* is the one you have to please. And besides, in a game, things usually happen so fast, no one, not even your coach, will likely notice where your weight is when your man suddenly catches a pass and thrusts forward. Your coach will want to see that you are ready to go with your man, to cut him off, to beat him to a spot.

The important point is that you learn to do these things and that you learn to listen to your coach. Even if your coach isn't the best in the world, five guys working together doing the "wrong" thing have a better chance of winning than five guys all doing their own thing because each thinks he knows best. **No team ever lost by playing the wrong defense. They lost by playing that defense poorly.**

The first rule of this book, then, is, "This book is a tool to help you help your coach." It is not a holy script to be used for arguing. There are a lot more bad players than there are bad coaches. Think of it. If players always executed properly, no one would ever find out a coach did something poorly.

Remember, you don't lose by playing the wrong way. You lose by playing poorly.

A FEW WORDS TO COACHES

Being the son of a basketball coach, I grew up reading everything I could get my hands on—books of plays, manuals on coaching and instructions on ten different kinds of passes and when to use three different heights of dribbles. Despite my diligent searching then and my continued interest in the game as a player, coach and camp director, I have never found a book geared to the player who could already play.

Let's face it, who ever really talks about medium dribbles and hook passes and rocker steps? To my knowledge, there's never been a winning team that spent time on seven different kinds of passes. A kid can learn those at camp and then "get his pants stolen off him" when he meets some athletes on a playground. So...

I wrote this book for players who can already play the game and want to improve and who need not a review of types of passes, but an explanation of fine points and concepts and a breakdown of the little things that great players *seem* to do "naturally." I wanted to write a book that players could take to bed at night and read in the off-season or just before a big game—and improve their own technique with. I wanted to write a book that would be an indispensable tool for the coach and interesting reading for the player. And finally, I wanted to write a book that *you* would recommend to your players because you know you don't have time to teach them all the things you would like them to know.

There simply isn't time for any coach to include in his two-hour practice sessions all the things he thinks are important. By the time you get your offenses down, your various defenses, out-of-bounds plays and so on, you are likely to find you have let slide all sorts of "things every second-grader should know automatically," (but your players don't).

You sometimes get to the point where your players are so conscious of running your offense that suddenly one of your players has the ball, and his defender darts by and falls, but the guy just throws the ball and continues the offense—it has never occurred to him to shoot a layup. And you start asking yourself, "What have I been doing all this time?"

It's tough for the coach and tough for the players. There's just too much to get across in too little time. Often a coach finds himself saying things like, "Don't do it because I said it. This is the way Mike Krzyzewski does it. This is the way Roy Williams does it." There's a need for a special authority, or at least for a new emphasis. No coach can possibly emphasize all the things that need to be stressed. In the course of intense practice sessions, players have enough trouble just psyching themselves into trying hard—they can't possibly absorb all their coach throws at them. Yet, there's so much they need to know, things the coach may never have time to mention, let alone emphasize.

So that's the reason for this book. Page after page of common-sense ideas about basketball. Not plays to run, not drills to use, but the concepts players need to perform well. The intent is to provide the conscientious player with guidelines he can review over and over to make more and more a part of his game. In the quiet and calm of his room, late at night, when you aren't urging and begging and anguishing over his deficiencies, a player might read over these concepts and make some of them (more of them as time passes) part of his daily habit of play.

No one can absorb all these concepts in one reading, but exposure to them should get more of them done as the season progresses—until someday one of your players is going to save *your* neck by doing something well that you never even took time to explain! (Wouldn't that be a miracle?)

"Good players just do that naturally," you might say. But you know they often don't. More often you are coaching only pretty good or mediocre players, and *they* don't do anything naturally. A very precious few athletes find ways to win games for you, and the huge majority finds ways to lose them.

I am counting on you to put this book in your players' hands, and you can count on this book to put into your players' heads some vivid ideas that someday will help you win some games you otherwise might have lost. I think you will find that few of the concepts conflict with your philosophy and many of them may be expressed in a way that will enable you to reach players you have so far been unsuccessful with in certain areas of the game.

Most of the concepts will be mere confirmations of what you already teach, but the slightly different angle or perspective may help fine-tune your players' concentration just a bit more. This book is a tool that should help your players help you. It is a giant checklist, you might say, of the little things, of the *STUFF Good Players Should Know*.

KEY TO DIAGRAMS

Blackboard diagrams appear throughout this book wherever they are useful to make the ideas clearer. A standard notation is used, as shown below.

DIAGRAM TITLES ARE BOLDFACED

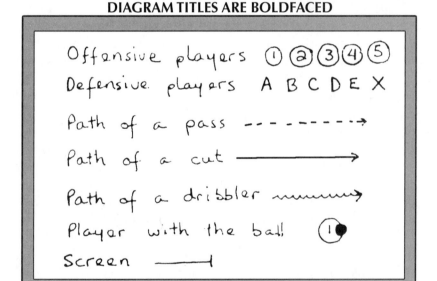

Here is standard basketball blackboard notation. (The diagram captions are in italics.)

Basketball players don't usually like complicated X's and O's and "blackboard stuff," so the diagrams in this book are easy to understand, included more to highlight a point than to make it.

SOFO AND OTHER TERMS

Many of the words used in this book, like SOFO, are made up. They are not a part of common basketball vocabulary like *overplay* or *backdoor*. But maybe they will be soon because it is useful to name concepts so they stick in your mind. SOFO is a good example.

Thousands of players go passively for offensive rebounds, and coaches often let players get away with that passive effort. Perhaps the reason is that defensive rebounds are expected or easier to get. But in most cases, the reason more offensive rebounds are not grabbed is simply that players don't try hard enough to get them. "Go in there and move around and try to get your hand on the ball" is not a very emphatic command and, therefore, likely to be ignored or overlooked when the whole game is considered.

But SOFO is definite. It means **S**pin **O**ff the **F**irst **O**bstacle. Spinning off the first obstacle requires that you go seeking the ball and that you try to avoid a block out to get it. After your team has taken five shots that missed, your coach and you have a clear-cut question to ask. Did you SOFO or didn't you? Go through the game films and don't count the offensive rebounds. (In some games, more are available than in others, and sometimes you get them by luck.) Count the SOFOs. If you are constantly spinning off the first obstacle, over the course of a season you are going to get a lot of offensive rebounds.

In this book, you will find many words like SOFO that aren't commonly used but that will be helpful. Use them and benefit from them and make up your own. The more general concepts that you can specifically tie into your mind, the better player you will be.

GAME STUFF:
The Fine Points of Basketball
from A to Z

A

1–Help **ACROSS**, not up

2–**AHEAD** near the end of the game…on defense

3–**AHEAD** near the end of the game…on offense

4–**ALIBIS**

5–**ALTERNATING** current

6–**ANTICIPATION**

7–**APPROACHING** the ball

8–Go **AT** defenders to get free

9–**ATTITUDE**

10–**AVAILABILITY**

1
HELP ACROSS, NOT UP

On defense, when you need to pick up a dribbler and help a teammate who is being beaten, remember to pick up or help *across* from your man, not *up* from him. This is simply done, if your man stays outside or merely stands still while you are helping. But if the man you are guarding is a good player, he will try to get behind you, down low for a pass over your head. Your job, even though you must help, is to stay across from your man, so that you can recover and get a hand in his face if the ball is thrown to him.

If you move across to help and your man moves down toward the basket, then you must move down toward the basket in order to stay across from your man. Don't permit your man to get behind you and receive a pass over your head. Help-defense *does not* require that you stop a penetrator's jump shot. (You cannot expect to stop every shot on the court, regardless of how good you are.) Help-defense *does* require you to get in the penetrator's way and stop his layup. Therefore, you move into the penetrator's path as quickly as possible, and you stop him as far out as you can while still staying across from your man (or down lower than your man, never higher or "up," which allows a pass over your head to the basket).

As long as you remember to **keep your man in your sight** while you help, you will be in good position. If you lose sight of your man, you are suddenly "up", not "across", and you will have to get back fast.

HELP ACROSS FROM YOUR MAN

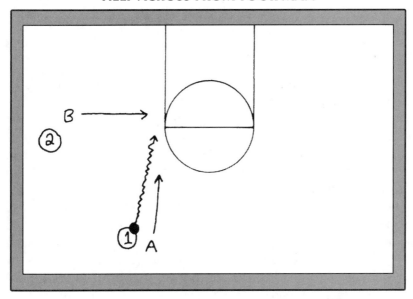

"B" can move straight across to get in the path of "1", because he can keep "2" in sight as he does.

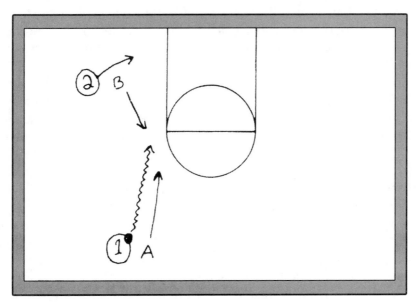

"B" moving up to take "1" allows "2' to get in for an easy basket.

2
AHEAD NEAR THE END OF THE GAME...
ON DEFENSE

If you are ahead and the clock is running out, the opposing team has to do two things: they have to score points quickly, and they have to get the clock stopped. Nothing would please them more than getting you to foul them. A foul will give them a chance to score—maybe even three points in one possession, and it will stop the clock. It will also give them a chance to set up a pressing defense and make it tough for you to get the ball inbounds.

Does one thing suddenly become clear about being ahead near the end of the game on defense? **Don't foul.** This does not merely mean in the obvious situation, when you are ahead by three with seven seconds left. This includes when you are ahead by five with four minutes left as well.

When you are ahead and the clock is winding down, your opponent will be getting more worried about the time than you. You might realize there is plenty of time for them to catch up (while you are wishing for the clock to hurry along). But the team that is behind may start feeling desperate midway through the second half. They will likely begin to feel more pressure on their shots—making them tougher to hit—and they will be reluctant to throw a lot of passes while patiently waiting for a good opportunity.

Because of their frame of mind, you have a big advantage, but not if you send them to the line to collect themselves and then end up watching them catch up while the clock is stopped. You want them to feel the time moving on, and you want them to have to earn every basket they score.

Usually, you will not have to play defense as long each time near the end of a game, since the trailing team will want to take a shot rather quickly. Therefore, you can afford to play particularly hard immediately, while keeping your concentration on not fouling (and yelling to remind your teammates not to foul). There is an excellent chance that the offense will put up their shot within five or seven seconds. Remember that, and urge yourself to be especially alert. You know you can give a huge effort if it is only going to be for a few seconds.

When you are ahead near the end, on defense, give that huge effort, and *don't foul*. Don't swing at the ball or try to block shots or get cute. Play good, solid defense and let them miss their poor-opportunity attempts.

3
AHEAD NEAR THE END OF THE GAME...
ON OFFENSE

Good players should not have to be reminded that no quick shots or long shots are needed when their team is ahead near the end of a game. But you should know exactly what your objective is:. Is it (1) "layups only" or (2) "any good shot from fifteen feet or closer" or (3) "no shots at all—hold it until they foul?"

You should know which approach your coach wants; and especially you should know *how* to play when you are holding the ball, waiting for a foul. Many talented players either stand around, since they know they are no longer trying to score, or they dribble in circles like the Harlem Globetrotters, thinking that is the best way to run out the clock. Neither way is playing smart basketball.

When you're ahead near the end and you're running out the clock, you need to play with the same decisiveness you would play with if you were trying to score. You *cannot* stand around and rely on passes that barely get to a teammate.

It might help you to think GO-GO, which means **G**et **O**pen or **G**et **O**ut, or even GWO-GO, which means **G**et **W**ide **O**pen or **G**et **O**ut. Being "sort of open" means you are standing someplace waiting for the ball. This is very dangerous when the other team knows it has to steal the ball and, therefore, is willing to gamble and lunge.

Because the defense will be going for the ball, you need to alter the way you expect to receive it. If you can't get the ball *going toward it on the run,* it is better to go backdoor and allow a teammate to come after it, *toward it and on the run.*

In passing the ball, you should think the same way. Give the ball to someone who is coming *toward you on the run.* Long passes or lob passes should be thrown with great reluctance—only when your teammate is so open that he has time to get out semaphore flags and signal to you. Sure, you might throw a successful lob someday and even score a layup, but you will be wise to look only for the short, crisp pass to someone close by running toward you. Then, someday, if that lob is *wide* open, throw it and enjoy the win.

Do not plan to dribble out the clock even if you are a very good dribbler. It is better to **dribble decisively and go someplace, then pass**

off, get the ball back and do it again. If you continue dribbling, you will soon get into a "keep-away mode" instead of an "attacking mode." You want to be the attacker, not the one who is being attacked. The longer you dribble, the more careless and tired you will become and the less decisive. You don't want to keep dribbling until they almost get one. Dribble, pass off, get it back and dribble again.

If you are not an excellent dribbler and not your team's main ball handler, you should stick with GWO-GO and try not to dribble at all, unless it is to move toward a teammate to shorten the pass to him. In this case, one decisive dribble ought to be all you need.

If you remain decisive, your opponents will become discouraged and start fouling. But if you are passive and careless and let them come close to stealing the ball, they will be encouraged to continue playing tough defense and even to apply more intense pressure.

4
ALIBIS

Nearly all mediocre players are great at finding reasons, excuses—alibis—for their failures. Some of these may even be correct. However, it is a stupid habit to get into. How much more rewarding is it to have an alibi than to simply say, and think, "We just needed to play better"? Do you really think you'll feel wonderful being able to place the blame somewhere else?

Placing blame and making alibis is really not much more than a simple bad habit. It is not something you really want to do. It is merely something you do.

Good players lose this habit, and good players learn not to look for alibis. They learn to accept responsibility. They learn to look inward. They learn to ask themselves, "What could I have done better?"

This is not to say that your coach is always right or that referees never make mistakes. But good players must learn to develop a *habit of mind* whereby they look inward for improvement and do not fear accepting responsibility even when they are not at fault. Because of his habit of mind, a good player expects obstacles and expects to find ways to overcome them. He wastes no time on excuses because he is too busy thinking up ways to overcome the problems.

5
ALTERNATING CURRENT

There are no hard and fast rules in basketball about how long you should hold the ball or how often. But you should be aware of the concept of alternating current. By alternating current—sometimes holding the ball and looking and trying to create a play, and other times giving up the ball immediately—you keep the defense offstride.

There are many players who hold the ball just about every time they get the ball, and there are timid players who always want to get rid of the ball the moment they touch it. Both are problems for a team, but ball-holders (even talented ones) hurt the team more than ball-throwers.

In general, a good player should know if someone is open near the basket; often it is possible to know *before* the ball comes to you, or at least it is possible with a glance that takes no more than an eighth of a second. Frequently, it is beneficial for your team if you get rid of the ball after your eighth of a second instead of always holding it and looking. This gets the ball moving and forces the defense to keep reacting to the ball in different positions.

There are no hard and fast rules, but especially against a zone it is wise to use an "alternating current" situation. **If the guy who gives you the ball holds it awhile, you should try to get rid of it immediately.** If the guy who gives it to you doesn't hold it at all, you might benefit from holding it and looking and taking advantage of an opening.

This is not mere magic; there is a very logical reason why this works. If the guy before you holds the ball and then passes to you a normal distance away (say 15 feet), the defense will need a slight adjustment to remain in good position. However, if you pass the ball immediately (say another 15 feet), that means the ball has traveled about 30 feet in less than a second. The defensive position that was fine a second ago must be drastically altered now that the ball is in so different a position, most likely all the way on the other side of the court.

Of course, you will find many exceptions and reasons why it might be great to hold the ball twice in a row or to throw the ball quickly twice in a row, and it would be stupid to argue with either. In fact, there are offenses built totally around the idea of throwing quick passes, and others where each player is required to hold the ball two seconds before releasing it. If you are running one of those offenses, fine. Run it and run it well. Both can be effective.

However, if no one has given you any rule about holding the ball, it will pay to think about alternating current. Not only should you hold the ball sometimes and pass it immediately at other times, but you should be aware of **doing the opposite of what your teammate does before you.** If he passes it quickly, you look and decide. If he holds the ball, you get rid of it quickly.

What if your teammates *all* hold the ball too much all the time? Better call a team meeting!

6
ANTICIPATION

This is a coach's favorite word and the hallmark of a good player. Can you anticipate what is *likely* to happen next? No one knows exactly what is going to happen, but it pays to be thinking and to be guessing *while* you are preparing for everything. For example, after a rebound, there is likely to be an outlet pass to the side. There may not be, but anticipating one and being prepared to intercept it is playing smart.

There are all sorts of things that come up during a basketball game, and the more of them that you can anticipate, the better player you are. For example, you're defending someone away from the ball, and suddenly the ball is dribbled baseline. Maybe the player with the ball will score a layup, or maybe he will pull up and take a jump shot, or maybe he will leap in the air and throw a turn-around jump pass back in the direction he came from. Maybe. But you should anticipate, if you can't cut him off yourself, that he will be cut off by one of your teammates, and then *you* will have to pick up that teammate's man. When the player with the ball drops a short bounce pass to an open man in the middle or across the basket, *you* can intercept it if you anticipate properly.

No one can anticipate every move in advance, but good players constantly are asking themselves, "Now what's going to happen? Now what're they going to do?"

7
APPROACHING THE BALL

Not many players have great moves, but often moves can look great when there is space to do them in. The majority of scoring moves are made when the ball is received with some space between the player with the ball and the defender; the defender, in trying to close up that space, becomes vulnerable to any tiny fake if he approaches the ball too fast or especially with strides that are too long.

Ideally, a defender should place himself so that he is already in good defensive position the moment his man receives the ball. When he fails to do that, his approach must be intelligent.

As you near the player with the ball, be sure your steps are **short, choppy steps** so that your feet stay on the ground and so that you are ready to react to whatever the offensive player might do. Naturally, long, fast strides are necessary to make up a lot of distance, but as you approach the ball six or eight feet away, take short, choppy steps and try to get to one side of your opponent so that if he does try to drive by you, you already know in what direction he will go. If you run straight at the man, he has the opportunity to go in either direction. It is best to run at his right hand (assuming he is right-handed; and if you have no time to think, that is a good assumption). Get to him as quickly as you can, knowing that he might try to drive past you on the left.

Mediocre players either let their guys shoot or lunge at them and let them drive by. But a good player thinks of two things at once: Get there as quickly as possible, and use short, choppy steps near the end of the approach.

Don't make the mediocre player's usual mistake of pretending he is hustling by running at the shooter, leaping into the air, swiping at the ball and then watching the rest of the action from out of bounds. Rather than trying to block a shot, it is better to run and jab a hand at the last moment in front of the shooter's eyes to distract him and then to block him out so he can't rebound. You may someday block the shot of a poor player, but you are likely to win that game anyway. The problem will be when you find yourself up against a good player, and then your bad habit will cost you the game.

Good players do not run and leap and take themselves out of the play. Good players always stay in the action.

Run at the right-hand, appear as though you are about to fly on by

27

him, but take those short, choppy approach steps, so you can cut the player off when he attempts to drive and block him off the board when he tries to rebound.

8
GO AT DEFENDERS TO GET FREE

When you are dribbling downcourt and there is a defender between you and the basket, go straight at him rather than show him which side you want to go to. By going straight at him, you "paralyze" or freeze him until you decide, just a few feet from him.

You can win a ten-foot race against anyone when you have a running start and your opponent must start from a turned-around, stopped position. This is precisely the case when you go at a defender and suddenly veer off—whether you are dribbling or cutting to receive a pass.

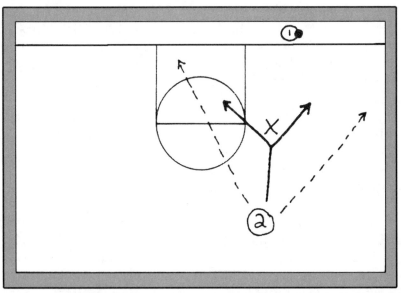

Cuts along the dotted lines are easily defended by "X," but the last second veer-off is not.

If a defender is playing between you and the ball, run straight at him and veer off at the last instant. By going straight at him, you force him to race you from that standing position. If you show him which side you are going to run to, you enable him to get a running start, too, and to stay with you.

9
ATTITUDE

Attitude, as most coaches say, is probably the most important aspect of the game. What is your attitude? All of us have a good attitude when things are going well, when we are the stars of our teams and winning big games.

But attitude goes beyond that. What is your attitude when your team is losing, when the referees are cheating, when your teammates won't pass you the ball, and when your coach is screaming at you for something that isn't your fault?

A good attitude is something you have to decide consciously to have. In bed at night, you have to be able to close your eyes and see yourself as the player you want to be under *all* circumstances. A good attitude is being calm under pressure; it is encouraging teammates even when the coach in practice is being particularly negative; it is requiring of yourself your peak performance at all times, which means actually touching the line (not almost touching it) when your coach says to run to midcourt and back. A good attitude is seeing yourself in advance, with your eyes closed, **performing to your utmost under all sorts of adverse circumstances**, and actually doing that when those circumstances arise.

Can you picture yourself in practice being screamed at by your coach for something that you know was not your fault, and simply accepting it, thinking over the point he is trying to get across and merely reaffirming to yourself that you will never make that mistake? Can you accept his screaming as a reminder instead of getting angry and losing your concentration? Not many players can do that. Not even a lot of good ones. But it *is* possible. The players who can are special. They are a joy to coach, they are great to have as teammates, and they help create winning teams.

A good attitude is very simple. It is doing your best at all times, keeping your concentration on your job, on the things you have to do to play well. It is easy to write down, but a lot more difficult to do.

Can you make yourself hustle when you're out of breath and your legs are lead weights? Can you keep encouraging your teammates even though you think some of them are ball hogs or lazy? Can you accept your coach's criticism and listen to what he is saying even when you feel sure he is wrong? Can you listen and think that maybe, just maybe, *you* could be wrong? Can you give your best under all circumstances—or are there dozens of things that cause you to lose your temper or hustle or concentration?

What is *your* vision of the ideal player and the ideal attitude? What is your vision of *you?* Close your eyes...

10
AVAILABILITY

One of the chief assets of a good player that the average fan rarely even considers, and which even the average player rarely considers, is the ability to play the game constantly available to the ball. A player who is constantly available defuses a lot of potentially troublesome situations and prevents a lot of teammates' turnovers.

Good players ask themselves constantly, "Can the ball be thrown to me now *with no problem?*" Many players have the tendency to "hide" or not come hard to the ball, thereby making passes to them difficult to throw. Other players have the tendency to wait until a teammate is double-teamed and in real trouble before it ever occurs to them to try to help out by running for the ball. A good player will sense the trouble *before* it happens.

For example, if you pass and cut to the basket and no one goes with you, what do you do? A typical answer might be, "Just run to the basket and wave your arms and wait for the ball." That might work against a poor team. But against a good team, if no one follows you, chances are your man left you for a good double-team opportunity, and even though you may be free under the basket, your teammate with the ball is in trouble and cannot get the ball to you. Your habit needs to be, **Anytime you pass and cut and no one follows you, curl back to the ball to make a short (six-foot) pass to you possible.**

What if a team has been playing a man defense and suddenly they switch to a trap or some sort of zone? Are you immediately six feet from the ball open for a pass, or does it take you an hour to recognize the change?

A ball is sailing out of bounds, and one of your teammates goes for it, grabs it but is falling out of bounds. Are you there, six feet from him, saying, "Here!" or are you watching from the other side of the court? Good players run routinely at any ball going out of bounds.

Good players always expect to facilitate things by being available for a pass—an easy pass, not a great, needle-threading pass.

How many teams have you seen attacking a full-court press with two or three guards struggling in the backcourt while two lazy big men stand down at the other end waving their arms, wanting the ball? It happens often, even to good teams, but it shouldn't happen to you.

Get in a passing lane in a seam in the defense. Don't wait for the ball to come to you. Always be in a position where the ball can be thrown to you easily. Never stand 40 feet from the ball and watch the action. Even when you are cleared out on the weak side, you should still be just a step or two away from the lane, about to break in any time an opening or opportunity presents itself.

B

11–**BACKDOOR** cuts

12–**BAD**–fake fakes

13–**BAD** shots

14–**BALL** defense

15–**BEG** for the ball

16–**BEHIND** near the end of the game...on defense

17–**BEHIND** near the end of the game...on offense

18–**BENT**–elbow pass

19–**BLOCKING** out

20–**BLOCKING** shots

21–**BLOCK** out details

22–**BOUNCE** passes go slowly

23–**B-U-B**

24–**BULLET** passes

11
BACKDOOR CUTS

Scoring a backdoor play against an overplaying defense is one of the best feelings basketball has to offer. The cutter has to get far enough out and wide enough to make the pass easy to throw. If the cutter stays in tight, the pass has to be perfect to get through.

Good players should already understand that. What good players, however, often fail to do is communicate with each other so that potential backdoor passes don't go sailing out of bounds because no one has cut for them.

The way to make sure this never happens is to make a rule: If the cutter takes two steps, that means he is going all the way to the basket. He can jockey with his defender and move his shoulders back and forth and try to duck behind the defender, but the passer should not have to guess whether or not the cutter is going. As soon as the second step begins, the cutter is going. If both the cutter and passer are sure of that, the cutter can be led and can score even when he is very well guarded.

Sometimes, a coach will make a rule that a player may not come farther out than a certain point to get the ball, so when he gets to that point, both the passer and he know that he must go backdoor. If the coach sets up backdoors against pressure in a certain way, terrific. But if he doesn't give you a specific rule, this two-step rule will be helpful.

12
BAD-FAKE FAKES

Since most players use bad fakes (hurried or incomplete ones) to try to get free, it is often possible to fake a bad fake in order to get free. This sounds almost like a tongue-twister and a contradiction in terms, but it makes good sense and it works.

Take for example a fake-and-crossover move. Since most players do it with a hurried fake to the left and then a hard drive-step to the right, it is only natural that defenders might expect the same thing from you if you lean a bit to the left and then take a big step to the right.

The difference is that *you* are not going right. Your plan is to go left after getting the defender off-balance as he "anticipates" your drive to the right.

By making the bad fake or faking that bad fake to the left, you get the defender thinking that he knows what you are going to do. He has reacted to bad fakes many times before, so he is ready for you, and there is a good chance he will leap out to the right to cut you off.

Then you can go left and score. The important part of the move is to lean left but to be sure not to move your left foot at all. Then, take that big drive-step to the right with the right foot. The defender will be there waiting for you, but he won't be ready for your crossover step to the left because no one uses this move.

A bad-fake fake can also be used effectively as a shot-fake. A seemingly poorly made shot-fake will alert a defender that you are going to drive, and your big drive-step is likely to have him reeling back on his heels. He will have no thought that the drive-step was really your fake and that you intended all along to go for the shot.

Bad-fake fakes work on all sorts of dribbling moves. Often you can appear to "tip off" the way you want to go by looking that way out of the corner of your eye, but in a way that you know the defender notices. You make a bad fake by leaning opposite of the way you "secretly" looked and then step *big* to the side you pretended to want to go to. The defender will be there with that sense of having you all figured out, and there is a very good chance you can blow right by him down the side you originally bad faked to.

The bad-fake fake is one of those moves that makes you look quick because if you don't use it too often, it usually will spring you wide open.

13
BAD SHOTS

Bad shots, probably more than anything else, lose basketball games. Yet, bad shots are ridiculously common. Go to any playground, and you will see more bad shots taken than good shots. Players seem to love taking bad shots.

Do *you* understand what a bad shot is? You probably think you do, but you probably don't. It might be easiest to illustrate this with a question or two.

Each time you come down the court, why don't you let a shot fly from midcourt? Most players readily understand why that is stupid. A midcourt shot is not a very high percentage shot. It is smarter to get closer and take a shot that has a better chance of going in. This makes good sense, and it seems like the whole world should agree on what is and is not a good shot. But agreement usually ends at midcourt because for some strange reason, players routinely think that all sorts of hooks, fadeaways, far-off jumpers and quick flings are good shots.

A coach will ask, "Why take a quick 20-footer?" And the player will answer, "I can make that shot, Coach." And yes, he can. A bit more often than he can make a fling from midcourt, but a lot less often than he can make a right-hand layup or an open 15-footer. So, why ever take a quick 20-footer?

Maybe you never should. The point is, if there is no shot clock, what excuse is there, especially in the first half when obviously there is plenty of time left, for taking a quick 20-footer? Why not wait for a better shot?

To some players, even good ones, these kinds of questions often sound ridiculous, and yet **winning teams** are most often the teams who **pass up** shots like these and **wait** for better ones. Only teams who have no confidence in their ball-handling should "jack up 20-footers" in the first half of a game. Otherwise, it makes sense to explore the defense and see if it isn't possible with a bit more movement and a couple more passes to get a 15-footer or even a layup.

For players, the toughest thing isn't so much to learn not to take fadeaways and hooks and flings but to learn the difference between a 45% shot and a 60% shot. There isn't a great deal of difference.

What *is* the difference between a 45% shot and a 60% shot? Not much. Both feel good, and both feel like they are going to go in. Both do go in rather often, yet 60% shooting wins games, while 45% often loses them. A bit more time. A step closer in. A bit more confidence and certainty about the one. A bit of this and a bit of that--not much, and not easy for a coach to make into a hard and fast rule. Yet, the 60% shot wins and the 45% shot loses. It is a subtle difference, a minor difference and almost no difference at all.

But then, neither is there much difference between two teams who finish a game 67-64. Only that one team won and the other lost.

14
BALL DEFENSE

For "good" players who look upon defense as a necessary evil to go through on the way to a score, this next section will be boring. There are a few major points you should be aware of when playing ball defense—too many to think of if you're just hoping to get by. These major points concern your position "in the bubble":

- your body position and weight
- position of your hands
- ☐get in his bubble "
- dictating the action of the ball
- the commitment you make to yourself

The Commitment You Make to Yourself. This last point is the most important, because if you aren't committed to stopping your man, and you don't have pride in making it difficult for a man to score, none of the other points will matter. You must begin with the sincere desire to be known as a good defensive player. If you have that desire to be a good defensive player, the other four points will be very helpful.

Your Body Position and Weight. All coaches seem to want players to get in a lower crouch than players want to get in. All players seem to want to stand straight up. So how low should you be?

A good rule to follow is: **Make sure your head is always lower than the head of the guy you are guarding.** If you stay lower than he is, you will be more ready to move than he is. If he lowers his head to drive, you need to lower your head even more to stay in front of him.

Players get blocking fouls when their knees are out, but look a bit longer. You will see that their heads are up, too. At the moment of the block, the defender's head is likely higher than the dribbler's.

Besides being lower than your man, you should have your *weight back,* ready to move when he moves. Get in your man's "bubble" (see below) and have your weight back. Players often stay away from their man, and then move forward when he fakes or looks to shoot or pass. So what happens? You get to the bubble, to the man, but now your weight is forward so that you can not possibly beat him to where he is going.

Imagine trying to win a 100-yard dash when one guy is in the starting blocks ready to burst forward and you start several feet in front of him, but you have to touch the starting line when the gun goes off. Obviously, you would be several steps behind after ten yards. Yet, apparently it isn't as obvious on defense, because in games at all levels, players stay too far away from their men and then they try at times to lunge forward, letting the man with the ball fly right by them. Why do players keep letting this happen?

If you want to win a race, you have to lean in the direction of the finish line. In basketball you have to lean in the direction of the basket because that is the where the guy with the ball wants to race to.

Position of Your Hands. Coaches always urge, "Hands up!" so their players will distract the offense and deflect passes, and players prefer to play with their hands at their sides. Because it is easier to move with hands at your side. (Sprinters don't raise their hands until they cross the finish line.) In guarding the ball, there are times to play with hands down and times to play with a hand up.

If you are guarding a dribbler, your hands need not be up, they should be down faking at the ball or helping your body stay in good position, on balance. The important distinction regarding your hands comes when you are guarding a player who has the ball but has not yet dribbled. If that player is out of shooting range, your hands can be down at waist or knee level, one to the side and the other stretched out to the ball handler's belt buckle. (The outstretched hand should be the same as whichever foot is forward. Left foot out, left hand out, and vice-versa.) The outstretched hand should be palm up, always prepared to slap *up* anytime the ball is held out in front.

If the player with the ball is in shooting range, you should have one hand up, almost touching your shoulder, poised to jab upward, so it is clear to the player with the ball that you are prepared to block his shot (though really all you want to do is distract him by getting your hand up near the ball and your arm in front of his face).

Never raise your body up to block the pass or shot of a player who has not yet dribbled. Stay low, keep your weight back, stay in that bubble and slap upward from the waist if he is out of shooting position, or shake your hand over your shoulder if he is in shooting position.

"Get in His Bubble." Though "bubble" is not a term commonly used by coaches, it is helpful in reminding you to play in good defensive position. Good defensive position means, unless your coach gives you some other rule, not so close that the player with the ball can step by you with one step, yet close enough that you can slap the ball if the man holds it in front of him. In other words, you are close enough to be able to bother him and to make him worry that you might touch his next pass or block his next shot or steal his next dribble. Not that you necessarily are going to try to block a shot or steal a dribble, but you should be close enough that the player with the ball is very aware of your activity and presence. **From eight feet away, regardless of what you do—dance, sing, or play a harp—you will not be the ball handler's primary concern.** Admittedly, the harp might confuse him momentarily, but not long enough to matter.

To play good defense you must consistently be in that bubble, invading that man's private territory. Ideally, even along with playing good helping defense, you should be in your man's bubble every time he gets the ball, the moment he gets it. If you can do that, you will be a constant irritation to him, which is exactly what you want to be.

You cannot expect to be a good defender if one day you try stealing the ball all the time because the player is not talented, and the next day you stay far away from your man because he is very talented and you are afraid he might drive by you. Good defense is a matter of learning to get in a player's bubble, in his private territory, and of being able to stay there. You are close enough to touch the ball if he has it in front of him, almost close enough to touch him, but not so close that you could bump heads if he pushes his head forward.

Why should you be in his bubble if he is 40 feet from the basket and out of shooting range? So that you can bother his ball-handling and make it difficult for him to take the ball exactly where he wants it or make the exact pass at the exact time he wants to make it.

Naturally, if your coach says not to pick him up until he gets in shooting range, don't. But if he doesn't give you a rule, or if you are playing in a pickup game, or if you are working out in the off-season, then get in your man's bubble and stay there. Try to be there simultaneously with the ball every time.

Don't be beside your man all the time. Don't be there when the ball is on the other side of the court. In this instance, you need to be in a position ready to help a teammate.

Remember: **The closer the ball is to your man, the closer *you* must be to your man,** because the moment he gets the ball, you want to be in his bubble, not on your way there. Be where you can worry him and bother him and make him aware that "Oh no, here you are again." You don't have to block a single shot or deflect a single pass. If you are merely in position all night long where you can be, and he can't ever manage to get away from you, you will be a great defender.

Get in that bubble and make sure your weight is back so you are ready to move when he moves. Your objective is not to steal the ball and block shots —it is to stay in that bubble all night long and irritate and distract and bother.

Dictating the Action of the Ball. A player with the ball can do three things: He can release the ball with a shot or pass (which your bubble defense and hand position try to make difficult) or he can dribble to the right or to the left. It is intelligent to take two of these three options away and battle for the third.

Your bubble defense takes the shot and pass away. He may still shoot or pass, but either will be difficult, which is what defense is all about—making things difficult. That leaves the dribble to either side. So if you overplay to one side, forcing the man to go to his left or to the baseline or to a helping teammate, you take away a second option, leaving him just one opportunity to try to beat you in the direction you have dictated.

The advantage of this type of defense is that you don't have to be prepared for anything and you don't have to worry about fakes. You know what the player is going to do. Either he is going to take a bad shot, or he is going to have to make a good pass by your hand, or he is going to have to force the ball in a direction where he is already overplayed—unless he decides to try to beat you in the one thing you are prepared for.

By dictating the action in this way, you not only make it easier for yourself, but also you make it easier for your teammates. With the opportunity for your teammates to see in advance where the battle is going to be fought—where the ball is going to be taken, they have a better chance of getting into effective helping position.

15
BEG FOR THE BALL

Good players beg for the ball, not so much with their mouths (though they do sometimes shout) as with their body movements and facial expressions. Good players want the ball, and that want is obvious to whoever has it.

The average fan would likely say that all players want the ball, and they do, but not like good players want it. Good players want it in a way that puts them always close by, always "popping out," always looking at the guy with the ball with a sort of desperation, as though two points would be automatically marked on the scoreboard just by completing the pass.

This whole desperate begging business would really seem like some sort of nuisance except that mediocre players don't—can't—do it, too. **You have to be a good player to know how to beg with your body** and your eyes and the muscles in your face. Good players don't have to say a word, but everyone knows a beggar when he sees one.

Do you beg for the ball? Or are you usually out on the periphery, hoping the ball comes to you? There is a huge difference between begging and hoping.

16
BEHIND NEAR THE END OF THE GAME...
ON DEFENSE

The rules of the game are different when you are behind. Now you don't "get anything" for staying between your man and the basket and playing good, solid defense. If you stay in good, solid defense, the clock will soon run out and you lose. Many players fail to adjust their thinking at this point. Now you are not trying to discourage shots so much as passes. You can't afford to let your man receive passes.

Often at the end of games, you see the losing coach urging, "Get 'em, Get 'em!", but nobody really gets anyone. The defenders let their men receive the ball, and then they make a show of useless hustle by crowding their man and reaching and swatting and huffing and puffing and so forth. But the show doesn't fool anyone. If you want to play good defense at the end, you have to make it very difficult, ideally impossible, for your man to receive the ball.

There is a time for fouling and making the foul look like an attempt to steal, so that you give up a one-on-one and not an intentional two-shot foul; but this is at the point of desperation, at the point of just hoping for luck. This point will come less often if you realize what adjustment on defense you need to make beforehand. If you realize that **your objective is to stop passes** and, if anything, give up the risky lob or backdoor bounce pass, then you will get your share of comebacks.

It is easy to find excuses, when you are tired and discouraged, for getting beat to the ball. Maybe you get screened out, or you have to help someone else or some such thing, but those excuses don't win games. Good players know their job is to prevent perimeter passes in spite of screens and other diversions. They know that hustle, once their man gets the ball, is too late.

When your team is behind near the end, it takes guts. Stick to your man and don't let him touch the ball. If anything, force him to get a lob going away from the ball. Sure, he might score, but you have to try. Standing back and letting your man break out and receive passes cannot win for you, so you have to take some chances. A team protecting a lead will not want to throw a backdoor lob anyway unless it is wide open, so you have an advantage. You know what kind of passes they would like to throw, so don't let them. Don't let your man catch the ball going toward it.

17
BEHIND NEAR THE END OF THE GAME... ON OFFENSE

The tendency of all players when behind is to hurry to catch up, but the best method for catching up is not the often-used long jumper.

Near the end, when your opponent is ahead, you will likely hear your opponent's coach telling his team not to foul. This should give you a clue as to the best way to try to catch up. **If there is ever a time to take the ball aggressively to the basket, it is near the end when you are behind.** At times, the opponent will nearly invite you in. At other times, the opponent might make a good show of defense, but generally, they will get out of your way if you are at all clever about the way you go in. It makes sense. If they are being told to avoid contact, and you go aggressively toward them (though not precisely head-on), the likelihood is that a path will be cleared for you. And if it isn't, so much the better because a foul will stop the clock and even give you a chance for a three-point possession.

So remember, resist the normal urge to flip up long jumpers at the end when you are behind. That is only playing into your opponent's hands. Take the ball to the basket aggressively. You'll get easier shots than you could ever expect to get in the first half.

18
THE BENT-ELBOW PASS

Another name for the bent-elbow pass might be "the greatest pass in the world," and yet few players use it. By using this pass, you can get the ball past a defender immediately, every time, without delay, without having to fake a lot or waste valuable time.

The pass is begun by putting the ball at your side, just above the waist, and then leaning a bit to that side and stepping to that same side. Your arm is not extended but bent. And *bent* is the key. Because then all you have to do is check the defender's hand on that side. If no hand is there even with the ball, you throw the bounce pass right past him. If the hand is there, you roll your wrist over and flip the ball just over your opponent's ear. The pass, though it doesn't sound like much, is like magic, because it works again and again. A defender simply can't get his hand up to his ear in time. In fact, the motion of having a hand beside the ear is so unnatural that **there is usually room to get the ball by his head, even if the defender has anticipated your pass.**

The key is the *bent elbow.* If you extend your arm and cannot throw the bounce pass, you have to cock your arm for the pass over the ear, which gives the defender time to react. But **if the fake is made with the elbow bent** (with the arm in a cocked ready-to-throw position the whole time), the pass over the ear can be thrown immediately and won't ever be blocked.

The usefulness of this pass can not be overemphasized. This is a weapon every player needs, but even most good players don't have. Guards especially will find this pass magical for getting the ball to the big man inside at the split second it ought to arrive.

This pass can be learned in a few concentrated minutes and used against anyone over and over for a lifetime. This pass is a great, great weapon. Be attentive to the details—there aren't many, -and learn to throw it and its value will prove itself a thousand times. This book has no more useful piece of advice. The world is filled with good players who have trouble passing a ball by a defender. With this pass, your troubles are over.

19
BLOCKING OUT

To block out effectively, stay low, keep your feet wide apart, back straight up, and your arms straight out to the side while your hands are up (and just out from the ears).

There are certain advantages to using this position. By being low and wide, you stay tough and are hard to move even by a stronger player. Also, you force the man behind you to jump when you do, or after you do, since jumping for the ball first certainly looks like he is fouling by going over your back.

By keeping your back straight, it is obvious to the referee that *he,* not you, is fouling. If you bend at the waist as many players do, it often looks as though you have moved under the man behind you and therefore the foul can be called on you. This is especially important if you are the one initiating contact. If you move to the man with your back straight up, the contact will be incidental and not be called. But if you move toward the man with your back bent forward, a bit of forward momentum will carry him over your back, and it will look as though you are guilty of the infraction.

By having your arms out to the sides, you can feel the man on your back with your triceps and you can hold him out without getting a foul called on you—as long as the referee can see your hands in the air.

This is one way of blocking out. It is not the only way, but if you are not given any specific method, this one will serve you well.

GOOD BLOCK OUT POSITION

Stay low, feet wide apart, back straight, arms out, hands up

The most important point of blocking out is not related to the hands, the arms, the back, the knees or the feet.

The crucial factor in blocking out pertains to the position of the *head*. The head must want to block out. The head must want to get in someone's way. The head must, as a matter of habit, enjoy getting in someone's way *every time* a shot goes up.

In drills, it is very difficult to block out well. Offensive rebounders have an assortment of clever spins and fakes and turns that are hard to handle. However, in games, these are hardly ever used. Hardly ever. Almost never. Or so seldom they don't even need to be considered. In games, what needs to be considered is *attempting* to block someone off the board every time. If you attempt to block someone off, most likely you will because in games there is rarely much time or effort put into faking and jockeying for position. The huge majority of offensive rebounders do nothing at all; the good ones go straight for the ball with no fakes and no effort to spin once they are cut off, and there are one or two guys in the world who hit and spin and fake and change direction—and these guys are superstars.

Go back and read how many superstars there are in offensive rebounding. One or two in the world and maybe a little guard somewhere that no one knows about because he's too small to get the ball even though he often gets to it. The point is, there aren't many "hitters and spinners" that you need to worry about. **Your primary concern needs to be with getting into the every-time habit of attempting to block out.** Why?

When you review game film after game film, regardless of the level of play, you find that the majority of offensive rebounds are gotten not by clever "hitters and spinners" but by players who simply move to the ball without anyone ever getting in their way *and* without anyone having made any *attempt* to get in their way.

Technique is not crucial. Do it the way your coach tells you, or if he says nothing, do it the way it is done in the line drawing. But do it. Do you understand? *Do it.*

The times you let your man get an offensive rebound will very seldom be when he outfakes you. Usually, his rebounds will come when you simply forget to block him at all.

20
BLOCKING SHOTS

A few great players average three blocked shots a game, and they are real forces and intimidators inside. There aren't many of these. About one per league, maybe two. Then, there is the rest of the basketball world—the guys that average one blocked shot per game and less, about 99% of the basketball players who play the game. When you think about these percentages and about how few shots are blocked by even great leapers, you have to start wondering what all the leaping is about. Or you might say:

> Show me a guy who averages
> one blocked shot per game,
> and I'll show you a guy
> who often gets faked out
> and hurts his team.

If you are anything other than one of those leaping superstars with great timing, you should consider a new rule you may never have thought of: **Don't ever again jump to block a shot.**

For every shot that gets blocked by a non-superstar, there are probably three times that he gets faked out. And the worst part of that is, the blocks usually come in the easy games which you would have won anyway, while the fake-outs tend to come against good teams when you really need good defensive habits. As much as you probably love the feeling of swatting a ball into the third row, you should learn to stay on your feet, intimidate and distract the shooter, and be ready for the rebound by blocking out and getting to the ball.

Remember, shot blockers are usually needless foulers and guys who get faked out too often. Unless you are really proficient—exceptional, you should seriously consider *never leaping to a block shot again.*

If you do decide to block a shot, do it only in the three-second lane where hopefully a teammate will leap right after you do (in case of a faked shot) and the two of you may cause a three-second violation. Outside the lane, even the best shot-blockers in the world should stay on their feet and intimidate, pretend, fake...but not jump.

You could be a great defensive player without ever blocking a shot in your whole life. In fact, you probably will be better if you don't, unless of course you are that rare, gifted superstar with timing.

21
BLOCK OUT DETAILS

On the jump ball circle, you don't often hear about the importance of good blocking out, but it is crucial as well as very easy. Many times, it is obvious to both teams where the ball is going to be tapped. If one team has a much taller player jumping, he will tap to a pocket where he has two men together. However, often, even though the ball is tapped between the two, a smart player from the other team will cut in between and steal the tap. He can easily be blocked out since he has no time to fake and jockey at all, but it is necessary for the players on the circle to realize that he must be blocked out. This is a perfect example where technique means almost nothing. Getting the ball is simply a matter of realizing that an attempt to block out must be made.

A BLOCK OUT SITUATION ON THE JUMP BALL CIRCLE

The X's must expect 4 and 5 to try to cut in front of them to steal this tap since it looks obvious that the ball will be tapped to that pocket. This should be an easily controlled tap for the X's, but it could result in a layup if the players in the pocket do not block out.

In a second situation, on the free throw lane, many players merely step into the lane instead of stepping against the man beside them. To be sure you get the long rebound, you have to step against your man and clear out some space for the ball to fall into. Many players get good block out position, but the only ball they can get is one that is falling through the net.

22
BOUNCE PASSES GO SLOWLY

BOUNCE PASSES GO SLOWLY

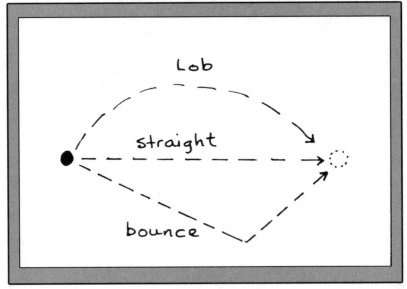

Simple geometry should make it obvious that bounce passes take longer to arrive than straight passes. Throw bounce passes only when there is someone to get under.

Everyone knows that bounce passes are good passes to throw inside to a man posting up, or to a cutter going backdoor, or perhaps on a 2-on-1 fast break, but a lot of players don't seem to realize that a bounce on the perimeter is a careless pass. It takes longer to arrive and, therefore, gives a defender a better chance for an interception.

Although a lob can be great for a backdoor cut, would you throw it to the teammate next to you on the perimeter even when there is no defender between you? Everyone answers no to that one. Even little kids don't throw a lob for no reason. Yet, stars often drop a bounce pass to a teammate *for no reason.*

Don't do anything *for no reason.* If there is no one between you and the man you are about to pass to, don't throw anything other than a crisp, straight pass to his chest.

The shortest distance between two points is a straight line, right?

Lobs and bounces are used to throw over or under people; otherwise, don't use them.

23
B-U-B

While not many coaches use the term "B-U-B", nearly every coach teaches this concept: **B**all-**you**-**B**asket. This refers to defensive position, and thousands of talented players often fail to comply with this rule. Wherever the ball is on the court, you should be closer to the basket than it is. If the ball is dribbled to the basket, you have the opportunity to stop the layup or pick up an open man should a teammate stop the layup first.

Even good players are often guilty of angrily asking, after a player has dribbled in for a layup, "Whose man was that?"

But to the coach, the question is a stupid one. The answer is, "It was *your* man." It was everyone's man. Everyone who is conscious of B-U-B, of being between the ball and the basket, should be able to stop the layup regardless of whose man the scorer is.

There are some exceptions. After a player has dribbled and therefore cannot penetrate to the basket, it is wise to overplay your own man even if that means getting farther away from the basket than the ball is. In certain overplaying defenses or against a stall, you might also be required to be out of B-U-B position. But the exceptions are not usually the cause for the rule being broken. Laziness is.

Whether at the midget, high school, college or pro level, you can watch over and over again the willingness of players to trot downcourt beside their man even though the ball is ahead of them. Few players realize the value of turning a 3-on-3 into a 3-on-4, but winning players do this routinely, and the logic behind it should be abundantly clear. Three-on-threes are easy to score and three-on-fours are difficult, yet players trot down, content to be even with their man instead of ready to help someone else.

FAILURE TO BE IN B-U-B DEFENSE

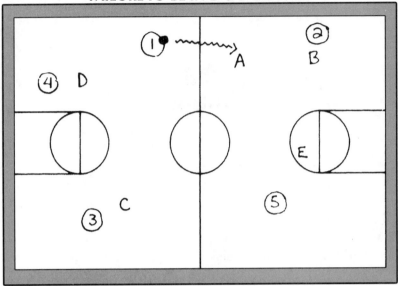

In this full-court man-to-man press, each of the defenders appears to be with his man. But this should be recognized immediately as very poor defensive position because "D" and "C" are not B-U-B.

GOOD DEFENSIVE POSITION

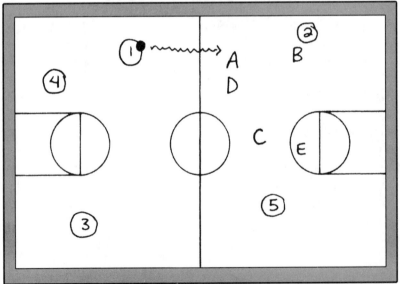

Note here the position especially of "D" and "C" Both players have passed up the ball. They are closer to the basket than the ball, ready to help.

Your thought ought to be: Always be closer to the basket than the ball; if you are not, then sprint as fast as you can to overtake it.

This rule of play is essential to good defense, yet few players adhere to it diligently. So-called good players are as often guilty of being behind the ball as are mediocre ones. But good **defenders are consistently ahead of the ball,** in B-U-B position, or are sprinting full-speed to pass up the ball when they are not.

24
BULLET PASSES

Soft passes and lobs are the most dangerous passes to throw since they allow the defense time to steal the ball. Bullet passes are not much better.

Many times it is the best athletes who throw bullet passes. In football, it is often a quarterback with an exceptional arm who is anxious to show it off. However, the result too often is a ball glancing off fingertips and being intercepted. The same thing frequently happens in basketball. A bullet pass is thrown, the receiver misses it, and the passer smugly feels that his teammate "shoulda had it."

The problem is *shoulda had its* never win games. To win games, you need to throw passes that people can handle. If you have a player with exceptional hands, fine; you can fling the ball at him, and he will usually get it and still do his thing. But most players, even good ones, have trouble with bullet passes. Firm, crisp passes are what is needed, not bullets. In basketball, there is no place for showing off how hard you can hit someone with a pass, and there should be no satisfaction in thinking *It was his fault* when a ball you passed is mishandled out of bounds.

Throw passes that can be caught, not ones that should have been.

1829

It looks like a year, but it's not.

It's a ratio—the diameter of the rim (18 inches) to the diameter of the ball (9 inches). Eighteen to nine. 18 to 9. The rim is *so* much bigger. You have to wonder how anyone ever figured he missed some crucial shot by only an inch.

C

25
TAKING A CHARGE

You don't need to be a hero to take a charge. When you get your body in position in front of the offensive player, protect yourself with your forearm across your chest. Stay in your defensive crouch and begin your fall just before the contact is made, taking all the contact on your forearm and not on your nose or stomach or chest.

Once you have learned how to take charges properly, you will enjoy taking them even against much bigger and stronger players. The crucial point is to *stay low*. By staying low, you assure yourself that you are not going to have to match strength with strength. If the offensive player has the idea of bulling you over, all he can look forward to is flying over you and tripping. There is no reason for you to be standing straight up and no reason for you to be called for moving under. If you have position and get low, you are entitled to that position. No hard-driving muscleman can bully you when all that his chest is going to hit is air.

There is one other point that is often misunderstood. People say that to take a charge you cannot be moving. But *moving* in that case means that your chest or knee is not allowed to suddenly get in the way. You are, however, allowed to be moving backward and, if you are staying in one place, you are allowed to move your feet—and you should. **By keeping your feet moving, you are prepared to alter your position slightly** in case the offensive player tries to cut by you instead of going straight over you. Of course, in altering your position slightly, you can not stick out a knee, but you can certainly move a bit more to one side *while moving back, too,* so that you again make it obvious that you got there first and have established your position.

There are two reasons why good players fail to take charges (assuming that all would like to). One is fear. They don't know how to take a charge without getting hurt, so they tend to get out of the way or go for a steal, unless it really counts or the charge just happens. The second reason is that they forget to stay low and keep their feet moving, and then at the final moment, when they could take the charge, they straighten up and brace themselves, allowing the offensive player to make a quick adjustment and go right on by.

There is no point at which you straighten up and brace yourself for contact. You stay low, you keep your feet moving and you begin to fall only after the offensive player makes contact with your arm. This habit of straightening up and bracing, which happens often even to players who generally stay well with their man, might be called a "Statue Charge" or a sudden pose as if for a camera.

Remember, there is no time when you stop playing defense and begin taking a charge. There is no time to suddenly pose or become a statue. Stay in the defensive crouch, keep your feet moving and take the contact on your forearm.

26
CLICK, CLICK, CLICK

All coaches probably have different names for it—maybe ping-ping-ping or tungo-tungo-tungo or maybe just "Move it quick!" But whatever the name, coaches and winning teams realize the value of having the ball click from one player to another.

A click is when the ball comes into your hands and goes out again in an eighth of a second. Not a second later, after you look around. Not a moment later, after you first check to see if you can get a shot. But *immediately.* You catch the ball, you throw the ball--like a second baseman on a double play.

The only way you can make a click pass is to **know before you get the ball what you are going to do with it.** That takes good court awareness. Larry Bird, one of the greatest players in the history of the game, was a master of click passes. Considering what a great shooter he was, it would seem as if he would have had an excuse for holding the ball and looking around all the time. But every game, he had dozens of click passes, passes that just barely touched his hands before he was sending the ball on its way to a teammate.

Naturally, if you have good enough court awareness to pass the ball immediately to a teammate wide open, that's great. But even if you don't, if you concentrate on throwing ten or twelve click passes per game, even if the passes don't go to the "right" man each time, you still will be helping your team. Click passes not only help team morale and look impressive, but even when they are thrown to the "wrong" guy, they still put enormous pressure on the defense because the ball is moving so quickly from one position to another.

You cannot be a good player just by *always* passing the ball immediately after you get it; but you would hardly ever hurt a good team by doing that, and you would help them often.

The point is that most players hold the ball too long most of the time. It is difficult to make this any more emphatic. You may miss an open man someday, and the fans or coach may groan for a moment, but you don't lose many games by clicking the ball. You lose them by holding it too much.

This is not to say that you should treat the ball like a "hot potato" and just flip it out of your hands without even knowing where a teammate is. But often you should get rid of the ball quickly, when you can.

Plan to get ten clicks a game. If you can talk your teammates into doing the same, your team will be much better. Click passes will put the ball in scoring position or dangerous position "like magic" against man or zone defenses. You will probably be surprised at how much easier it is for your team to score by this simple effort. Click, click, click. Get ten.

27
WHEN THE CLOCK IS STOPPED

Mediocre players use this time to rest, to complain, to limp, to frown at referees, to look around at the crowd. The problem is that many talented players use the time when the clock is stopped for the same purposes. But there is an endless number of valuable things a good player can do while the clock is stopped if he is thinking and really trying to be as much of an asset to his team as he possibly can.

On the free throw line, remind someone to block out the shooter, remind the big guys to block out aggressively, remind the inbounds passer to get the ball in quickly. These are obvious things, yet so often they go unsaid, and so often there are breakdowns in one of these areas.

To go further, though, a good player is constantly singling out people and whispering in a teammate's ear: "We need to draw a foul on their big guy next time" or "I'll look for you this time cutting across the lane, make sure you come hard" or "Let's really hurry on the break this time. I think we can catch one of 'em loafing" or "Make sure you turn and come back to the ball after you screen," or "C'mon, we gotta hit the boards," or "Let's get a layup next time down."

Singling out a teammate and giving him extra encouragement often works wonders, yet it is so seldom done. If you are about to take the ball out of bounds, tell someone you'll be looking for him. Get your teammates doing their best. Praise someone for a play he made a minute ago. Urge tougher defense.

When there is a break in the action, and you can't think of anything to say to anyone that might help the team, you are either a very selfish player, or you know very, very little about basketball. *Good* players use the time when the clock is stopped to make the next play work better and to make teammates try harder and concentrate.

If you use part of this valuable time for frowning and complaining and foot-stomping, it would be difficult to call you anything other than a stupid player, even if you are talented and a high scorer. Chances are you are not a winner.

28
AGAINST GOOD TEAMS, COMPLETE PASSES

There is a simple way to beat any opponent: Complete your passes. How often have you heard players say things like, "Gawd, we could never beat them. They're too good." Have you ever stopped to think what it takes to win a game? If you did, you would probably never go into a basketball game with a negative attitude.

Football is different. In football, if you are playing a bigger, tougher team, they are going to push you around and beat you up, and they can make themselves win. But **in basketball, no one can make his team win.** Everyone has to hope that the other team makes themselves lose. In basketball, you aren't permitted to tackle anyone or hurt anyone or roughly grab the ball from anyone. **Even the great coaches of great**

teams can only say, "Keep the pressure on them, and they'll make mistakes."

Yet, if the other team doesn't make mistakes, if the other team concentrates on completing passes until it gets an easy shot, it is going to be a close game, perhaps decided at the end on a last second shot and on luck.

Of course, this doesn't usually happen. Good teams force other teams to get nervous and to try to throw passes they shouldn't be throwing or to try to make shots that they can't make. But finally, it will be the other team that makes the mistakes, not the good team that makes themselves win.

When you go into a tough game, your job is to hold onto the ball until you can throw it to a teammate. That's all. If all of you do that each time, eventually one of you will get a layup or an easy shot that any fourth-grader can make. You complete passes, and your team wins.

However, that's not all there is to it, is it? It is difficult to complete passes. And it is difficult to make the shots once you decide to take them. Therefore, it pays to become a good ball handler and a good shooter. And yet, it also pays to realize that all it takes to win is the ability to complete passes until one of the five guys on the team gets a shot that he can make. When you look at it that way, you realize that it doesn't take miracles. In most games, it takes merely a little precision, a bit better judgment, a shade more concentration. "Don't throw *that* pass." "Don't take *that* shot." Hold onto the ball until you get a shot you are excellent at, or until you can make a sure pass to a teammate. A **sure pass,** not any old pass. **Not a "maybe" pass.**

In most games, the losing team could have won if they had just concentrated on completing passes and not trying stupid shots and plays. If you concentrate on completing passes, especially against a good team that is pressuring, you won't need to think about finding scoring opportunities. Complete passes will create them for you, and somewhere along the way, before the thirteenth pass, someone will find himself with the ball in position for a fourth-grade shot.

Do you know why this doesn't happen more often? Because players don't sit around thinking up ways to complete passes. They go to a playground and work on 360s and behind-the-back passes, and in games they wait and hope the passer makes a good pass to them, instead of moving to make a pass to them easy to throw.

You may not initially like the idea of putting your concentration on completing passes. But in a tough game, the effort will pay off.

29
CONSISTENCY

The ability to be consistent is what separates a good player from a mediocre one. When your coach starts saying things about you like, "No one can beat him baseline" or "No one can keep him off the boards," you are a good player. Mediocre players are the ones always pointing out the times they do something good. But good players *expect* to perform certain tasks over and over again *routinely*.

You don't expect praise for never giving up a layup, you just do it because it's do-able. Things that are do-able, you do, over and over again, every time. Good players have an every-time kind of pride, and that is what coaches call "consistency." That, not 360s and slam dunks, is what separates good from mediocre and winners from losers.

Strangely enough, season after season, teams called "great" get four or five or even ten victories a year by *only a few points* over teams called "mediocre" or "bad." Think of that. *Great* teams often beat *bad* teams by only a few points. That's one turnover, a tip-in somewhere, and a free throw made or missed one way or the other. That's a tiny defensive lapse maybe tucked away someplace in a fold of the game that the fans never even saw, could have been early in the first half (of all places!), or some play snuck in from out of bounds or on a jump ball someplace.

You've got to think hard about that to realize what it means. A few points, a couple of plays, a 45% shot someplace instead of one more pass and a 55% shot—not much difference between a 20-game winner and a team with a losing season. It should give you a healthy regard for complaining, dissatisfied coaches and for words like *precision* and *concentration* and *hustle*. Such a tiny thread in 32 or 40 minutes of basketball separates good from bad, and yet, some people win consistently (by a few points) while others lose consistently (often only by a few points, too).

There is probably only one way to cross that tiny little thread and get on the winning side. Be consistent. Develop a ridiculous attention to detail, to doing things right, to making every practice count, to concentrating on every shot. It is not easy to be consistent. Because that's what "good" is.

30
COUNTERING CHANGING DEFENSES

Your coach has to help you counter changing defenses by giving you offenses to run against various defenses, or by giving you an offense that you know you can run against both a man-for-man and a zone. But you still have to recognize the changes, and besides, a team often may try to fool you by showing one "look" while actually being in another defense.

The best way to counter any confusion over what defense your opponent is using is to run through the lane to the other side (or send someone through to the other side) and swing the ball. You might want to call this a *cut and a swing.* If you have an offense that includes a quick cut and a swing of the ball, then use it and you will know immediately what they are playing. Are they going through with that cutter, playing man, or are they letting him cut and picking up, playing zone?

A defense can be cute when a point guard or any player is standing around in a nondangerous position with the ball and doing nothing. But regardless of what defense the other team is in, if you send a cutter through and swing the ball and threaten, that team will show you immediately what they are up to, or, if they are still in the process of disguising, there should be openings all over the court.

"Should be?" you might be saying, "but what if there aren't?" If you cut from one side and quickly swing the ball and threaten from the other side, and you still don't know what they are in, then it has to be a zone—or else *you* don't know the meaning of "threaten."

In fact, **if you know how to threaten, every defense is a zone.** This thought might not initially make sense, but it is simple when you think about it.

Every time you get the ball, if you can beat one man enough to force another to help out, then whether the other team calls it a zone or not, they are playing you three to four—a zone—or else they are leaving a man open, in which case their defense is neither man nor zone, it is "poor!"

In other words, if you can threaten a defense, it doesn't matter what they call their thing, they are in a scramble to prevent you from scoring.

Don't try to recognize a defense by studying it from afar. Call an offense or make a movement with a cut in it, and pass the ball and threaten. You can never go wrong by taking the ball forward and engaging two defenders. When you have a 4-on-3, you don't care what defense they are in.

31
CRITICISM

If you have a good coach and you are a good player, most likely you have already learned that the only intelligent response to criticism from your coach is to accept it, keep your mouth shut and try to learn from it. No one, especially tough competitors, can ever be expected to *like* criticism, but you certainly must be able to take it and learn from it.

If your natural spirit of rebellion prevents you from learning while you are being criticized, you might try getting a student manager to jot down the negative things that are said to you during a practice. You will probably be surprised to find out, an hour after practice when you are showered and gone from the gym, that even a coach you don't like has said some things you can benefit from, *even if one time he said the guy was your man and it wasn't.* So someone scored, and the coach said it was your man, and you know it wasn't. Big deal. *Could* you have gotten him? Would a better player than you have switched off and taken that man anyway, even though it wasn't his man?

This is not to say that a coach's criticism is never wrong, but it *is* to say that you can probably learn from just about every criticism even when one is wrong in a particular instance.

A good player can go a step beyond that. When was the last time (this is if you are already out of the complaining, rebellious stage yourself) you told a teammate who argued or frowned at the coach to quit acting and play ball? When was the last time you told someone, "Don't worry about it" or "Don't take it so personally. Keep doing your best." Sometimes you need to be firm, sometimes you need to be encouraging. It depends on the situation and also on whether you are the toughest guy on the team, a senior the others look up to or a frail sophomore who shoots every time you get the ball.

Regardless of what your situation is, **criticism is going to be a large part of any basketball experience if the goals are excellence and winning.**

If you haven't gotten accustomed to criticism enough to have already developed *a useful response* it is time you start making some giant steps toward changing and finding one.

No one ever said you have to like criticism. You merely have to learn from it with your mouth shut. There isn't enough practice time to allow for your various explanations and refutations. "Suck it up" as the saying goes—it's part of the game.

D⁴

Sometimes
especially outside
when it starts to get dark
and everyone has gone home
and you've played all day
and you're there alone—
you, a ball, and the court—
the feeling is a combination
of meditation
and dream
and love.

D

32
DANCE

Dance is a word used to refer to a simple four-step routine that should be an every-time habit of all defenders when a shot goes up. No thought should be required. All four steps should become reflex, automatic. They are:

1. Hand up, yell *hey!*
2. Turn around and block out
3. Move toward the basket
4. Fast break

The process could easily be put to music, and the rhythm should lead to consistent execution. Hand-block-seek-go. Hand-block-seek-go. Hand-block-seek-go.

There is never a need to do one without the other. When your hand goes up, your mouth yells *hey!* and your body turns to block. These first two steps are one fluid motion. The next motion, oddly, is often omitted. Players fail to go toward the ball, especially those who usually do not grab the rebounds. They get in the habit of standing and watching, and they lose many tipped balls they could get during the course of a season. All five players should be on the move toward the basket until someone gets possession of the ball. You cannot hope to react to the ball if you are standing while it is tipped around. You need the momentum of going toward the ball to be able to grab it when your opportunity comes.

The final part of the hand-block-seek-go is left out even more often than the seeking of the ball. Players act as though they need a kick in order to realize it is time to break to the other end of the court. The moment you see one of your teammates get possession of the ball, you turn and sprint. If the defense is back, you may decide to slow down. But it is foolish to start slowly. A fast start is very possible and often successful, and it need be nothing more than a habit, an extension of the defensive rebounding *dance*.

33
DEFENDING A STRONGER PLAYER

When you are guarding a stronger player, especially when he has the ball, how do you combat his pivots and his movement to the basket? How do you stay close to him and apply pressure without getting an apparently accidental elbow in your eye? It can be very difficult to apply pressure and hold your ground unless you can protect yourself in the process. Protecting yourself is the key ingredient, because no player is permitted to make contact intentionally. Intentional contact will result in a foul and a turnover, so a strong player who uses his strength merely to run over you or push you is of no particular concern. He is a poor player and will soon be out of the game. The problem is with the good player with strength, more strength than you.

The best way to guard a strong player with the ball is to **keep your forearms up in front of your face.** Keep your hands just to the side of your head or almost in front, with your palms out (facing forward) and your thumbs near your eyes. This is a very natural position, almost like Ali in rope-a-dope, except that your palms face forward, so that you are ready to put your hand up on a shot or to deflect a sudden pass. With your arms next to your body like this, you feel comfortable moving quickly, yet your hands are ready for anything.

The great advantage is that now you can take the pivoting and the swinging elbows and all the aggressiveness of your opponent *on your forearms,* the one place where you don't really mind getting hit. Your nose is no longer at target for an "accidental" elbow, and you need not shy away from an aggressive pivot. You can stay in your opponent's face without fear and without backing off an inch.

Also, by having your hands in the air, visible to the referee, it will not look as though you are responsible for any contact. So any fouls will likely be called on the offensive player as long as you maintain good body position.

This forearms-in-front-of-the-face defense is especially useful in guarding someone inside who is about to turn and take the ball to the basket, in applying pressure in a double-team or after the offensive player has used his dribble. You may find this defensive position useful even when you are guarding someone not as strong as you, but certainly it will be extremely valuable when you are facing a very physical, aggressive player who has great strength.

34
DESPERATION SHOTS

Did you know that even a so-called slow baseball player can get from home plate to first base in about four seconds? (The fast ones do it in three and a half.) That might seem like an insignificant fact for basketball players, except that the distance from home plate to first base is *farther* than the distance from basket to basket on a full-sized basketball court. A court is 94 feet long from baseline to baseline; the bases are 90 feet apart in a baseball diamond.

Are you beginning to guess the point of all this? Game after game, a player with the ball in the backcourt throws up a 60-foot shot because there are only three or four seconds left. Do these players not know that you merely need to get the ball out of your hands before the buzzer sounds in order for the shot to count? Or is it that they think baseball players are a lot faster than basketball players? Would they take the ball upcourt and maneuver for a better shot *if they could wear spikes?*

Whatever the reason they have for "jacking up" a 60-footer with four seconds left, don't you do it. Take the ball upcourt on a full-speed sprint, and get yourself a chance to shoot a shot that you really might make. Plan on shooting with a second left, or less.

If you aren't sure that you can do this, go to a court one day, and take a friend with a watch. Start at the free throw line in the backcourt, and have him count off the seconds, 5...4...3...2...1.... You will be surprised how far you can go, how you even have time to stutter-step and fake and still get to the other end for a good shot. Do this just one day, and you should never again fill the air with a throw at the basket with three seconds left—that is, unless you decide to stop for a sandwich before shooting.

35
DOUBLE-TEAMING ON DEFENSE

Double-teaming poorly is nothing other than very stupid basketball. Committing two defenders to the player with the ball of course leaves three teammates to guard four offensive players, an easy scoring situation *if* the ball is allowed to be passed to the open man.

That "if" is crucial to the two players double-teaming the ball, and it gives them one critical assignment. They must make the player with the ball feel intense pressure, so that he is not free to look around and decide who he would like to throw the ball to. To apply intense pressure, keep your feet wide apart so that the player with the ball cannot step by and beat the double-team. Keep your arms up and waving to distract a pass, but do not jump to block it. Stay on your feet, ready to recover quickly if a successful pass is made.

Although coaches teach the double-team differently (and most don't teach it at all; they simply say, "Get on him. Get all over him. Pressure him. Make it tough."), there are some considerations which are useful if your coach has not specified how he wants it done.

In the backcourt, it is possible to get many steals by allowing the player with the ball to split the double-team and then steal the dribble. Your thinking here is, "Be sure his only possible movement is toward the other double-teamer, and be ready immediately to run with him when he splits the double-team and dribbles up the court." Players in the backcourt are likely to be thinking "dribble" if they are able to split the double-team.

If the split comes as a surprise to you and your defending teammate, you are in trouble, and the other team has a 5-on-3 break. However, if you both force the player with the ball toward each other, *knowing* that a split is the only possible way he can get out, and if you both are *ready* to run alongside him, he will have to be much faster than you to be able to dribble out. In most cases one of you will have an excellent chance of stealing the ball as it is dribbled up court between you.

DOUBLE-TEAMING IN THE BACKCOURT

Here, a dribbler may be allowed to split the two defenders, a risky play for the offense, with the ball still 80 feet from the basket.

In the frontcourt, when you are in a half-court trap, or simply double-teaming out of a man-to-man, you might alter your thinking to this: "Be sure his only possible movement is toward the nearest sideline. He may not split the double-team, but must have only the possibility of dribbling around it, toward the sideline."

If the trap occurs very near the sideline, the double-team is even more effective, since the sideline acts as a third defender. Also, when there is only a half-court to work with, three defenders have a better chance of defending four offensive players, *especially when they know that they only have to defend the narrow side of the court.* When all five defenders know in advance where the ball will be forced, the defense is easier to play effectively.

DOUBLE-TEAMING IN THE FRONTCOURT

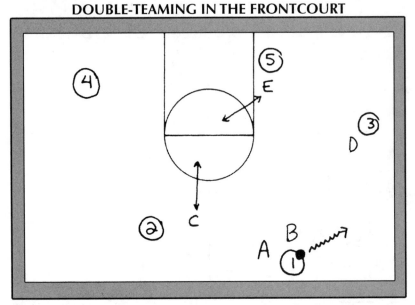

In the frontcourt, a split is more dangerous and may lead to an immediate score. It is better to force the ball to the nearest sideline.

When there is a trap near the sideline, the three others must know that the double-teamers *will not let the player with the ball turn back to the middle.* By knowing this, they can leave a man open on the other side of the court without worrying that he will be the eventual receiver.

If *you* are on defense but not double-teaming, know where the ball is being forced. Prevent the most logical outlet passes, and don't allow a pass for an immediate layup.

A double-team is not something an individual player can pull off effectively just by leaving his man and rushing the ball. The double-teamers must know what they are trying to accomplish, and the three other defenders must be prepared to react accordingly.

36
BEATING DOUBLE-TEAMS

Double-teams must be tough to beat in football. Two big linemen can run at you and stick their helmets in your stomach. But, in basketball, where no one is allowed to touch you, there is no reason that double-teams have to bother you. It is merely a matter of how you think. If, at the moment you see a double-team form, you think, *Oh no, a double-team,* you are likely to panic and throw a lob pass somewhere that someone can intercept.

Your thinking should be, *Oh, here's a 4-on-3 opportunity.* All you have to do is be strong with the ball, be patient, stay low, pivot and look. If you think "tough" and protect the ball, one of your teammates will have time to get open for an easy pass, and your team will have a 4-on-3 scoring opportunity.

What if one of your teammates does not get open for an easy pass? What if they do not run aggressively seeking the pass? The answer is one you should know in advance, before any double-teams ever arise, before the game even starts. **Know which of your teammates is the easiest to throw to.** What does "easiest to throw to" mean? It means the toughest kid, the kid who is most aggressive, a competitor who wants the ball, who likes to get it and who doesn't mind a scuffle or getting his body on the court for a loose ball. Before you go into any game, know who your tough kid is and tell him, "Anytime I get in trouble with the ball, I'm gonna throw it to you."

When you do get double-teamed and in trouble and realize that you need to be getting rid of the ball, call the tough kid, see where he is coming from and then throw the ball where he has a good chance to get it. If you can give him an advantage, so much the better, but if you have to throw it "up for grabs," then fine; you've chosen a good guy for the "grabs."

BEATING A DOUBLE-TEAM

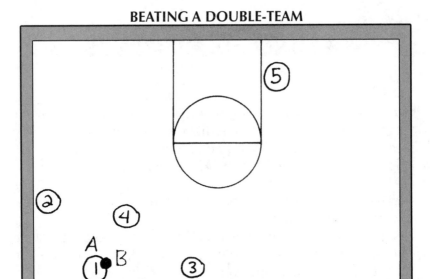

To beat a double-team, bring three players into prime receiving position, six to ten feet from the ball, spread out. With two men on the ball, the defense cannot bring three men up to guard all three receivers or they will be leaving a player wide open under the basket.

A trapping team cannot afford to use up all five defenders within six feet of the ball, and they won't, which is precisely the reason that *going to* the ball makes sense. One of the players near the ball will be open as long as two teammates don't stand next to each other and let one defender guard them both.

37
DRAG A FOOT

There is a "trick" used commonly by the pros to get closer to the basket without a dribble. It's an easy trick, but seldom done by any but the very best amateur players. This is the habit of dragging what will become the pivot foot while receiving the ball.

The average player is generally quite content to move out to the ball with both feet, while the pro will keep one foot as close to the basket as possible and stretch out to the ball so he is just barely able to reach it. Where he gets the ball, once he moves back to his pivot foot, is often six to eight feet closer to the basket than the player who "hops" out and takes the ball without thought for the offensive play to follow the catch.

This pivot-foot-drag is especially useful in receiving the ball on the low post since it may allow the receiver to swing around past the defender without the need of a dribble. The foot is actually "dropped" back just as the ball is about to enter the player's hands.

DRAGGING A FOOT ON THE LOW POST

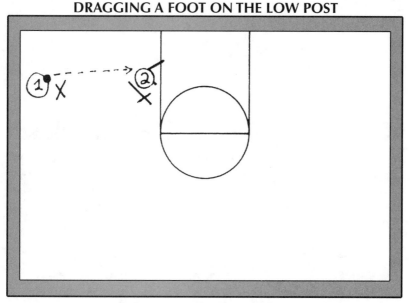

Dropping a foot will permit "2" to shoot a layup without need of a dribble.

Another situation where the *drag* is useful is against a zone defense. When standing between two players to receive a pass, it is possible to stretch out one leg and an arm and give a target for the ball and then step through the defenders (again, without need of a dangerous dribble) once the ball is received.

No special talent is needed to be able to make use of dragging a pivot foot. You merely have to want to get the ball closer to the basket and think about doing it anytime you are standing in a position where you expect a pass may come. Pros use this move so often it is surprising that it is seldom seen on other levels, though of course there are some college players who do it well.

DRAGGING A FOOT AGAINST A ZONE

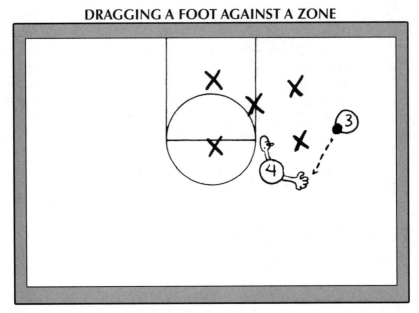

In this drawing, you can see a hand stretching out, presenting a good target for the pass, while a foot is dragged, or kept as close to the basket as possible. As soon as "4" catches the ball, he can step up between the defenders without having to use his dribble to get there, putting tremendous pressure on the zone.

38
THE USE OF ONE DRIBBLE

A dribble is like a burglar alarm. When the opponent hears or sees one, especially a good player, he will get himself in defensive position, a help-and-recover position so that any scoring effort made by the dribbler will be difficult. Against a good team, when all four players off the ball hear that signal, it will be very difficult to score, even if you can beat your man.

For that reason, and despite the fact that reverse-dribbles are useful at times (especially against poor defensive teams), you should learn to score from everywhere with one dribble. That means, when you get the ball in shooting position (at a distance you can shoot from), you should expect to be able to get to the basket in one dribble. This can be done—and is done by good players all the time. It is a matter of wanting to get there in one dribble, practicing and developing the habit. One dribble is explosive, and one dribble does not signal the defense. By the time the defenders see a need to alter position, you are already shooting.

Concentration on scoring with one dribble will pay other dividends. You will rarely be surprised by a defender jumping in front of you, and you will learn to fake your opponent out of position using necessarily quick, violent, effective fakes instead of moseying around hoping for an opening or relying on scoring with indirect moves to the basket. Scoring the drive comes to be seen as going *past* your man, not going *around him*.

The problem with scoring on backyard moves involving reverse dribbles, spins and several dribbles after you get the ball is that these are less effective the better the team is that you play against. Your time is better spent perfecting a style of play which will be effective anywhere, anytime, against anyone.

The mediocre player will likely say, "But if I restrict myself to one dribble, I don't get many opportunities." The good player will admit to himself, "I haven't learned to fake well enough yet." One-dribble moves will provide you all the opportunities you will ever need. And once you learn to use them habitually, you will find that your fakes are so effective and your moves so explosive that once in a while you can take an extra dribble or two—just for showing off!

39
DRIBBLING TOO MUCH

Most basketball players, even the ones who usually don't dribble very much, dribble too much. Drives to the basket that should involve just one explosive dribble are most often made with two or three dribbles, too many to score against a good defensive team. And players stalling or freezing the ball often let themselves be doubled-teamed or fouled because they want to keep pounding the ball to the court instead of quickly passing the ball off.

For many point guards, the problem of one extra dribble is the failure to pass at the right time because of the desire to show off that dribbling ability one more time. For big men inside, often even one dribble is too many. A move should be able to be made effectively without any dribbles at all, so the defensive guards have no chance of stripping the ball on its way up from the floor.

Analyze *your* game. Chances are you often take unnecessary dribbles.

Sometimes, unnecessary dribbles may not seem as though they hurt you, but they always end up hurting a team. Unnecessary dribbles give opponents extra chances to steal the ball or get into the defensive position they want. This lack of purposeful activity encourages the offense to stand around instead of developing precision cuts and perfectly timed passes. Your teammates cannot get a feel for when to cut if *you* are in the habit of taking a few needless dribbles, or even one needless dribble, when you have the ball.

40
DUCKING OUT OF SIGHT

Coaches always tell their defensive players, "See your man and see the ball." And that should tell you, if you want to get open on offense to go somewhere that your defender can *not* see you and the ball. Often, you can do this by ducking and leaning to your defender's back side but hardly moving your feet. The advantage of ducking out of his sight is that you disorient him. You make him wonder momentarily if you have cut backdoor, and you get all his attention—and often his feet—going after you, and then you can react accordingly.

Players trying to get open to receive a pass too often *jockey* back and forth, working very hard but not really going anywhere. Although they think they are confusing the defender because they are faking one way, and the other way, and the other way, and the other way, the defender can guard them by merely standing still.

Choose to go backdoor or choose to come out for the ball. And just before you choose, ducking out of sight, **disappearing low and behind your defender's head will often get you free** by several steps. It works simply because defenders are not accustomed to guarding someone who *disappears!* Either they lose sight of you, giving you the opportunity to thrust out while they are not prepared to move as you do, or they overcommit (thinking you've gone backdoor) and are badly faked out when instead you are suddenly coming out for the ball.

E

41–**EATING**

42–**EFFORT**

43–Guards get to the **ELBOWS** for offensive rebounds

44–**EQUIANGULAR** triangles

45–**EXCUSES**

41
EATING

What you eat makes no difference. If you play on a team that has carefully prepared training meals, wonderful. Thank whoever it is that provides them. But don't make the mistake of going into a game with a negative attitude because you ate too much or too early or too little or too late. Great games have been played on full stomachs, on empty stomachs, on spaghetti, on hamburgers, on diets, on hunger strikes.

What you eat is not a crucial factor. If you are lucky enough to get a steak four hours before the game, great, super, wow. But don't ever let yourself be heard grumbling or even thinking about how hungry or how full you are.

Good players can always play well. The food is incidental, psychological and unworthy of your attention. It might be wise to eat a while before you play, so your nervousness has less of a chance of causing you an upset stomach near game time. It might also be wise to eat something within a day or two of playing a game, so you feel energetic.

But just remember one thing: If you ever blame a game performance on something concerning eating, that's just a bunch of garbage.

42
EFFORT

I hope that you aren't one of those guys walking around thinking you give 100%. Because you don't. You loaf. Everyone loafs. And the guys that come closest to giving 100% know this better than the others. No one gives 100%. There are so many things you can do in a basketball game, so many opportunities to help out a bit more on defense or to overplay a bit more, or to run back faster or block out better...the list is endless.

Good players know after a game, even a game in which they played well according to the papers, that they could have done more, could have hustled better, could have made a few more things happen *if only they hadn't rested at the wrong time,* if only they had put out just a little more.

It is not simply a matter of conditioning. Of course, good players are going to be in good condition. A good coach gets even mediocre players in condition. It is simply that **you can always do more.**

Your only chance to approach your potential is to strive constantly to do more—always with a nagging sense of inadequacy, of having loafed and failed. Satisfied players are rarely good ones.

43
GUARDS GET TO THE ELBOWS FOR OFFENSIVE REBOUNDS

Give a guard defensive responsibility against a potential fast break, and half the time or more you end up with only four players playing on offense, especially on rebounds. This is as true in college as it is in high school, and it shows that often even a so-called heady little guard isn't thinking about what contribution he can make (in addition to merely doing his job).

Unless the defensive team is in the habit of releasing a sprinter/cherry picker without even waiting to see what the shot does, there is no reason for a guard on the shooting team to drop back in the midcourt area and watch the game. Guards everywhere do this, and coaches often forget to correct them. But there are a lot of tipped balls and long rebounds that fall somewhere near the free throw line or a bit in front of it. These balls are easily scooped up by any alert guard who decides to hang around and see what happens instead of just drifting backward.

When the shot goes up, two guards can go to either corner of the free throw line and lean toward the basket while watching for any possible defenders wanting to leave early and score an easy layup after a long pass.

Most teams do not automatically release someone, so the majority of the time it is possible for the guards to go to the free throw line corners, called the *elbows,* and wait. If the ball rebounds long, one or both can go for it; if the other team gets the rebound, they can get back.

GUARDS GET TO THE ELBOWS FOR OFFENSIVE REBOUNDS

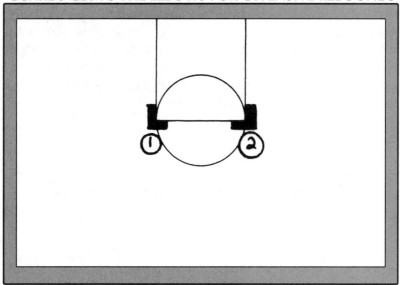

Lean toward the basket and look for cutters. Don't stand 40 feet back if you don't have to.

Remember, no one is saying you should stay up at the elbow if a cutter has run down the court. Then it makes sense to go with him, and the rebounding situation is four against four. The stupid thing is drifting back for no reason, guarding no one and watching as four rebounders battle against five.

Guards can, and good guards do, wait and watch and decide according to the circumstances, not drop back and watch 50 feet from the basket. Just because you have been given *back responsibility* does not mean you have to be back. It simply means you have to be able to beat anyone else back.

Some players may ask, "What if I look for the rebound and decide I can get it, but I don't, and the other team scores a layup?"

The answer to that is simple. Stay back. If that happens to you consistently, you have poor judgment. *That* could only happen once a season to a good player, and it can certainly happen once a season from wherever he chooses to stand. It has happened enough times that a guard back by midcourt sees a ball batted out toward the top of the key or beyond and finally decides he should get that ball, then tries, fails, and the other team gets by for a layup. So the distance you are back is no assurance that the one exception won't happen, unless you are committed never to try for any ball regardless of where it goes.

The intelligent thing for a good player to do is to get himself in a position where he can be most useful and do the most possible things. As far as offensive rebounding is concerned, that position is on the elbows, very ready to get back with a sudden cutter and very ready to leap for a long rebound. In playing against a 2-3 zone, it is especially easy for the guards to slip in for long rebounds; you should seek them always and go for them when your judgment dictates.

44
EQUIANGULAR TRIANGLES

Equiangular triangles are useful for remembering how to receive a ball when playing against a zone defense. Too many players forget to alter their position as the ball moves and the zone shifts, but thinking of equiangular triangles (triangles having three equal angles) should help you to move where you can be most effective.

Against a zone, you want to receive the ball each time in a position where *two* defenders feel they need to take you. Then, theoretically at least, every time you have the ball you have four teammates to throw to who are guarded by only three men. By keeping the ball moving, to places where two men must scramble to take the ball, the zone will soon get distorted out of shape and someone will be wide open for a shot.

EQUIANGULAR TRIANGLES

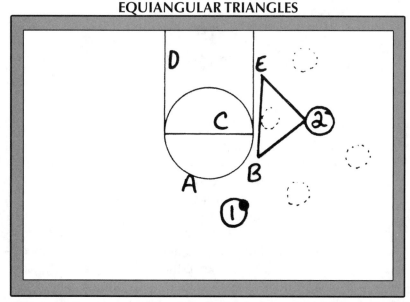

Offensive player 2, to stand in the perfect position to receive a pass, forms an equiangular triangle with two defenders, so that both think they must take him when he receives the ball. Number 2 should not be too close to "B" and "E," nor even with either of them where it would be obvious which one should take him.

The dotted circles show positions too close to the defense, too far away and matched up beside only one defender. None of these positions puts pressure on the zone, but 2's position does.

Players make the mistake of standing and waiting for the ball without regard for placement between defenders. A pass to them is very easy for the zone to guard since it can easily match up with each player on the offensive team. Quick passes are of no value when the zone does not have to move swiftly to cover them.

Stand between two men, not so close to them (as in a sandwich) that the ball cannot be thrown to you and not so far away that you are no threat to either of them. Try to maintain a position so that you are one of the points of a triangle that has all equal angles. This will mean that you are always in a position to receive the ball, yet close enough to the defense to force them to commit two guys to you immediately.

45
EXCUSES

Excuses have already been covered under "Alibis," but this subject is so important, it seems worth repeating.

Excuses are for mediocre players. Forget them. There are thousands of excuses available to all losers. To have a good excuse is to have what every other loser in the history of the world has had. Don't make the ridiculous mistake of thinking that your particular brand of excuse is somehow more valid than the last 20 million that have been uttered. You can hope your mother will believe you and maybe your girl friend—or at least they may sympathize and keep their mouths shut if they don't, but everyone else knows an excuse when he hears it.

Your particular excuse is just as stupid as everyone else's. There. Now you know it. Now you are free to accomplish things, and to work, and to concentrate.

Forget about excuses. They are enormous wastes of time and words.

THE WORLD IS ROUND

Athletes go through school playing "mere games" and preparing for life, for becoming doctors and lawyers and so forth. And doctors and lawyers wait for five o'clock so they can leave work, maybe catch the game of the week on TV and sit around and talk of the good old days—when they were young athletes.

F

46
FAKING ON DEFENSE

Faking on defense is something rarely done except by good players. Most players are merely hoping to *get by* on defense; they aren't really trying to create anything. A player who does fake on defense stands out as a good player. As with offensive faking, *how* the good player fakes on defense is not as important a consideration as *does* he fake on defense. Look at some of the situations where faking on defense will be helpful.

When your man has the ball, fake at him to try to get him to commit himself too soon. For example, you may fake with your hands to give him the feeling that you are too close, too worried about his outside shot. Then when he drives for the basket, you are prepared since you know you are purposely acting overaggressively. In the same way, you might fake to one side to encourage him to go in the other direction. You give the impression that you are overplaying one side, while knowing that you are trying to get him to go to the other.

When you are not guarding the ball but are on the ball side of the court, many times you can fake at the dribbler as though you are about to double-team, even though you know you are planning to stay with your man. By doing this, you may get a dribbler to pick up the ball or discourage him from trying to penetrate to your side.

When you are playing a zone defense, often you can pretend that you are about to dart out to intercept a perimeter pass, even though you know you are going to stay inside and prevent a pass to the middle. With this movement, you may get a player to throw a pass right into the area you are concentrating on (since he thinks you are about to leave it). At least you may slow down the movement of the ball on the outside and prevent a rapid swing of the ball from one side to the other because the passer has to worry about what you are going to do.

When you are playing a man on the low post, you can give the impression you are about to dart out and intercept a pass into him (by playing on the side of him and lunging out a bit the moment the player with the ball looks in) even though you know that your primary concern may be to stay between your man and the basket.

On the jump circle, it is often possible to discourage the jumper from tapping to a certain man (even a bigger, stronger player who could certainly get the ball from you). Stand there looking aggressive as though you are about to jump in front of him the moment the ball is tapped.

There are times in a full-court press when a back man can "play possum" and pretend he is not ready to cover someone, thereby encouraging a pass to be thrown that he is prepared to intercept. All of these situations, and there are many more, require thinking and effort— probably the two primary requisites of good defense.

Ask yourself about *your* defense. Are you conscious of faking often in a variety of situations? If you aren't, don't fool yourself—you don't play well. If you do, then you are very likely a good player, and you should be constantly looking for new situations where fakes can be effective.

How can fakes help in defending a 2-on-1 break? How can fakes help you slow down a fast breaking team's quick outlet passes? You should be able to find ways to fake in almost every defensive situation.

47
FAKING ON OFFENSE

Fakes, almost all fakes, work great in games, and there is a very good reason why. Most players, even a lot of good ones, don't fake, or at least not very often. As a result, very few defenders have had the opportunity to react to fakes, so when they meet one in a game, they fall for it and get faked out.

The most important rule on faking is, "Use fakes!" Need this be further emphasized?

You don't fake enough. Fake more. Fake more than you do now. Fake, fake, fake.

Lead fakes (fake passes that lead the defense away from your pass) are especially useful against zone defenses. They require no particular ability or effort. Players just forget to use them.

Foot fakes are extremely useful when you have the ball in scoring position and you haven't dribbled yet, but the biggest problem with these is that players tend to hurry foot fakes and walk with the ball, and referees love to make that call. You have to be careful.

If you are going to step one way and cross over, make sure you step-and-step-again *with the same foot.* Don't drag that back (pivot) foot at all because referees can't wait to blow their whistle on this move. This is so true that **it isn't even wise to try a fake-and-crossover move in the second half of a close game** unless you have already used it earlier and the referees have learned that you can make the move without walking. It doesn't do you any good to note a day later on the game films that you really didn't walk. **Don't surprise referees with new things at the end of a big game** when they are as tense and anxious as you are.

As for the fake-and-crossover itself, to do it well and make it work, be sure you don't just move your foot. Move your head and your shoulders and your hip and the ball, and do it all violently so it really looks as though you are going that way. *Violently* does not necessarily mean quickly, at least not like lightning. **Defenders need time to go for your fakes.** Don't make the mistake of making your fakes so fast that defenders, even those who are very willing to be faked out, don't have time to go for them.

Once your body is down, coiled and ready to spring to the other side, be sure that you do spring from the down-coiled position instead of lifting your head and coming back before crossing over. The important thing is to keep your head down and your shoulders down over the ball so you take full advantage of your opponent's movement. This way you can protect the ball and place it on the floor exactly where you want it.

The biggest mistake players make in faking is that they think they have to get through the fake quickly and get on with their real purpose—their move to the basket, and the result is a poor, unconvincing fake. Stay low so you can maneuver precisely. You may think that by staying low you are sacrificing speed, but **players who fake and put the ball on the floor far out in front of them, just a few inches off the floor, are very difficult to guard.**

The fake-and-crossover and lead fakes against a zone are two of the more common offensive fakes. There are, of course, many other situations where faking is useful. Don't worry too much about how to fake. Concentrate instead on your opponent. Keep trying to get him to do what you want him to do. You can learn by trial-and-error on the playground or in the backyard. Think about using the fakes you know, and work to incorporate more and more fakes into your normal game.

48
FAKING SHOTS

Shot-fakes work great. It is wonderful fun to watch an opponent go sailing over your head after a faked shot, just as it is fun for him to leap and put your shot into the ninth row. In fact, it is so much fun to knock a ball into the ninth row, that the mere possibility of it will make most defenders try for it again and again without even considering how often they are getting faked out and made to look stupid instead.

The good thing for shot-fakers is that this situation is not likely to change. Fans don't hate a defender who leaps out of position nearly as much as they love one who occasionally knocks a ball into the stands. So, since players do love to please fans, there will always be players who are anxious to leap and make you look good if you have the patience to fake before you shoot the ball.

The essentials of the shot-fake aren't difficult at all, though most inexperienced players incorrectly imagine a shot-fake being a motion with the ball toward the basket. **A good shot-fake is a bend of the knees and a look at the rim with the ball cocked at the chin.** From that position you can do anything—shoot, drive into the basket or throw a quick pass. It is a mistake to go through with the upward motion of the ball. (You think a blocked shot is bad; imagine the disgrace of a blocked fake.) A cock at the chin and a look at the rim is all you need to make the defender leap provided you are in a position of danger. Of course, if you are not, the greatest motion in the world, including an actual shot itself, won't make the defender budge. If you cock and look, and the defender doesn't move, it's time to go for it. Take the shot.

The most important thing with a fake-pass or a fake-drive or a fake-shot is that you **fake to a position that will gain you an advantage if your opponent doesn't go for it.** Step to a position so that you can drive right from there if the defender doesn't move. Fake a pass in such a way that if the defender doesn't stick his hand there, you can pass right from there. And fake a shot in such a way that if your opponent doesn't go for the fake, you are ready to shoot immediately with no other movement.

Some coaches call the inside shot-fake a "pump fake," since all you do is make a quick pumping motion with your body while the ball stays by your chin and your knees stay bent. You are ready to shoot immediately after the fake, or even during the fake if it is clear that the defender has no intention (or capability) of blocking your shot.

49
FAST BREAK FANCY

Many players dream about dribbling downcourt on a 2-on-1 break and going up in the air and flipping a behind-the-back pass to a teammate for the score. Wow, whatta play! The fans go wild, and the coach goes, *"Oh no!"* because while the fans are thinking *wow*, the coach is thinking, "The more difficult plays you make in a season, the more turnovers you will have." For every great pass you make, you are likely to have a turnover pass as well.

A 2-on-1 is an *advantage* situation. When you have more players than they do, you don't need a great pass or a fancy play. You simply need to give the ball to the player who is unguarded. The same is true of a 3-on-2 or a 4-on-3 break. These situations don't require great plays. And not only do they not *require* great plays, a great play shows the coach that the player used poor judgment.

There are simple ways to score the 2-on-1 and the 3-on-2 break, and these simple ways can work over and over again **with simple, sure passes.** Why use passes that often fool your own teammates as much as or more than they fool the other team?

Learn how to score the advantage fast break situations the simple ways, the ways your coach gives you (or the ways in this book if he doesn't), and then do that in games. The best way to turn on the fans is to win, and winning is most easily done when simple plays are performed simply. If you have an urgent need for the spectacular, get your coach's permission. Chances are if you ask him before a game, he will let you throw a behind-the-back pass on a 2-on-1 break at the end of the game after you are ahead by 20.

Remember: The best way to win is by learning to do simple things simply. Advantage fast breaks are not complex. Don't treat them as if they are.

50
FAT DEFENSE

"**F**AT" is a made-up word for "**F**ake **A**nd **T**hreaten." This is the kind of defense you need to use when you are not guarding the ball but the ball is being dribbled toward you, or when you are trying to stop a fast break and hoping to get the dribbler to commit himself. You might also use FAT defense in a zone, while you are trying to guard two men, or when you want to guard a man inside but give a man outside the impression that you will not let him shoot.

FAT can be anything that indicates to the player with the ball that you are about to do something that you are not really about to do. Defensive players usually play too passively. A good defensive player must learn to stay with his man while still making fakes and threatening the ball and getting the ball to commit.

FAT should help you to remember that a good defender is not content just to run back on defense alongside his man. Get back and face the ball, and be prepared to fake and threaten the ball to discourage a pass or a penetration. Defense cannot be played passively if you want to win.

51
THE FIRST-PASS SHOT

Most players, even lazy ones, give the impression they are ready to play good defense during the first five seconds of any defensive play. Most of them have been drilled enough that they are even willing to turn and block out the man they are guarding, if he happens to be near them when the shot goes up. As a result, any shot taken after only one pass is likely to be well defended, and followed by five men blocking out for the rebound, and prepared to fast break immediately. What could be easier? Two to five seconds on defense, no cuts to guard, no man to chase, no screens to get over or through, no fakes to worry about. One pass from the point guard to the side, and the shot goes *up*.

It should be obvious, when you think about this, that the first-pass shot should be refused—even if it is a good shot, so that the same shot can be taken later when each defender is not in a position to block out and immediately fast break.

In a midget league, everyone is so happy to have a scoring opportunity that the ball flies upward at the first sign of daylight. But good players can always find some daylight, and the daylight after several passes and cuts will yield a much better scoring opportunity *and* defensive capability than if the shot is put up after the first pass. (This of course applies to offense against a set defense, not fast breaks where the advantage situation may not come up again and where the rebounding opportunity is even better than it would be in a five-on-five.)

There are, in addition, the added benefits of better teamwork being fostered by more than one pass each time down on offense. But that is a byproduct. Even if the team "agrees" with the shot and the shooter, and even if morale would not suffer as a result of some first-pass shots being taken, good players will refuse them anyway. The percentages favor that refusal. Very, very seldom is a first-pass shot rebounded by the offensive team.

Special note to point guards:
It should go without saying that dribbling downcourt
and shooting anything but a layup—with no passes at
all—should be avoided completely.

52
FLEET

Fleet means quick-moving, and here it is also a made-up word for "**FL**oored fe**EET**." Feet on the floor, on defense. If you happen to be a great leaper, your coach may give you a different rule from the one that follows. But if you are anything less, you should follow this rule conscientiously.

Never leave your feet on defense, not even to block a pass, not even to block a shot. For every pass you block by jumping, two will get by you, and you will be slow getting to a good defensive help-position because you are not FLEET when you are in the air. You have to wait until you come down to move. For every shot you block, twice you will foul unnecessarily and another time or two the shooter will miss but be able to run by you for the rebound since you can not block out in the air. You have to wait until you come down.

A great leaper might be permitted to jump occasionally, and then again a great leaper might just be the guy who needs this rule more than anyone. Because great leapers have the tendency to want to show off their leaping ability, consequently they are frequently in the air and not in good defensive position.

By staying on the floor, you stay FLEET, always ready to move, ready to respond immediately to each new position of the ball. Do you have to let people shoot? Of course not. You get a hand in the shooter's face just like always, and you attempt to distract the shooter, and you try to make him think you are going to jump for his shot. If the offensive player is so clever that, even though you are crowding him and distracting him, he still puts the ball up right in your face and hits that shot consistently, then it might be time to run over to the bench and ask your coach if just once you can put his ball in the ninth row since he has the idea you will not jump under any circumstances.

Seldom, however, has there been such a clever offensive player. Even more seldom are there players who can hit consistently from outside when there is a hand always threatening to touch the ball as they bring it up to shoot (and waving in their face as they take the shot). If there is a player that good, most likely he will score on *you* regardless of what you do!

Jumping is not a valuable skill on defense (unless you are a gifted, intimidating center). Even in a defense such as a 1-3-1 trap, it is wise not to jump to try to touch passes. Keep your hands up, forcing lob passes or bounce passes (slow passes) and then be ready to move immediately to get the best possible defensive position.

Don't jump. Never leave your feet. Keep your feet on the floor at all times on defense. Stay Fleet.

Are there exceptions to this rule? Yes. On a last-second shot where there will be no rebound or no new defensive position to get, you will want to distract the shooter as much as possible or even touch the ball, so okay, jump, but make sure you don't jump into the man and foul him. Jumping is an aggressive move, and referees will be "whistle-ready" when you do it even if you don't touch the man. "With the body!" referees like to say. The foul was with the body, and that happens most frequently when the body is in the air.

In the three-second lane, you or your coach may decide that it is worth jumping to block a shot since the offensive player has only three seconds to do something. Perhaps, even if he does fake you, one of your teammates will have time to get there to jump and block his shot when he finally takes it. If your team has the habit of converging on the man with the ball in the lane, then theoretically one of you could go in the air after each fake, and the shot could never be taken.

With or without the exceptions, the facts are that players who are in the habit of leaving their feet are also in the habit of being out of defensive position and in the habit of fouling unnecessarily. Blocked shots and passes usually occur in easy games you would have won anyway, and the success that you feel, the easy layup or the crowd applause will tend to reinforce your jumping behavior and encourage you to do it in tough games where you won't touch the ball anyway, but your poor defensive position will hurt your team.

Most guards should never leap. Keep your feet on the floor. Like it or not, you are not tall. You do not command the skies. Rather than try to show that you can compete with the big boys, stay low and fast and command the floor, getting to big guys' dribbles and getting underfoot to draw charges.

Great leapers should avoid the tendency to show off that ability at the wrong times. Show it off rebounding, not on defense. And on defense, learn to stalk your prey. Slyly wait. Stay in good defensive position, and seek that one great opportunity to block a shot. Then the rest of the game you can get the same result (or even a better result) by simply intimidating but not shot blocking. A missed shot rebounded is more valuable to your team than a shot knocked into the third row. If you learn to stalk your prey and don't go for fakes very often, you will force a lot of too-quick shots that miss. And you will still get your share of blocked shots on layups and other plays when you see that you can touch a ball after it is already in the air. You are not told never to jump, but to **jump less often, only when the ball or shooter is already in the air.**

Forwards and centers who are not great leapers should concentrate their attention on not letting their man get the ball inside in the lane. Never leap on defense, except perhaps when the ball is in the lane. Wave and intimidate and fake at the first thrust, and jump straight up on the second. Never do this outside the lane. It is better to distract and maintain rebounding position. But in the lane, give a huge-fake-on-first-thrust, then jump-straight-up-with-hands-straight-up.

53
FLING

"**F**ling" is the name for a play that scores against a zone just about every time, but players fail to look for it. Not that it can always be done—it can't. But when it is possible to throw the ball from the side of the court to the corner of the free throw line, it is usually possible to fling the ball to a teammate on the other side of the foul circle for an easy shot. It works like magic because the nature of zone defenses is to put more defenders on the side of the ball than there are offensive players.

Zone defenses make it difficult to get the ball to the high post from the side. However, when you finally are able to get it there on a pass from the side, very often the post man tries to go one-on-one (even though it's a zone), or he passes the ball back out from where it came. It is not a natural move to **turn with your back to the basket and fling the ball out to the other side,** but players who learn to make that move give their teammates baskets constantly.

The natural thing to do is to turn and face the basket (not a bad habit at all) and perhaps look for a baseline cutter. Occasionally, this *is* open, so players do not learn to look for the fling. Yet, good players will want to be aware of it because that pass is consistently open and yields not only an unguarded 15-foot shot most of the time, but it also yields a good offensive rebounding opportunity since the entire defense concentrates more on shifting to the other side of the court than on getting position for the rebound. The fling pass is such a high-percentage scoring opportunity that many top coaches don't even want their high post men facing the basket when they receive a pass from the side. The fling is just too good to pass up.

FLING AGAINST A ZONE

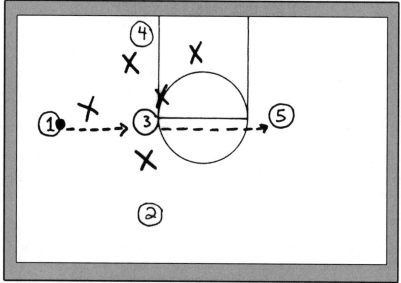

The "fling" is an easy scoring opportunity against almost all zones. The ball goes from one side, 1, to the high post, 3, and immediately to the other side, 5, for the shot.

Naturally, on a chalkboard, it is possible to draw in defenders to make the play look easy or difficult. But the defenders in the drawing aren't too far off from where they will be in a game. The defense will make it difficult to get the ball to 3, but if you can get it to him, the pass to 5 is easy nearly every time.

The main thing to remember? Expect to have to receive the ball on the run, going toward the ball, and then pivot with your back to the basket. Otherwise, you will have to throw the ball through a defender carefully instead of being able to fling it to the open man on the other side.

54
FORGET FADEAWAYS

Though players, even great players, love shooting fadeaways, the game of basketball would be none the worse off nor would any teams have worse records, and a lot of teams would have much better records, if the fade-away jump shot were simply banned or called a violation.

In the final three seconds of play, there may be a reason for a fade-away sometime, but even then, in most cases a two-shot foul could be drawn and maybe a three-point play scored if the shooter would take the ball straight up instead.

Players who rely on fadeaways apparently don't know that fadeaways are poor-percentage shots, and they probably don't know how to fake very well either.

It would be possible to include tables and percentages to prove the case against fadeaways, but that shouldn't be necessary. Talk to any winning coach and find out what he thinks about them. He will tell you they lose games. Is that simple enough?

Even though you may be good at fadeaways, forget fadeaways.

55
"DON'T GET FOULED!"

This phrase may confuse a lot of players, but it doesn't confuse many coaches. It is a phrase a coach might use in practice when you go driving into the basket and miss a short shot. The coach says, "Don't miss those easy ones. You gotta hit those."

"But Coach," you say, "I was fouled."

And the coach responds, *"Don't get fouled!"*

What did he say? Is *he* crazy? How can you help it if you get fouled?

The point is, you *can* help it. **You can learn to play in a way that fouls don't bother you.** You don't take shots that a slight shove will bother, and you don't dribble near enough to the sideline so that a small bump will put you out of bounds. Good players don't do things that depend on referees' decisions. When you go for a shot, you have to assume that no foul will be called. When you dribble the ball someplace, you have to assume you will be bumped and be prepared for it. You can't play hoping the referee will notice *why* you missed or *why* you stepped out of bounds. You can't rely on referees, you must rely on yourself. Do things decisively, forcefully, prepared for the bumps and fouls that may or may not be called.

When you play good, solid, decisive basketball, you understand the phrase, "Don't get fouled." You don't take the ball to some vulnerable place. You don't get yourself in some whirling loop-dee-loop shooting position. You learn to beat your man so decisively that he can't even get close enough to foul you.

Some players are thinking, "Yeah, but what about when I get the ball under the basket? How can I keep from getting fouled down there?" Okay, sure, of course there are situations where you cannot prevent someone from fouling you. In fact, under the basket, getting fouled is precisely what you want to do. You want to take the ball up strong, right up through the defender's nostrils. To have a chance to stop you, he *must* foul you. That's great, but that is not at all what "Don't get fouled" applies to.

Good players should know that inside play demands toughness, the willingness to seek contact and the ability to score despite the foul, while play away from the basket requires intelligence and good judgment, playing in such a way that reaches and bumps can have no effect on the action.

56
FOULING A SHOOTER

Very seldom should a shooter be fouled. When you foul a shooter, you give him a chance for three (or four) points, and often you give two (or three) easy foul shots to a guy who was not likely to make his shot anyway. In those cases when a big man gets the ball under the basket, and you know he is a very poor free throw shooter, and it is late in the game, then if you decide to foul rather than give away the sure two points, be sure you foul decisively. Grab the shooter's shooting arm forcefully. Nothing looks much worse than half-hearted attempts or lazy fouls that not only don't bother the shot, but also give the scorer another shot from the free throw line as well. Fouling lazily or hitting the nonshooting arm or pushing the body is a three-point invitation, and three-point plays spark teams.

Do not give three-point plays. **Either foul the shooting arm decisively or don't foul at all.** Early in the game, it is probably better not to foul at all. The foul shooter will not be so nervous early in the game and, therefore, has a better chance of hitting his free throws. Also you will be putting your opponents in a bonus situation sooner, and you will put yourself one foul closer to the disqualifying five. Better to get your intentional fouls at late in the game when you know you have fouls to spare, when the other team is already in a bonus situation and when the circumstances tend to make the free throw shooter feel the pressure and be more likely to miss.

The trade-off early in the game, stopping two sure points in exchange for two free throws, probably is not worth the possible consequences. Late in the game, the trade-off might be well worth it, and your awareness and quick fouling decision could save your team the game.

57
FOULING BAD SHOTS

This situation happens enough, at least once a game, that it needs its own separate explanation even though the details are very simple. **Never foul a difficult shot.** Game after game, players go driving into the basket and get themselves underneath or stretched out; their only opportunity to shoot is some off-balance, whirling, loop-dee-loop throw. Then some eager but stupid defender swings at the ball and fouls. In a flash, a two-percent shot has become a two-shot foul, almost certainly one point and very possibly two.

If they want to hang themselves, give them rope!

Don't try to prevent a shot that you are happy for them to take.

Let them. Whirling, loop-dee-loop throws don't go in that often. But they are constantly fouled.

Don't *you* do that.

If your opponent wants to take a low-percentage shot or a long jumper off-balance, let him. Sure, he may score one sometime. But it won't happen often.

Let people shoot their bad shots. Don't send them to the free throw line.

58
FOULS ARE ERRORS

Players often fail to realize that fouls are errors. Not just because five of them will put you on the bench, but because they allow mediocre players to score points on unmolested 15-foot shots.

Someone dribbles down the court, you reach out, get called for a foul and think, *Oh well, no big thing.* It is early in the game or second half, they only get to take the ball out and the game goes on. The problem is, several minutes later, after several of the team members have a similar "harmless" foul, some mediocre player who doesn't have a single move in his repertoire gets bumped on a rebound and goes to the line for a one-and-one. And *you* don't even feel responsible as the awkward guy struts up to the line and hits two. When you foul, you are in the habit of thinking, *Oh well, that's only my first,* instead of, *I just gave them two points.*

During the course of a half of aggressive play, there are likely to be several unavoidable fouls, but not usually enough to get the other team in the bonus situation unless there are careless, needless-error fouls, too.

The next time you make one of those early "oh well" fouls, remember that you may be giving the opponent two points they otherwise never would have gotten. Don't be smug simply because it isn't obvious to the fans that you gave those points that eventually lost the game.

Good players know the importance of not fouling.

Except in very few cases, fouls are errors.

59
"MUST FOUL" SITUATIONS

If you get to the point in the game when your team is behind and you must stop the clock and hope they miss free throws, be sure you foul intelligently. The difference between a two-shot foul or a one-and-one and two shots *and* the ball is obvious and enormous. For this reason, you must make sure that your intentional foul looks unintentional. You can do that by thinking **steal** and by going for the steal aggressively, knowing that if you can't get the ball cleanly, you are willing to **chop the arm off** at the elbow to be sure you make contact.

Go for the steal, not for the foul, but know that you are going for it very aggressively so that you either get the ball or the whistle blows. *Do* go for the ball. By going for the ball, it will certainly look as though you are going for the steal (because you are). If your intent is merely to foul, very often it may look just like that, like you are trying to foul... *two shots and the ball!*

Go for the ball. Who knows? You may even surprise yourself someday by getting it without fouling and winning the game. The important thing is to go for the ball. If an elbow or wrist gets grabbed in the process, so be it.

NEED A CRYSTAL BALL?

Any lapse of effort, temper, or concentration due to a missed shot, a bad pass, a referee's call or any other every–game event is not only costly to your team, it is also an absurd lack of foresight on your part. What do you expect?

G

60
GETTING THE BALL

Players shouldn't be shy about asking for the ball. This does not mean getting open one time, yelling for the ball, not getting it, and then walking around pouting the next few minutes because someone wouldn't give you the ball. The "He's a ball hog" theory is correct a lot less often than the "He just didn't see you that time" theory; all too often the problem is that you didn't look very open.

No one should expect to get the ball even half of the times he is open. You should expect something more like one out of ten. Therefore, you should put a definite plan into effect that can help you get the ball more often.

Forwards and centers who don't feel they are getting the ball enough need to make special efforts to change that. Number one, tell the guards to get the ball to you, and you will get it right back to them. That's a good way to begin. Every player likes knowing he has the possibility of passing the ball, shaking his man and then getting an immediate return pass. So that ought to get the guards wanting to throw you the ball. After you pass back a few times, you can mix in a few fakes and do your own thing, and you should be able to end up with a good mixture of passes and shots along with being generally spotted more often when you are free.

However, even if you have guards who are receptive to throwing you the ball, you still need to "train" them. You need to help them learn when you are open. You do that by calling for the ball whenever you get free. You don't keep yelling and getting disgusted and making faces. You simply get free, crisply shout the player's name who has the ball and do that again and again. You ask for the ball. You don't plead for it. Get free, shout crisply and move away again. If you are willing to be patient and to keep getting free and shouting for the ball, soon your guards will learn to see you when you get free.

Running around quietly makes no sense. You do need to make the fact that you are free clear to the people who can throw you the ball.

To make sure your guards don't get irritated with you, tell them that you don't expect them to throw you the ball every time you yell, but that you just want them to know that you are there if they need you or want to pass.

Guards, too, need to ask for the ball, especially in the outlet areas after a rebound, or at the foul line when the defense has converged on a big man who has the ball inside. Again, clap or shout crisply. Make the man immediately aware of where you are, but with the understanding that you don't expect the ball necessarily to be thrown to you.

Remember, above all, that you will get the ball only a small percentage of the times you are free. Don't waste your time pouting over times they don't pass to you. That is like complaining about spilled milk. What's done is done. Forget about it. Spend your time looking for the *next* pass, not complaining. Not receiving passes when you are free is a fact of court life. If you don't understand this, you don't understand the game.

A player with the ball would first like to score. Second, he wants to dribble and not lose the ball. Third, he will try to run the team's offense, and finally there is his girlfriend in the stands, his friends, his personal goals, his post-game plans and maybe even his poor vision. Like it or not, no player is intent on getting you the ball except as a distant priority— especially if you're in the habit of complaining when you don't get the ball, you miss it or fail to go after it aggressively when it is thrown to you, or you strut back like a superstar after you do get a pass and score. None of these reactions will help you get the ball more often. If you want to help alter the passers' priorities though, try these reactions:

1. Compliment a pass all the time.
2. Throw the ball back often to the guy who throws it to you, and do it immediately so it sticks in his mind that you often give it right back.
3. Move to get open constantly, so players with the ball get in the habit of you being open.
4. Yell, but don't nag, to let them know when you get open.
5. Go aggressively to meet the ball when it *is* thrown to you.
6. If a pass is thrown to you and you don't get it, say you "Should've had it" **even if you think it was a bad pass.**

Don't do this last one for the sake of nobility. You are free to be your normal, selfish self here. Saying you should've had it is solely for the purpose of getting the ball more in the future. Who cares whose fault it was? The play is over, and the coach will have his opinion of who was at fault regardless of what you say to the passer. You say "My fault" to the passer for one reason—so he continues to look for you, feel good about you and *want* to give you the ball.

Do all these things and you will certainly get the ball more often and likely enjoy playing the game more too.

61
GNAW-POCKET DEFENSE

When a dribbler gets by you, there are two possible reactions. The most common is to turn and watch as his rear-end gets farther and farther away from you. The other reaction is to realize you are getting beaten, **turn quickly and low and get your mouth down where you could gnaw, or bite, his pocket** if it were sticking out. By this second reaction it is possible to get a lot of steals, especially if you force your man to his weak side because his tendency (thinking he has passed you) is going to be to put the ball back in his strong hand, precisely the side you are on. Very possibly, his first strong-handed dribble will be right in front of your face where you can swipe it without having to reach across his body or foul.

The only reason there are not more steals from behind like this is that players who are lackadaisical enough on defense to let themselves get beaten are usually too lackadaisical to think about recovering aggressively and "gnawing that pocket," hoping for the dribble in front of their nose. The chance of getting the ball with this type of maneuver is so good that this can be used purposefully at the end of a game when you are behind when you need a steal. (See "How to Make a Game-winning Steal," entry #69.)

Under normal game conditions, a steal is not the point of gnaw-pocket defense. You *must* get in the habit of beating the ball downcourt and of chasing the ball furiously, desperately, any time it beats you.

Think of the enormous difference in the defense based on the two possible reactions. If you get beaten and just watch as the rear-end disappears, your teammates picking up will have to decide whether to leave their men free near the basket or give your man a short jumper. Either way, the opposing team will probably score.

However, even though you get beaten, if you gnaw-pocket beside your man, your teammates can easily see that they do not have to stop the short jumper. If he stops, you will have time to get a hand in his face. They also can see that he cannot go one way (the side you are on). That means all they have to do is prevent him from driving all the way in for a layup while being ready to recover out to their own men. This kind of help-and-recover situation, where the dribbler's path is obvious and limited, is often drilled on by most teams and quite well-defended in many cases. The best a team can get is a jumper with a hand quickly in the shooter's face, not at all the high-percentage opportunity that the turn-and-watch-the-rear-end-disappear situation presents.

62
GOALS

Scientific experimentation has shown conclusively the value of setting goals. If you have to prepare and mail a thousand letters, and if someone else who works exactly like you has to do the same, you can get your letters done faster by having your thousand in stacks of ten and the other guy's letters in one stack of a thousand. If he has the stacks of ten and you the one stack of a thousand, *he* will do his faster. Scientists have proven this phenomenon many times with corn shucking and wheat harvesting and stamp licking and many, many other activities. People work more efficiently when they have goals to work toward, even if they don't know they are racing. Somehow, **the idea of just getting ten done and then starting over is more appealing to the human psyche** than the prospect of doing a thousand. By doing ten, there is a feeling of accomplishment (however small) that inspires (however slightly) a person to work better as he starts the next ten.

This proven fact cannot be overlooked in regard to your practicing basketball, playing pickup games in the summer or walking out to a court to play the big game of your season. Having specific goals will help you attain your ultimate objective—to play good, winning basketball—more easily.

When you walk onto a court to practice alone, you shouldn't just "shoot around." You should count your shots and have definite objectives. "I will shoot free throws today until I hit 45 out of 50." Walk out there knowing what you are going to work on, and do it.

If you are playing in a pickup game, don't always play your "same old way." If the competition is easy, make yourself do everything left-handed. (And don't tell anyone, if you happen to get beaten, that you were only using your left hand. Learn not to save face but to get better.) If there is an excellent player in the game, try to guard him and keep him from touching the ball.

Or go into a game concentrating on an area you aren't good at. For example, play the whole game concentrating on getting offensive rebounds. Count how many you get. Or count how many steals you get or how many balls you are able to touch on defense.

Too many players go to the courts and play and never get any better at their weaknesses. Pickup games are the time to experiment. Once you get into your regular season, you can't afford to experiment. You have to polish the skills you have and show that you know how to play within your own limitations. In pickup games, you try new moves, not during your season. So go into pickup games prepared to try new things and knowing which things you are going to try.

During your regular season games, you still need goals. Go into games wanting to cut down on the number of turnovers you had last game, get your hands on more balls, call on yourself to set better screens or shoot a better percentage. You should have no problem finding things to concentrate on. What does your coach criticize you for every day in practice?

Are you in the habit of writing down your objectives before each game and then after the game writing down what happened, how you came out? Why not? Do you think it isn't necessary? Players who really are trying to improve will do these things, and they will improve faster than you. This is why coaches are in the habit of saying, "We take 'em one game at a time." The best way to have a good season is to have a good game *now*.

Don't walk out onto the court, whether for practice or a game or a summer pickup or when shooting alone, without having definite objectives in your mind. The best way for you to be a lot better player a year from now is for you to do a little better tomorrow than you did today.

63
GREAT PASSES FROM THE LANE

Every coach wants an unselfish team, and every player enjoys playing on one. But the time to be unselfish is *not* when you get the ball in the three-second lane. When you get the ball in the lane, it is Nostril Time (see #96), time for you to get strong, time for you to go for it. Score!

There are exceptions of course. If, at the instant you get the ball, three defenders surround you and you are ten feet from the basket, not right beside it, it is best to flip the ball out to a teammate and *leave the lane.* You would like to stay there for rebounding position, but you shouldn't. A pass from the lane signals the referee the way a red cape attracts a bull. Even if you can cut into the lane, get a pass, flip it back out and have the shot go up in two seconds, it is not worth the risk. Referees tend to think this cannot be done in less than three seconds, so they blow their whistles. And they're usually right.

Any time you catch the ball in the lane, plan on shooting. Go all the way. Go for broke. If you start to go for it, then decide you can't get a good shot and begin to make a great pass, the chances are excellent that your great assist will be accompanied by a whistle. If you know immediately that a shot is not a good opportunity, get the ball out to a teammate and *you get out, too.*

Referees will not call you for a lane violation when you are in there two and a half or three seconds if you don't have the ball. But if you get the ball in the lane and pass it out, you may get a violation called for just two seconds. Anytime you get the ball in the lane and pass it out, show the referee that you are hustling to get out. Any less effort is likely to result in a whistle, even if three seconds haven't gone by.

64
GREAT PLAYS

Beware of great plays.

Common sense might seem to tell you that great plays are what make the difference between a good player and a mediocre player. But most coaches would disagree. More often, they would say, great plays—or the attempts to make great plays—are what make good players mediocre. Since this seems to defy common sense, a few definitions might be useful. What is it that separates a mediocre player from a good player? Both are in many ways the same. Both could have about the same speed and quickness, the same strength, the same height and weight, about the same shooting and dribbling ability. Often, the only difference comes with regard to great plays.

Many players are mediocre because they try to make great plays. They want to score a fancy layup, and they miss it. Or they try to throw a lightning-quick pass to a cutter six inches ahead of his man, and it goes out of bounds. They try to hit a fade-away jumper, and it goes off the rim. Or they go for the game-winning steal, but they miss it and the other team puts the game out of reach. Mediocre is sometimes just another name for at erratic or inconsistent or "always striving to make great plays."

It may surprise you to learn that good players don't strive for great plays. Great plays come to them occasionally, but only when they are in the process of concentrating on their job, trying to do all the little things right.

Take Michael Jordan for example. He made a lot of great plays, but his value, even more important to his team than all those spectacular dunks, was that he didn't miss many dunks. He was consistent. On the plays where a spectacular dunk had a good chance of missing, Jordan "happened" not to try it at all. *"Ah,"* said the fans, *"he should've dunked that one."* But he didn't dunk every chance he got. He dunked the ones he could dunk, and he didn't attempt the ones he could not. If it was 50-50, he didn't try it.

Good players don't like those odds. Good players are not gamblers—they are performers. That is why **great plays are not what make an outstanding player. It is knowing limitations.**

A good player knows that he doesn't need a slam dunk in the final seconds to be credited with winning the big game. If he can stop his man from scoring and go down to the other end and get a good shot, he can win the game just as well. And more often. He isn't running around searching for a way to look spectacular; he is out there trying to get a job done, doing "whatever it takes." If somewhere along the line he gets a chance to do something spectacular, fine, that's icing on the cake, a bonus. But he doesn't seek it out. His concentration is on the little things, playing the game right, getting good defensive position, being there for rebounds and always taking high-percentage opportunities, whether shooting, passing, stealing or penetrating.

A lot of players are potentially good. They try hard to show everyone how good they are, how many great plays they can make. Along the way they make some great plays, but they also make a lot of mistakes. They go quickly from good to mediocre, and many of them spend their entire basketball careers hearing coaches say, "You *could* be good." But they aren't.

Good players are those guys who get the job done, who do the little things and who are always looking to do just a little more. They have the habit of usually making things appear quite easy. Often, they can be pretty boring since their pride is in playing intelligently. They don't like looking stupid or missing dunks that should have been easy layups. They would rather have fans go away disappointed that they didn't do anything spectacular than to hear someone saying their stupid play lost the game. Good players have a pride about things like that. It's not just that they don't want to be labeled "erratic." They really don't want to make any mistakes at all.

65
GUARDING THE CHERRY PICKER

If you are a guard, a cherry picker is your responsibility, and it is important to understand that there is no need to take yourself out of the offense because of your fear of giving the other team a layup. If your opponent is interested in leaving early to begin the break, you have to make him pay for that gamble. You often can do that by urging your team to be a little more patient on offense, throw a few more passes and score the five-on-four.

There is plenty of time to run back on defense after the shot if you are ready to do it. There is no need to take yourself out of the play and stand at half-court. Stay in tight, look for the opening to score, look to exploit the cherry picker's lack of concentration on defense and be ready to go when he goes.

It is easy to guard a cherry picker. The problem is that very often a team gets so worried about a man leaving early that both guards play the game always backing out of scoring position. After each shot, the other team has a 4-on-3 rebounding advantage (which ends up being more damaging than the baskets the cherry picker is able to get).

You cannot allow your team to get into a 3-on-4 (or even 3-on-5) attack out of fear. Play your normal game, and be especially ready to cut into the middle after your team gets an offensive rebound or a loose ball. In this way, *you* can be the one who gets the easy baskets, even though they won't look as impressive as a breakaway layup all alone.

Remember not to back up to midcourt for any reason. If you are at the free throw line and the cherry picker goes, you go, too. Be ready to come back quickly and get open if your team keeps possession. Cherry pickers are rarely concentrating on how quickly they can get back into the defense, so if you are alert, you can exploit that bad habit over and over again.

66
GUARDING A POTENTIAL SHOOTER

Too many players fool themselves into thinking they have played good defense (despite their man making a shot) because they got their hand within an inch or two of the ball when it was shot. But how close you come to the ball has nothing to do with how well you defended that shooter. The crucial consideration is what are you doing while the shooter is *deciding* whether or not to shoot.

If you are standing there passively or playing possum and waiting for the block as the shooter decides to go up for a shot, then you will have no effect on the shot unless you touch it. Coming two inches from the ball is the same as coming two feet (or eight feet) from it. If the shooter expects to get the shot off and he shoots it accordingly, with confidence, it has nothing to do with you. Coming close to the ball after it is released may fool you, but it won't fool your coach. Your activity is too late.

If you want to have an influence on a shot, **if you want to make a shot difficult, you have to get the shooter's attention while he is deciding to shoot.** It is when he is deciding that you need to get him thinking about you, thinking that you might get there to block it, that you might touch the ball at his chest, or you might crowd him and prevent a complete follow-through. If you get him thinking about you, there is a good chance he will hurry his shot or not concentrate as well, and more often than not, he will miss.

No player is so good a shooter that he simply makes whatever he can get off. All shooters are at their best when they *know in advance* they are going to be able to get their shot off.

For this reason, a small man can often defend a taller outside shooter better than a guy who is the shooter's size. It is not a question of whether or not the little man can touch the shooter's ball. Very possibly he cannot. But can the taller shooter get free to set himself and bring the ball off the floor the way he likes to? Many tall players would rather go against a guy their size, a guy they have confidence they can fake out, rather than have to worry about a smaller but quicker man who tends to get underfoot and break up their rhythm with quick jab fakes and fast hands dangerously near the shooter's dribble.

The crucial point is to worry the shooter before he shoots, while he is deciding. Once he goes up, it is too late. A player is likely to complete the shooting motion with the confidence and concentration he began it with.

A good defender has to interrupt that rhythm and concentration by gaining that shooter's attention with jab fakes, violent movements— whatever it takes to get the shooter's attention on you and off the shot. You don't need to touch a shooter's ball to make him miss. You merely need to gain his attention. Confident shooters make high-percentage shots, while distracted shooters, even great ones, shoot poorly. Everyone *knows* that.

But what is *your* style of defense doing about it?

H

67
HIDING

For all the complaining that players are apt to do about not getting the ball enough, one of the biggest faults of most players is their failure to come to the ball against pressure. "Hiding" is more relaxing, and that is what players tend to do. They get 25-40 feet from the ball, and they stand there waiting for it to be thrown. Sometimes, they even wave their arms and frown, but whether they know it or not, they are hiding.

Few players realize how often they hide. They seem to be readily available when no help is needed, and they are very concerned about getting their share of the shots against a team that is applying no pressure. But where are they when the going is tough? Where are they when the ball is being double-teamed? Where are *you?*

If the ball is being double-teamed, or if your teammate has picked up his dribble and the defender has gotten in his face—**if you aren't ten feet from the ball, then you are hiding.** You cannot be found. A player being pressured by two men or having no dribble left cannot be expected to find you 40 feet or even 25 feet away. A 25-foot pass takes too long to get there, and an alert team will have an excellent chance of intercepting it. Run *to* the ball.

Hiding against pressure (when your team especially needs you) is the worst form, but it is not the only form. Game after game, players go trotting casually to the offensive end without a glance at their point guard dribbling downcourt and without recognizing the semi-fast break scoring opportunities. Often, their defenders aren't even looking at the ball and aren't ready to defend a quick burst of speed toward the basket. But the quick bursts don't happen very often, because players are not constantly seeking the ball.

In just about every game, there are easy baskets to be gotten that don't even require basketball ability. There are 3-on-3's that easily could become 4-on-3's except that someone hides instead of seeks. And there are 3-on-3's where nothing happens except that the dribbler waits for all five and sets up an offense. Why do even good shooters fail to realize that by running and making a sharp cut, they could get the ball in a great scoring spot?

These answers seem to be attributable to sheer laziness—and angry coaches claim that constantly—but it cannot be that simple. Because well-conditioned players with good attitudes do it, too. They hide. They jog behind a trotting defender or alongside him when a sprint could result in an easy score.

Someday, play in a pickup game with the sole objective of trying to see how many times you and an alert guard, or you and a forward who is willing to run, can score easy baskets. You may not score them or throw the assists, but you should see how many times it could happen.

There are dozens of baskets to be scored out there on the courts just waiting for you to come out of hiding.

68
GET OPEN INSIDE WITH THE HOOK STEP

Players often make the mistake, when they want to get the ball on the low post, down near the box, of jockeying for position rather than planting and being firm and forcing the defender to make a definite decision.

By planting and being firm you can give the passer a definite target. With the hand closest to the defender, you nudge a bit; with the other you present the target by holding that hand up and away from the defense.

Now the defender has to decide: Does he let you get the ball, or does he try to get around you enough to get a hand in the passing lane?

Let him make his decision. When you jockey and move your feet back and forth, your teammate with the ball will be uncertain where you are going to be when he passes. By planting and being firm, you give that definite target and, if the defender tries to get his body around far enough to have his arm in the passing lane so that he can touch the pass as it comes to you, you have set him up perfectly for the hook step.

Assume you are on the low post and you are holding out with your right hand (the defender is on your right overplaying), and your left hand is up in the air giving the target. If the defender is making the pass to your left difficult, **take one long hook step** with your left foot, **turning your back to the defender as though you want to block him out for a rebound.** However, instead of keeping him on your back (which you can do if there are no defensive helpers in the lane making a lob over your man's head possible), you make another quarter turn while holding the defender off with your left hand and now present a target to the passer with an outstretched right hand.

In other words, you do a 270—not a 360. You begin facing the side of the court. Your first step turns you around (a 180 to block out position). Then, you bring up your right foot (a quarter or 90-degree turn), so you finish the move facing midcourt.

This hook step move is not nearly as complicated or difficult as it may sound to a player who has never tried it. The diagrams will make it clear if it is not already. It is an excellent move used by almost all good post men. It is especially effective against an aggressive defender who tends to overplay a bit too much and therefore is easy to hook step. Just when he thinks he is getting his body around in position to deflect the entry pass, you hook step him and put him in a very poor defensive position.

The crucial point to remember is to begin by planting firmly, establish your position and present the passer a good target. Once you do that, it is up to the defender to decide. Does he let you get the ball, or does he move around to front you, giving you the opportunity to hook step and get him on your back? If you stay low and in a crouch and hold him off (with your arm, not your hand), he will not be able to prevent the pass to your outstretched hand unless he moves so far out that he makes the hook step possible.

Every post man, and any guard or forward who wants to be able to post up a smaller player, *must* know how to use the hook step. With this maneuver, no one man can ever keep you from getting the ball inside. If you do not know this maneuver, make sure you learn it. If you know it, use it.

GETTING FREE WITH THE HOOK STEP

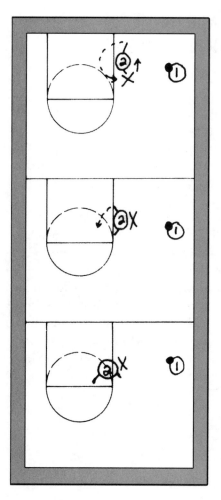

First, "2" sets up low and gives the passer a target with an outstretched left hand. But as the defender tries to move over to make that pass difficult, "2" swings his left foot around, putting his back on the defender.

With the defender on his back, facing away from the ball, "2" moves his right foot up and holds the defender out with his left hand.

"2" now has his back to the basket as he holds out and asks for the ball with an outstretched right hand.

69
HOW TO MAKE A
GAME-WINNING STEAL

This defensive maneuver really might get you a game-winning steal someday. Because of the psychology behind it, it has a better chance of working at the end of a game than it does at the beginning when there is no pressure. If you use this play early in a game, you are likely to get out of position, get beaten and get taken out of the game by your coach. It is not good basketball to be lunging for steals early in a game, and since the player with the ball is not likely to be particularly nervous early, this play is not likely to be effective. End-of-game nervousness and **that altered psychology of protecting a lead rather than trying to get one is the circumstance under which this works best.**

Assume you are behind by a point or two or three, and you are in the closing minutes. At a time like this, **you can get away with a steal attempt because the team with the ball is not so intent on taking advantage of a defender momentarily out of position.** Their chief concern is running out the clock. So, even if you miss your attempt, you are unlikely to hurt your team, and you may very well get the ball.

SETTING UP THE STEAL

Get far over to the dribbler's strong side, drift back with him and "influence" the ball to his weak hand without applying pressure.

You know that any player, even an excellent player, would like to have the ball in his strong hand in pressure situations. Therefore, what you want to do, at the end of a game when you need a steal, is to **create very suddenly a pressure situation,** and you want to know exactly when you are doing it. If you can surprise the dribbler with the suddenness of the pressure, he will not have time to respond intelligently—he will respond instinctively. **His instincts will tell him when he meets sudden, unexpected pressure to get the ball immediately in his strong hand.** Knowing this, you can prepare a response and perhaps beat him to it.

Try it like this: Let your man get the ball and pick him up full-court. Give him a lot of room, and move far over to his strong side, giving him a safe, wide-open path up the court to his weak side. At first, you are so far from him that he can even advance the ball upcourt with his strong hand if he wishes, but as he advances the ball, you get a little closer to him, so that he dribbles the ball with his weak (usually left) hand. At this point, you are in a "token pressure" situation**, applying just enough pressure to get that ball in his weak hand but not enough to give him a cause for worry.** You are just close enough that he doesn't feel safe dribbling with his strong hand, but he still feels very safe dribbling the ball with his weak hand (with his body between you and the ball). It is

121

from this safe, secure position that your steal attempt comes.

At a point you decide on, **lunge violently to his weak side.** Go from passive to violent in a flash, **but don't go for the ball.** This first lunge is only a fake, only to create that sense of sudden, unexpected trouble that makes his response instinctive. After you make the violent fake, **don't wait for his reaction. Throw your body to his strong side** while watching and reaching for his strong hand. There is an excellent chance that he will put the ball right out in front of you as he tries to get it in his strong hand.

VIOLENT LUNGE FAKE

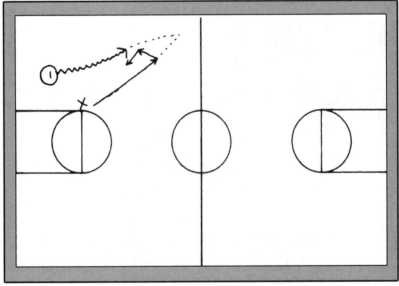

Drift back on a diagonal path which takes you gradually closer to the dribbler. But before the logical point of confrontation, surprise the dribbler with a sudden lunge to his weak side. Then go straight for his strong hand.

This maneuver has won games and gotten steals and certainly is worth trying. Usually, even if your fake or your lunge doesn't work, there will be time to recover since the player with the ball is not primarily interested in taking advantage of a sudden five-on-four.

You can try out this maneuver in pickup games to get a sense of when to fake and how big to make your fake, but remember, without the same sense of pressure, the dribbler in a pickup game is much more likely to see the weak side path you are giving him and take it aggressively in order to pass you. If he does this, all is not lost. (You may even purposely set up this situation by letting the dribbler *think* you have been badly beaten.) If you are ready to run with him, you can catch up and very possibly get a swipe at the ball when he tries to switch to his strong hand and go for the middle of the court. (See "Gnaw-Pocket Defense," entry #61.)

89%

No one gives 100%. Forget all this talk about 110%, 120% or 200%. All players loaf. Even great ones. Push yourself, fight yourself and make yourself hustle more and more. There is always more you can do.

I

70
IMAGINARY LINES

How many times have you seen someone drive baseline and step on the line on the way to scoring a layup that, of course, will not count? How many times have you seen a player dribble on the sideline when bringing the ball upcourt against a full-court press? How often have you seen someone get called for a three-second violation because his heel or back foot remained in the lane after he thought he was out? How many players have you seen catch a pass while standing on an out-of-bounds line? How many over-and-back violations have you seen where someone caught a pass but wasn't quite in the frontcourt yet?

All of these situations happen too frequently. The reason is that players fail to use imaginary lines. Imaginary lines are lines you draw yourself, lines that you imagine are there even though they aren't actually painted on the court.

Paint those lines in your mind—three feet in from the real lines, all around the court, and eight inches to a foot around the three-second lane. Then use those lines. Play just as if your lines were the referees' lines. If you are trying to beat someone on a dribble and you get to your imaginary line, stop or go back the other way.

Someday, in a big game, when you get bumped and the referee doesn't see it or call it, instead of having to go home a loser, talking about how you were pushed out of bounds, you can go home thinking how nice it is to win. Maybe you'll even enjoy thinking about the one time you got pushed over your imaginary line but not far enough to put you out of bounds.

There is no need to have more than one career turnover due to stepping on a line or being "forced" out of bounds.

IMAGINARY LINES

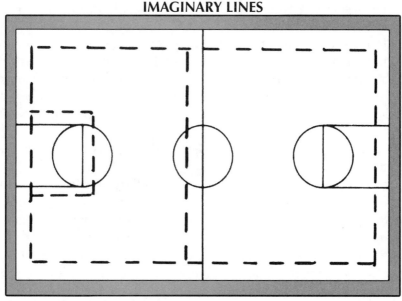

Play with imaginary lines, and your turnovers will be imaginary, too.

71
IMMEDIATELY OR NOT AT ALL

This phrase and concept is so important that it is used as at title rather than as an explanation under "One-on-one" or "Taking the shot." The concept is very simple to understand, but few good players understand the importance of it.

If you decide to go one-on-one, do it immediately after you get the ball, or don't do it at all. There is a very good reason for this. The longer you hold the ball and look around or jockey for position, the more time the defense has to get in good help-position to stop you and clog the lane. If there is an opening to go one-on-one, your best chance is immediately, not after you hold the ball for several seconds.

The same concept applies to taking a shot from outside. If you are free and in your range, take the shot. If you aren't, don't take it. But don't stand there deciding and then shoot. **Anytime you have stood there deciding, decide not to shoot.** Why? Because tentative shooters are poor shooters. If something about the situation causes your instincts to delay, something about your instincts is likely to disrupt the smooth flow of your shooting motion.

Players shoot at their best when they get the ball, and they know as it comes that they are going to shoot. When this happens, your rhythm is right, and "all systems are go." But if something about the play makes you reluctant, your rhythm is likely to be off. If you need further proof of this, watch some games. Players who hold the ball and think and decide usually miss.

A good rule to follow is this: **when in doubt, pass.** Or, if you have held the ball, pass.

Seldom does a team lose for having passed up open shots. You lose by missing shots, by shooting too fast, by taking bad shots, by shooting tentatively. Passing up a shot rarely hurts and often it helps. If ever you pass up a shot and you think, *I should have shot that one,* your rhythm will be in gear for the next time. When you get the ball, you are very likely to have the confidence and the smooth flow that will enable you to put up your best possible shot.

Most certainly, never hold the ball deciding and then shoot because a fan yells "Shoot!" Make your own decisions. Go one-on-one when it feels right, and take the shot when it feels right. But do it immediately or not at all.

If you are thinking now, *But it takes me a while to recognize the situation. I can't know as soon as I get it what I should do,* you are not a good player yet, and you really don't deserve to be taking shots or going one-on-one. For a team to win, contrary to fan opinion, it is *not* necessary that each guy be taking shots and going one-on-one.

If you are playing in a league with no shot clock, all you need is a little patience and movement, and eventually one of the team's best players will get a good shot at the basket. The more you play, the sooner you will recognize situations and be able to decide when you have a good opportunity and when you don't.

If you are at the stage where you still have to hold the ball and look in order to decide whether or not you have an opportunity, you don't deserve to be shooting and trying to score yet. You can use yourself better by concentrating on moving to keep your defender busy, screening for your teammates, handling the ball well, playing good defense and rebounding.

The players who take the scoring initiative should be those who know at the instant they get the ball that they have an opportunity. If they do have one, they should take it immediately or not at all.

72
RESPONSE TO AN INJURY

Many baskets are lost during the course of a season by players who fall or who get hit in the face and then stand there or lie there and think about the pain. Everyone may sympathize with your injury, but going motionless for a moment or two is a mere bad habit.

It is possible to develop the habit of jumping up or "playing basketball" immediately following an injury. Even following an accident such as a broken leg (although many reactions to this will be, "Oh, come on now!"), it is possible to jump up and hop on the other foot. There are several reasons for this.

1. An injury seldom hurts more standing than it does lying down. If it is a hand or face injury, it does not hurt more while running than while standing.
2. Most injuries involve immediate pain that subsides very rapidly whether you run or not.

So it is wise to treat an injury initially as a non-injury. If the pain persists, you could have something serious. If it does not, you were wise to keep on going.

Even a serious injury is not made any worse by the *habit* of jumping immediately back into action. If your leg truly is broken, you will not put weight on it despite your developed habit, and you will be quite capable of hopping off the court or lying back down *after* the whistle blows.

Naturally, if you are injured so badly that you cannot move or cannot get up immediately, this will not apply. In this case, no habit is going to make any difference.

Have you ever been poked in the eye during a game? The tendency is to stand there and close both eyes and put your hands over your hurt eye. But that is just habit. Holding your eye does not decrease the pain, nor does standing there. You are perfectly capable of opening the unhurt eye and running down the court. You are simply not in the habit of doing that, though you can be if you work on it.

No one, not even a Marine drill sergeant, expects you to go on playing with a bone sticking out of your skin. But what happens a lot more often is you lie on the court nursing an injury that will be gone moments later. There is no excuse for that kind of habit.

Getting attention for minor injuries is the province of mediocre players. Save *your* attention-getting for slam dunks and tough rebounds, alert steals and clever assists. Treat all your injuries like minor ones destined to be gone soon. Most of them will be just that, and the major ones will be so obvious that it won't matter what you do.

73
PASSING THE BALL INSIDE

If you have a big man who is good at scoring inside, you ought to try often to get him the ball on the low post. The best place to pass to the low post man is from the side or corner, not from the middle or anyplace past the free throw line.

Any pass thrown from beyond the free throw line is a bad angle pass. A bounce pass is too easily overplayed and deflected, and it must be thrown away from the defender and therefore away from the basket. A lob from out there takes the low post man toward the baseline and under the basket or behind the board.

The pass from the side, on the other hand, can be thrown away from the defender and still allow a direct turn to the basket for a shot. And a lob, rather than heading for the out-of-bounds area, is up near the basket where the low post man can go up after it and still have a chance to score on the other side of the basket (if no helpers are preventing him).

The rule is: If you have a low post man you want to get the ball to, take the ball down the side of the court, and **penetrate the foul line extended.** From there, it is a simple matter of getting the ball past your defender and away from the defender on your low post man. Most good players can do this without much difficulty since the ball usually does not have to be passed cleverly. It merely needs to be lobbed softly over your defender's hands. (The bent-elbow pass is also effective here. (See "Bent-elbow Pass," entry #18.)

One problem that often comes up and presents difficulties happens when your defender does not pressure you but instead plays between you and your low post man (or back farther, standing in front of your low post man). Often, in this situation, the player who has the ball in the corner does nothing but throw the ball back out. He may figure a shot from the corner is not a good-percentage shot, and the pass into the low post man looks impossible as a result of the sagging defender.

To create an opening in this situation, whether playing against a man-to-man defense or a zone defense, take one aggressive dribble forward and act as though you want to shoot. This will force the sagging defender to move forward to guard the shot, and it will leave the low post man wide open for the pass. Rarely will the low post man be fronted in this situation, since no team is likely to put two men in front of one offensive player. If the sagger fronts the low post man, the man guarding the low post man will be content to stay behind him. When your aggressive dribble and shot-fake bring out the sagger, the low post man is left free.

Crucial to this play is that you look at the basket as you move forward. Otherwise, you will not draw out the sagging defender.

Be prepared to shoot if the defender will not come out at all. Or get your best shooter on that side, so the defense either has to give up a high-percentage shot or permit the pass to the low post. Rarely should you take the shot from the corner, even if you are a fine shooter. You can get a lot closer than the corner and force the defense to make a decision.

74
INSIDE DRIBBLES

Players give all sorts of reasons why they take dribbles when they get the ball close to the basket. They are off-balance, so they need to dribble to keep from walking; their feet aren't in position to go up strong; they get more power going up in the air when they have to pull the ball off the floor first. Probably you know even more reasons why you do it. And you can recall dozens of players you have seen, even pros, who do it.

Fine. So sometimes you *can* get away with dribbling *inside*. Sometimes you can even get away with it against good teams. But most of the time, when you meet a good team, when you need your inside moves the most, you get your inside dribbles stolen by little guards sagging in and helping.

The point is, whether you can get away with it or not, you should **develop a sense of pride in your ability to score inside without having to**

put the ball on the floor at all. You should learn how to get on balance without need of a dribble, and learn how to go up strong without need of a dribble.

Once you learn these things, then if you get a chance to score where it is obvious that a dribble will make it easier, dribble and score! But if you are an inside man, make sure you learn to score without the dribble first. Too many players have never learned how to get their balance and make a move inside without dribbling; as a result, they are not effective when they meet a team that sags well to help.

It is possible to learn to fake, to score off two feet and off one foot, and to make many many moves without using a dribble inside. Forcing yourself to score this way exclusively in pickup games and in summer practice, will pay dividends during the season and will get you in the habit of using a dribble only when it is necessary.

In nearly every game at every level, two or more should've-been-layups are never taken because the ball is batted away when it never should have been dribbled in the first place.

Learn from this statistic and learn to score inside without dribbling.

LUCK?

Being behind near the end of a game is like hitting the wall in a marathon—trying to pry loose the ball from a team smelling victory and from opposing fans getting boisterous and jubilant. But what sublime feeling—to keep the pressure on, to keep trying, to push yourself just a little bit longer—to make a game-winning steal. It takes a great player to do that, and despite the way it may look, it is never luck.

J

75
JOCKEYING TO GET OPEN

Leave jockeying to horse racers. Too many players expend a lot of effort trying to get loose when all they are doing is moving their shoulders and taking one step one way, one step the other way. They think they are working very hard, but they go nowhere. They would do better to lean one way, and either go hard that way (at least three steps) or go hard the other way. Get open or get out of the way, but do not stand in a prime receiving position moving your body back and forth a step at a time going nowhere and clogging the area.

Many players walk out of gyms thinking some opponent is a great defensive player who stuck to them like glue all because they didn't go anywhere. It rarely occurs to jockeyers that a defender can guard them by standing still and doing nothing.

Remember, you don't get open with head and shoulder fakes and quick pumping feet. You get open by running hard in one direction and hard in the other direction. You can also get free by leaning against a man or stepping between his legs before breaking out. If you cannot get open immediately, go violently backdoor and clear out the area so that someone else can run into it.

Whatever you do, make a decision and go hard. If you are beaten in one direction, turn and go back the other way. You can't possibly get beaten in two opposing directions, unless your defender is *so* much better than you that none of this will help you anyway!

76
JUMP BALLS

It takes only one intelligent player to make sure the whole team is lined up properly for a jump ball.

If you are the jumper, great—you can stoop down and tie your shoe to make sure you have time to get everyone in the right positions. If you are not jumping, act quickly or discuss with your teammates the value of shoe-tying to make sure the set-up is correct. Most important, check two things:

1. Make sure *they* don't have any place to tip that would give them an immediate layup or 2-on-1. Nothing is much more demoralizing or unnecessary than giving up a layup on a jump ball.
2. Make sure your team has an offensive readiness so in case you get the tap and the other team is "sleeping," you can take advantage of them.

Those two rules are very simple and never change: Can we stop them? And what can we do to score? Under ideal circumstances, you should get the ball and advance it to a cutter for a basket a second or two after the tap—not by accident but by knowing in advance that you are looking for that particular cut.

Beyond those two considerations, there is the question of who looks likely to get the tap. If your team looks likely to get it, make sure there is a place to tap it where you know your team has the best chance of getting the ball. This would be either to a pocket, where you have two of your players standing together, or to one of your tough, aggressive players who has only one defender beside him (so the ball can be tapped to his other side).

It usually doesn't hurt to tell the jumper directly who to tap to. Opponents are usually unaware of first names, especially nicknames. And besides, even if they know where you are going to tap the ball, there is no reason they should get it.

Remember, if you are the player about to get the ball, or if you are one of the two players in a pocket, **be sure you block out the man beside you.** Do not let an opponent steal a tap by cutting to the spot where the ball is going. If it looks as though the other team will win the tap, or if it is not clear who will win it, **don't give them an obvious opening to the tapper's left.** Most players tap with their right hand, so taps to the left are much easier to make.

When a right-handed tapper tries to tap to the right, he loses several inches, much strength and a lot of control. Forcing a back-handed tap gives you a much better chance of getting the ball than if you allow a back tap, a forward tap or a tap to the left.

JUMP BALL WHERE YOU EXPECT TO LOSE THE TAP

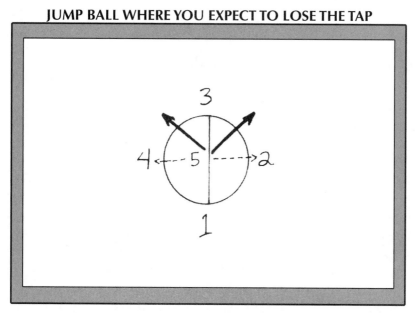

The arrows show the places where 5 can tap the ball effectively (assuming he is right-handed), so these areas must be guarded. A tap to 1, or between 1 and 4, or 1 and 2, is very difficult.
Never permit pockets shown by the two long arrows.

A good player can see all of this in an instant:

Prevent them from getting an easy layup. Have an offensive attack in mind yourself. Look for a pocket or a tough kid to tap to. Don't give them an obvious tapping situation on their tapper's left nor straight ahead or back. If they look sure to get the tap, force them to tap to their tapper's right; look to cut there to steal.

One final jump ball suggestion. If you feel certain your jumper will get the tap, take one man off the circle and put him downcourt on your offensive end. They will have to send a man with him to prevent an easy layup, and therefore (with only three men on the lane) they will not be able to trick you with any stealing cuts. If your three men are spread out on the circle, your opponent must either give you an uncontested opening or try to play each man closely, giving you an easy block out situation where no rotation to steal will be possible.

A SURE-TAP SITUATION FOR 1-2-3-4-5

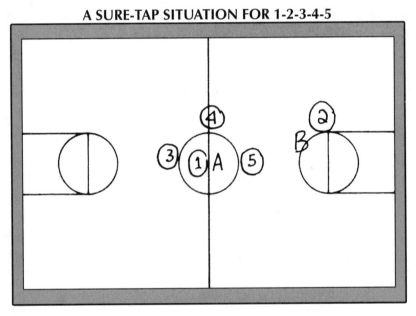

There is no place you can put C-D-E to make this tap difficult.

77
JUMP SWITCHING

J ump switching, as opposed to passively changing men, means that you jump out violently on the man with the ball. You don't wait for him—you go out and get him.

A jump switch commonly occurs when a dribbler tries to use a screen. The defender guarding the screener jumps out and takes the dribbler with one very specific objective: He wants **to prevent any dribbles in the direction of the screen.** In other words, the defender jumps out on the dribbler and either stops him immediately or turns him back in the direction he came from. He does not play passively so that the dribbler can dribble past the screen and continue on. You do not want the ball to continue on, because this allows the screener to roll free to the basket for an easy pass.

GOOD PASSING ANGLE ON THE SCREEN-AND-ROLL

By letting 1 get past the screen, 1 has a good chance of getting an assist to 2 cutting to the basket with "A" on his back.

The value of the **screen-and-roll** as an offensive weapon is well known, but it **rarely works if the ball is stopped at the point of the screen.** When this occurs, the roller must catch a ball coming directly over his head, and he must take his eyes off the basket and off the people in front of him as he cuts. This "straight angle" cut is very difficult to score from because the defense can set up to draw a charge while the cutter's eyes are diverted. It is much easier to score off the roll when the ball is coming from an angle past the screen, and the roller has the man he has screened firmly on his back.

If this is not clear, you need only try it a few times to realize that the straight angle cut is not a good-percentage opportunity. Unless your coach tells you otherwise (perhaps to prevent mismatches and so on), it is useful to jump switch anytime your man attempts to screen for the ball.

AN EFFECTIVE JUMP SWITCH

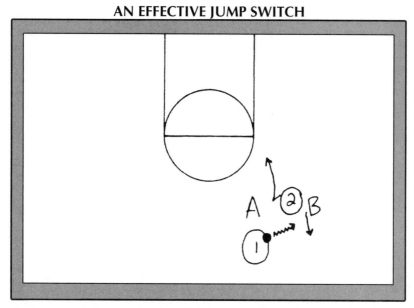

By aggressively jump switching, "B" prevents 1 from continuing his dribble, and therefore a pass to 2 rolling to the basket will have to be thrown directly over 2's head—a difficult play to make.

The crucial point to remember is that you must be right up against the screener (or the man who the dribbler plans to use as a screen) to be prepared to "jump" soon enough to stop any dribbles in your direction. "Right up against" means **forearm in his back**—not pushing, not holding with your hand, just resting your forearm there, ready to jump out.

Never sag on a screener unless you want to give the other team outside shots. If you do sag, you cannot be in a position to jump switch.

Too many players are content to stay off their man, especially when it is a big, tough non-shooter standing at the high post. "Why stay on him when he can't shoot from there?" It seems like a reasonable question, until a hot shooting little guard knocks your best defender into that big man and gets an unmolested easy jumper on the other side of the screen while *you* (Why play him close? He can't shoot from there!) stand six feet back and watch. For this reason, you guard a screener closely regardless of what kind of shooter he is, unless you don't fear the outside shot of anyone on your opponent's team (in which case you won't need intelligent basketball for that game anyway).

DEFENDING A SCREEN-AND-ROLL

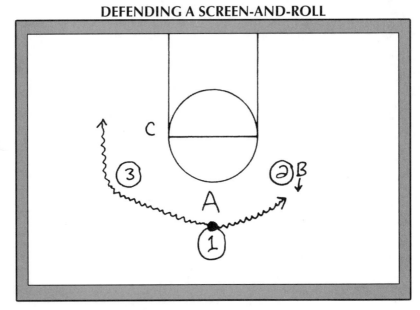

If 1 dribbles to the right to use 2 as a screen, "B" is in good position (forearm on the back of 2), ready to get out and stop the dribble at the point of the screen.

If 1 dribbles to the left to use 3 as a screen, "C" (who is sagging off) is in bad position and will not be able to stop 1 from dribbling "A" into the screen and continuing down the side toward the basket.

What do you do after you jump switch? You can retreat quickly, back to your original man, once you have turned the dribbler back or stopped his dribble, or you can keep the man you switched onto and let your teammate get your man. This after-the-jump-switch situation will usually be decided by your coach. If he leaves it up to you, yell "Switch!" and simply switch men, unless by doing that it would put you on someone much bigger or smaller than you, leaving you and your teammate in a mismatch situation.

In the case of a mismatch situation, it is often better to scramble back to your original man once you have stopped the ball. If you get some defensive help from your teammates, and especially if you have stopped the dribble at the point of the screen, recovering to your man won't be nearly as difficult to do as it may seem.

YEAH!

There may be no more complete satisfaction in the world—personally, socially, psychologically, or emotionally—than a well-executed play with sharp passes and cuts, perfect timing, a swish and applause, and that feeling of collective, spontaneous *Yeah!* on the way down the court to play defense.

K

78–KUP

One of the marvels of organization, or of scarcity-abundance theory, is that something that stands alone tends to be valued or at least seen or remembered. A scarecrow in the middle of a field tends to be noticed. Whooping cranes tend to be valued, as do other vanishing species like fierce competitors and offensive rebounders who spin off obstacles and try every time to get the ball.

For this reason, the letter *K* has only one entry, and this entry is Krucial. You Kan't play well without it. It really should have been in with the Ps, but it seems worthwhile to set it off, alone.

78
KUP

KUP stands for **K**eep **U**p **P**alms. *Keep* your palms up on defense. If you try to steal a dribble or a held ball, do it with your palms up, in a way that you could balance a "kup" on your palm, not turn the kup over. If you try to touch a shot on defense, do it with your palm facing the sky, not the ground.

Players draw unnecessary fouls by reaching, palm down to the floor, for dribbles or by swatting, palm down to the floor, at shots. And players walk around courts during free throws shaking their heads and mumbling that they never touched him.

Because of that, it would help you to accept right now this new definition of a foul.

A Foul is

Any time you make contact
with a player on the other team
and the referee blows his whistle,
or any time you *look like* you make contact
with a player on the other team
and the referee blows his whistle.

Understand this definition, and prepare yourself to play accordingly.

You do not have to foul to get called for a foul; you merely have to *look like* you fouled. Therefore, a good defensive player does not waste his time mumbling about never having touched someone; he spends his time learning not to look as though he touches someone when he doesn't, and even how to look as though he hasn't touched anyone when he has. When you swat downward, it *looks like* a foul.

When you get in the habit of playing palms-up, KUP, defense you will find that you can get away with making contact often because when you reach palms-up, it does *not* look like a foul. KUP will also help you stay on balance and in good position on defense. The habit of reaching palms-down causes you to lunge and put all your weight forward, and then get beaten. But reaching palms-up does not cause this same tendency. A down-swatting motion tends to throw your body off-balance while an up-swatting motion keeps your body on balance.

Stand there right now and try it and see. Imagine there is something you want to swat at, just out in front of you, just beyond your reach. Notice how hitting down throws your body off balance.

A good way to remember KUP defense is to imagine that the floor has eyes. Never let those eyes see your palms. Play so that those eyes always see only the backs of your hands whether you are reaching for a steal, getting your hand in a shooter's face, or even when you are blocking out for a rebound. Don't let those eyes see your palms. Keep your palms up. Keep Up Palms.

"GOOD PLAY!"

Most players never even dream of the beneficial effect they can have on the quality of play (and life) of their teammates by little comments, gestures, pats on the back and encouragement.

L

79
LONHOBIRS

LONHOBIR is a made-up word for good shot selection—a thing that almost all players are terrible at. The word takes the first letter of each word of the following phrase: Shoot **L**ayups **O**r (shots with) **N**o **H**and (up) **O**n **B**alance **I**n **R**ange.

You've got to wonder (unless time is running out) why anyone ever takes anything but a **layup or a shot with no hand in the face on balance and in good shooting range.** If you can't get the shot you want, pass off. That seems easy enough, yet players instead want to flip up a scooper or let go a flying hook or a fade-away jumper. What for?

"But Coach," you hear players say, "I'm good at that shot."

"Sure, but you're better at shots with *no* hand in your face. You're even better at shots when you're on balance. You're even better at shots when you're a little bit closer."

Why take a fade-away when you can pass off and try again? Why take anything but a very high-percentage shot? The guess might be that players are selfish, and they want to score, and they are afraid that if they don't shoot when they have it, someone else will. But that is not the answer. One-on-one games prove that.

In a one-on-one game, you not only get *every* shot, but the more shots you make, the more shots you get to shoot since most players play one-on-one with a "make-it-take-it" arrangement. Yet, even in one-on-one games, players repeatedly take poor, low-percentage shots instead of being patient and waiting for a better opportunity. There is no explaining it except as being a lack of awareness. Most players just don't give much thought to percentages.

Learning to make a shot with a hand in your face is not nearly as important as learning to pass up such shots and learning how to get shots with no hand in your face. Of course, layups and inside shots are not included in the "no hand" rule. You should be able to make those with *ten* hands in your face.

For a quick review, some questions.

What excuse do you have for shooting shots off balance and out of your "sure-shooting" range?

Why do you shoot when there is a hand in your face?

Why won't you pass off and wait for a higher percentage opportunity?

And the best question of all is, why do you ever take a bad shot in a one-on-one match?

Sometimes, even good players make very little sense.

80
LOOK DOWNCOURT

Any time you get the ball, and often *before* you get it, look to your basket. It is astonishing that players need to be told such a thing, yet players fail to do this constantly.

Often there are men free near the basket (Isn't that where *you* go when you are free?), but the player with the ball doesn't look at them. Frequently, a so-called great pass is made, and all it took was someone to look.

There is nothing clever or complicated about this instruction. It is something everyone can do, but **very, very few players do it every time.**

It *can* be done every time, so make it a habit. Overdo it in some pickup games if that will help you remember. And then do it in games. Every time.

81
LOOK 'IM IN THE EYE FIRST

When a big man gets the ball in the three-second lane on a pass or maybe on an offensive rebound, often he sneaks up a quick shot. He tries to get it up there before the guy near him has a chance to block the shot *and* before that guy has a chance to foul him. The problem is, there is a better chance for an aggressive shooter to draw a foul than there is for even a very tall center to block a shot. So a quick sneak shot is not a very intelligent play.

When you get the ball near the basket, turn toward the defender between you and the basket and look at him. See what he is going to do. If he is going to jump, let him; then you go up. And if he wants to stand there, let him. Then you go up strong.

The important thing to remember is **look him in the eye first and then make your move. There is no reason to sneak up shots inside,** no reason to shoot before you know where you are in relation to the basket and the defenders. Take the time to look at the defender, freeze him and go for it. For every shot that gets blocked, you will get ten fouls. The exchange is well worth it. Besides, any shot-blocking center will tell you that it is easier to block a fade-away or a sneak shot than a shot that goes right up past his nose.

Look him in the eye first, then go for it.

82
LOSING

No one is quite sure about how a player is supposed to act after a loss. It doesn't seem necessary to cry for a week, especially since you are likely to have another game within that time. Yet, it doesn't seem quite right to walk off the court laughing either. Naturally, some losses will be more bothersome than others, and, just as naturally, *every* player will lose sometimes. Therefore, it seems intelligent to prepare a response in advance for those unhappy times when the inevitable happens, you lose.

First, after you lose, you should think. Thinking should keep you from

151

laughing and probably from crying as well. Neither laughing nor crying is likely to help you much for next time, but thinking is always valuable. Did you give your best physical effort? Were you fully tuned into the game mentally? What things could *you* have done better? How could *you* have prevented the loss? What would you do differently if you had it to do over? What did the other team do to confuse you or to make it difficult? Can you use that on someone else in the next game?

There are a lot of questions to ask yourself, and those should come in place of the more common comments like "The referees were terrible," "The coach was stupid," or "If only Jones hadn't tried that stupid shot."

No one loses a game singlehandedly. There are unfortunate circumstances when a player misses a shot at the end with his team a point behind, or he travels with the ball or kicks it out of bounds. People may say *he* lost it. But he didn't. *you* lost it with that one turnover at the beginning, that bad pass, or that failure to talk on defense in the first half that gave the other team an easy basket.

Second, get out of the habit of blaming referees and coaches and others, and *think*. Don't decide until the next day what your verdict is. A lot of times, with emotions high after a big game, things get said that aren't meant and aren't true. But, mixed in with disappointment, anger and fatigue, it is easy to say things that won't seem so intelligent the next morning.

Third, get in the habit of saying you aren't sure what happened or why you lost. Say you need time to think about the game. And then do that. Think about it. Go back over every play, everything you can remember—not forever, not even for a week, but certainly on your way off the court, in the locker room, on the bus home, and that night in bed. That ought to be enough.

Then, there should be some jokes in the morning that will be funny again, and it will be time to be getting ready to win the next one, to encourage others and to go on living. It's only after the game you should think about it. Think so much that there isn't time to laugh or cry.

If you don't think about it when it is fresh in your mind, it is difficult to believe that you really want to be a good player.

Good players think. Especially after a loss. That's how they learn not to lose very often.

83

LOW POST PLAY

Whole books could be written about playing and scoring inside, but the basics are simple, though often ignored.

1. Set up in a good position.
2. Give the guard (or passer) a good target with your hand.
3. When you get the ball, take what the defense gives you... dynamically.

LOW POST SCORING POSITION

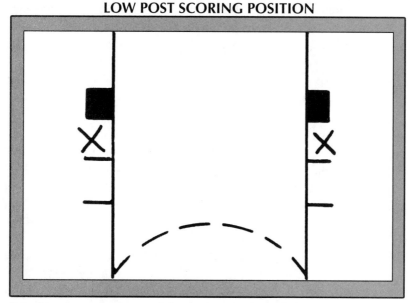

Stand between the box and the first mark on the lane.

1. Position. Stand on the "up" side of the box. This allows you to receive a pass and turn to score on the baseline side as well as to the middle. If you position yourself too close to the baseline, it is easy to get behind the backboard, and then the backboard helps the defender.
2. Target. Many players get free down low, but they fail to ask aggressively for the ball and show the passer where they want it. Be sure you set up and are strong. Hold the defender out with a firm forearm and make it clear where you want the pass

153

to be thrown with your other hand (the hand farthest from the defender).

3. Take what comes. Don't fight the defender; use him. If he forces you to the baseline, take the baseline aggressively with a quick drop step and (at the most) one protected dribble, so that you get to the basket with your feet in position to go up strong. If you get the ball with the defender on the baseline side, one step into the middle for the shot is all you need. Or take a quick drop step to the middle, use one protected dribble, and then gather yourself on two feet and go up strong.

    Whatever you do, do it immediately and with power. The low post is no place for sneak shots or for cute moves. Power is the key, even if you are not a strong player. Any player can make a powerful move inside because the defense is not permitted to grab your arm. It is not a matter of how strong you are, but how aggressive and strong the move is.

    Don't fool yourself into thinking that trick shots and fadeaways, even if you are good at them, have any place in a low post man's game.

4. One more tip. If you get the ball and the defender is directly behind you, or if you aren't sure exactly where he is, look immediately to your strong side. With the ball held firmly at your chin, find out how he is playing you. If you can step anywhere to that strong side, do it and get the body momentum you need to go strong to the basket. As you go, keep **your non-shooting elbow high (above your head) and "roll" it toward the defender as you shoot.** If you cannot go to that strong side, you ought to be able to "drop" the other foot (if you are right-handed, drop your right foot) and get by your man on that side. A defender should not be able to contain both a strong side move and a drop step to the weak side.

    Be sure you go up strong with any shot you take in the low post area. (See "Look 'im in the Eye First", entry #81.)

84
LUNGING

Have you ever noticed that good boxers don't miss very often with wild swings while inexperienced boxers are constantly missing with big swings that look like they could knock out an elephant if they connected? It doesn't pay in boxing to swing wildly or lunge forward and get off balance. A boxer is too vulnerable when he is badly off balance.

And so are basketball players. Good ones don't lunge and get out of position very often. It is the mediocre player who tries to show the coach he is hustling by making flamboyant attempts to steal or block shots when obviously it is too late. How many times per game do *you* dart out to steal a perimeter pass and go by your man after he has received the ball? How many times do you run at a shooter and go sailing by him after failing to touch his shot?

These lunging errors should happen only a few times per season, not a few times per game. The problem is, basketball players don't learn this as quickly as boxers. When a basketball player lunges out of position, it only results in a five-on-four situation, and the eventual shot may seem to be someone else's fault. Too bad basketball players can't get a solid rap to the chin when this happens. If they could, they would learn faster.

For every time you lunge and miss, you should have about five or six steals. That's an adequate ratio, but it's strange. The great ball hawks don't have many "dart-on-bys" while the non-stealers are usually the lunging leaders. Taking yourself out of a play with a lunge more than *once* per game is too often, and even "once" assumes that you are getting five or six steals.

Learn to play good, solid defense without lunging. Get the other team aware that you are always a factor, always someone who may touch a ball or get his body in the way.

"SORRY, FOLKS"

The most discreet, gentlemanly way of telling 10,000 hostile fans to go to hell is by walking up to the free throw line with ten seconds left, ahead by two, and calmly, oblivious to their taunting and screaming, sinking both ends of a one-and-one without even batting an eye.

M

85
A MAGNIFICENT MOVE FOR
A QUICK GUARD

Most players, and even coaches, would say it is not intelligent to go right when dribbling left-handed, or to go left when dribbling with the right hand. But for a quick guard who doesn't have to worry particularly about protecting the ball, this move is nothing short of magnificent. It can be used over and over again, and there is no move in basketball that is tougher to defend.

TO START THE MOVE, A RIGHT-HANDER BEGINS ON THE RIGHT SIDE OF THE COURT. WITH THE BALL BEING DRIBBLED IN HIS RIGHT HAND, HE SIDESTEPS AS THOUGH HE IS PLAYING DEFENSE WHILE "DIAGONALING" TOWARD THE FAR CORNER OF THE FREE THROW LINE.

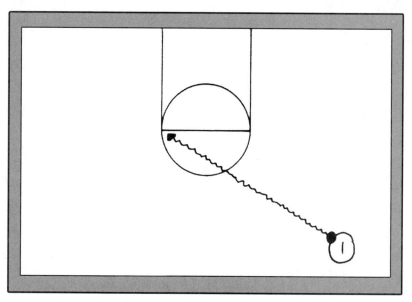

The dribbler's objective is to get inside the circle to shoot the ball or make a play. By sidestepping, a quick two-foot stop for a jump shot is always possible, and the feet are always in position to take advantage of a defensive mistake.

THE BEAUTY OF THE MOVE IS WHAT HAPPENS WHEN THE DEFENDER TRIES TO CROWD THE DRIBBLER AND PREVENT HIM FROM GETTING TO THE CIRCLE.

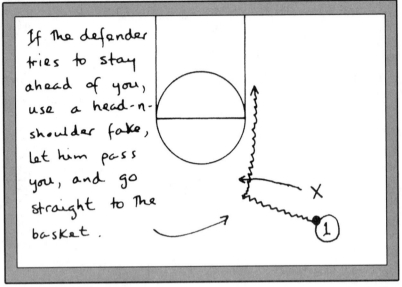

If the defender tries to stay ahead of you, use a head-n-shoulder fake, let him pass you, and go straight to the basket.

When the defender gets too close, the dribbler simply keeps the ball in his right hand and steps straight to the basket past the defender.

There are three great advantages to using this move.

1. The ball stays most of the time in the strong hand.
2. The head is up the whole time, seeing all developments (unlike the reverse dribble), and the chance for surprise by some other defender is therefore nonexistent.
3. By sidestepping rather than running, the dribbler is prepared to take advantage of the slightest over-reaction by the defender.

While sidestepping his way to the scoring position he wants, the dribbler gets in a rhythm with the defender, making it easy to make a head fake, which gets the defender to step one step too far. What initially seems like a dangerous move to make, because the ball is exposed to the defense, is actually *the* move that puts the most pressure on the defender. The dribbler's feet and the ball are always in position to take advantage of the slightest defensive mistake.

THE SAME-DIRECTION SWITCH DRIBBLE

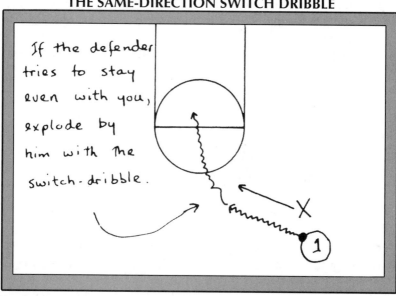

If the wordings the defender (handwritten in image:)
If the defender
tries to stay
even with you,
explode by
him with the
switch-dribble.

1

If the defender goes for the ball, which is right in front of his face (and lagging behind each of the sidestepping thrusts of the dribbler's front foot), the dribbler speeds up in the direction he is already going. As he speeds up, he makes a low switch dribble to his left hand to go by the defender.

Most defenders have a strong tendency to go for the ball, rather than stay ahead of the dribbler; therefore, they are very vulnerable to getting beaten badly. Naturally, a switch dribble right in the face of the defender is not something that every player can do. But for a quick guard whose bursts of speed keep the defender wary, the switch dribble in front of the body is not impossible at all.

If you are the kind of quick player who plays and dribbles low to the ground, this move will free you from the whole world. You will be able to use it every time you want to. It is extremely difficult to contain a player who can control the ball and the defender with this kind of move. It must be remembered, though, that this move will not work at all for a slower, higher dribbler. He will more likely have the ball swiped before he gets a chance to change rhythms or switch dribble in front of the defender.

One additional, important point: the dribbler should **sidestep at a fast, not leisurely, pace.** The fast pace makes it difficult for the defender to jockey and fake you into committing yourself. At a fast pace, all the defender can hope to do is stay with you. There isn't time for him to fake. You must learn to make a head and shoulder fake on the move, and drive straight for the basket as the defender moves beyond you in "the rhythm that was."

For a quick guard, practicing this move will pay enormous dividends.

86
THREE KINDS OF
MAN-TO-MAN DEFENSE

There are three basic ways to play man-to-man defense, and a good player should be aware at all times of which he is playing and why. If the coach tells you to play a certain way, you play that way. But if he only tells you "man-to-man," you need to be sure which of the three he wants.

The three basic ways are:

1. total overplay pressure
2. passive or no pressure (content just to stay between your man and the basket)
3. give-'em-a-chance-to-make-a-mistake pressure

It is possible to introduce all sorts of other situations, like how far out to pick up your man, how aggressively to guard a potential shot, how much help to give your teammates or when to double-team. But all these things are decisions your coach will usually make for you or the game and circumstances will determine. A poor ball handler will be guarded more closely, a slow player will be guarded more closely and a great shooter will be guarded more closely when he is in shooting range. These are individual circumstances; let's get back to the three basics of team defense.

1) Use total overplay pressure when you are behind and your chief enemy is the clock. If you are behind by three and there are ten minutes left, your chief enemy is not yet the clock. A lot will happen in ten minutes, and you can still win if you play good basketball. The clock is not a key factor.

The clock *is* a key factor when you are behind by five with two minutes left. If you play normal defense, the other team is likely to stall and let the clock run out. You need the ball, and every pass they throw puts you closer to defeat. When you are behind and the clock is your chief enemy, you need to "get all over them." Don't let your man touch the ball. You must force your man to go backdoor or force a risky lob. Don't be content to trail your man and allow perimeter passes to be thrown. All perimeter passes must be cut off. If your man catches a pass, it must be on the way to the basket, *not* on the outside.

2) The other extreme, passively playing between your man and the basket, you would expect to play when you are ahead and want to make sure you don't foul or give a layup. Passive defense is easy enough to explain. You simply stay away from your man and force him to shoot from outside.

Total pressure when you are behind, passive defense when you are ahead. This makes sense, but it isn't the only way. Your coach may think it best to keep the pressure on when you are ahead, and stay in the defense that got you there. (If the other team is poor at ball-handling or slow, but very good at shooting, this would especially make sense.) In the same way, your coach may decide to stay in a passive defense when you are behind if the opponent has shown no inclination to hold the ball.

3) The defense between total overplay and passive is the give-'em-a-chance-to-make-a-mistake defense. This should be your most commonly used defense, or at least the one you use most often when you are practicing on your own in pickup games where no coach is demanding anything. Give-'em-a-chance-to-make-a-mistake means just that. Play close enough that they have to worry about you, close enough that passes are not easy to throw back and forth, close enough that a dribbler cannot simply stand there and bounce the ball or take the ball exactly where he wants to at the speed he wishes to go.

If you are behind by one with three minutes left in the game, which defense would you play? Certainly not passive. And not total overplay (unless your coach thinks you are much quicker and can get away with it). The likely defense is the "mistake" pressure.

Three minutes is a long time to hold the ball, especially with the pressure on, the crowd screaming and the clock winding down. There is a good chance that the team with the ball will walk or throw a bad pass or mishandle the ball *if you give them the opportunity*. You can't sit back and play passively and merely deny the layup and hope for an error. You have to give them a chance to make the error. Without going wild or triple-teaming, it is very possible to force a mistake if you stay near your man and don't allow anything to be done easily. Basketball players, in general, are quite willing to make a mistake, but not when you allow them to dribble unmolested and receive a pass anytime they break out for it. It *is* possible to guard against the layup or easy shot and still be applying enough pressure that the other team may turn the ball over.

Make sure you understand the three types of defense, and especially know—if the other team is stalling at the end—whether you need to be in a total overplay (when your biggest enemy is the clock) or in a "mistake" pressure where there is still enough time to hope for a turnover or a missed shot.

Finally, ask yourself what *your* normal pickup game defense is. Are you passive like the majority of defenders? Or do you always go for steals, sometimes getting them and other times giving up layups? Or are you a good player, always putting on enough pressure to give them a chance to make a mistake yet being very stingy about giving up easy shots?

87
MENTAL TOUGHNESS

Mental toughness is not something you have on game day. It is a habit of mind that becomes a part of your pride and your self-image. It is something you carry with you everywhere: patience in a line of traffic, attentiveness in a classroom, a nobility on the practice floor. It's a quality of mind.

What do you care if you are fouled going for a shot in a pickup game? What do you care if the court you are playing on isn't very well-lit or if the temperature isn't just right? What do you care about how well your uniform fits?

What do you care about referees' calls, length of practice or the criticism you get? There are thousands of potential complaints, and there is also a certain kind of nobility that surmounts it all. *you* don't need to worry about all the tiny things, the minor problems, the childish complaints.

Develop a noble quality of mind. Learn to do your best quietly, methodically, without regard for tiny problems and adverse conditions. There are players who ignore all the negatives and give every game, every practice, everything they do their best shot. *That* is what mental toughness is. *That* is what every player should strive for.

88
MISTAKE RESPONSE: HUSTLE-CAT

Probably one of the most absurd sights in a basketball game is that of watching a foot stomp or a head down or the hands grasping the head because a player has missed a shot or made a mistake. The game of basketball is filled with mistakes. Even superstars make many mistakes every game. They miss shots, get turnovers and make defensive errors every minute or so. So what's all the fuss about a mistake?

A mistake is a common event in the game of basketball. It happens all the time. Good shooters miss shots; good passers toss the ball off legs and throw it out of bounds; good defenders get beaten backdoor or beaten to the ball. Since it happens to everyone in every game, it hardly seems like cause for footstomping or fingersnapping or headholding. When it happens to you, you should be well prepared. **You make mistakes all the time. You should be used to them by now.**

And by now you should have prepared a more useful response than some gesture that says to the world, "Oh look at me. I have done something wrong, and I am suffering anguish." What a waste of time and energy. What a needless lapse. What a losing lapse.

When you make a mistake on offense, you should do exactly what you would do if you had scored on offense—make the swift, abrupt transition to defense, and play the best defense possible under the circumstances. *That* is the only response that makes any sense at all in a fast-moving game like basketball.

What possible excuse can you give for taking time to make some gesture of disgust or disappointment or anger? There is no time for gestures that do not help the team. Besides, even from a purely selfish point of view, these gestures are stupid. Your gestures merely tip off the fans, and the coach as well, that *you* made the mistake. **If your particular brand of gesturing is unique or flamboyant, your mistakes are likely to be remembered not for themselves but for the gesture that always accompanies them.**

A far more intelligent response to your mistakes would be to **try**

to call attention off yourself as soon as possible. Why stand there and announce to the world that *you* messed up? Even your own coach may forget your mistake if you quickly involve him back in the action of the game.

For example...Say you throw a long pass that is intercepted. Instead of standing there fretting over your misfortune and calling attention to your pass, call your teammate into action, the guy you were throwing to. Because, regardless of whose fault that pass was, the point now is that *he,* not you, is out of position. *He* needs to get back on defense. The ball has passed him up, and *he* needs to be chasing it. Therefore, by yelling and urging him to chase the ball ("Get back! Take 'im!"), you alert your coach to the fact that there is defense to be played, and no time for crying over spilt milk.

This type of reaction is "Hustle-CAT" defense. The CAT means "**C**all **A T**eammate." Any time you make a mistake, don't stand there and fret and gesture. Hustle-CAT. **Hustle immediately, and call a teammate into action.** Yell out the new situation. By doing this, you will not only be calling attention off your mistake, you will be helping your team.

89
MOMENTUM

Momentum isn't just someone's fantasy or a figment of some play-by-play commentator's imagination. Teams do tend to score points in clusters, when the fans get revved up and energy levels rise. Players' emotions ebb and flow, and it *is* true that a player is more likely to hit a shot after his team has hit four in-a-row than when they've missed four in-a-row and they are falling behind.

For this reason, it makes sense to respond to momentum. If your team is "hot," go with it, keep the pressure on, keep shooting, let the game flow. But don't let the game roll along when the other team is getting the best of the flow.

A good rule of thumb: **When the other team scores two consecutive baskets, slow down the game, throw more passes and keep them on defense longer** until the momentum breaks. A running-gunning game may be your specialty, but if you've missed twice and the other team has scored, you need some change in the rhythm of the game. Changing a game's adverse rhythm is important enough that you usually would even want to pass up an early open shot just to keep the other team on defense longer and make them earn all their points.

90
MOVE YOUR MAN

Whether you are a point guard dribbling and looking for an open man, or a forward wanting to drive in for a layup, the important thing that you must do is move the defender who is guarding you. It is not enough to merely keep the ball from him. Nor is it adequate to hope to fake him out by using a move you've practiced on a playground. Your purpose, very definite, is to move him. Make him go places. Make him do things. Make him move to guard you.

If the guy who is guarding you must move to guard you, he will be vulnerable to fakes and quick changes of direction, and you will be able to get yourself free for a shot. But if you are lazily searching for an opening and hoping to create one with a sudden burst of speed, you don't understand what it takes to be an offensive threat.

A real offensive threat moves his man. He makes that man do things. His man is constantly being forced to go here and there and then recover and come back.

Do you move your man when you have the ball? Many players, even those who move around a lot, never move the man who is guarding them and never force him to scramble to cover them. Take time sometime, preferably in a pickup game, to look at the guy who is guarding you. Is he scrambling to cover you? Or is he able to stay on you by casually gliding from place to place?

Good players make their defenders scramble, sometimes just for the sheer joy of knowing they can. Good players *move* their defenders, and *then* they decide what to do to try to score. They don't go through some motion that worked in the driveway and hope it will lead to a score.

Move your man. Then try to score.

91
"MY FAULT!"

Get in the habit of taking the blame yourself.

Too many times in a game a pass is thrown, the receiver misses it, and he tells the passer to get the ball higher next time. Then the passer says, "Catch the ball!" and they both run back on defense angry at each other and hardly prepared to work together to stop the other team from scoring.

What an immensely different feeling to miss a pass and hear the passer say, "Sorry, bad pass." And what a feeling for that passer to hear, "No, I should've had it." In this case, both players are determined to do better next time, to pass better and catch anything; and both are prepared to play good team defense in the meantime.

This kind of attitude, of taking the blame yourself, does wonders for team morale and will help you win games.

N

92
NERVOUSNESS

Before the first game of the season, or before a big game or any game, you are likely to feel nervous. Your hands may be shaking and sweaty, and you are likely to have an anxious feeling deep in your stomach. Every player experiences these kinds of feelings to some extent. Often, the players who outwardly seem the most calm and in control are actually those experiencing the most inner turmoil.

What matters is not that you feel nervous, nor that you find some way to hide it. Many players make themselves more nervous by trying to think about other things, trying to tell themselves they aren't nervous and trying very hard to give the impression of utter calm and even nonchalance. But you will probably control your nervousness better and be sure that it helps rather than hurts your performance by **enjoying your nervousness instead of trying to hide from it.**

When you are eating before a game, or watching a preliminary game and waiting to go to the locker room to get dressed, or sitting in a classroom hours before "the big one," let yourself feel your nervousness fully and be grateful that you have it. Do you know how many people live their lives day after day without ever having the opportunity to feel nervous? They get up and rub their eyes and throw water on their faces, they get something to eat, they drive to the office and they do their work—and some even do important work exceptionally well—and yet through it all, they have hardly experienced any emotional highs the way you feel before every game.

Sports contests have that unique ability to raise people, fans as well as players, to emotional highs that they rarely get outside the arena. When you think about this and understand it, your tendency should be to really enjoy the opportunity you have. Be nervous, enjoy the fact that you have a game to play, a contest to win, a challenge to confront that is right out in the open, in front of people who care whether you succeed or fail.

When you stop and think about it, when you consider whether you would choose a life free of nervousness and challenges and crowds of hopeful or jeering fans, it is clear that you would choose nervousness. You would choose to lay your body on the line in front of crowds. And you would choose to fight for victories' highs even knowing you might get defeats' disappointments instead.

All that this means is that nervousness is part of the life of an athlete. Every athlete trains for the big game, the big confrontation, that special time when the fans will be gripping their programs and biting their nails and sitting on the edges of their seats. The athlete chooses this condition and strives for it. Regardless of whether you succeed or fail, you have to enjoy the opportunity and all that goes with it.

The next time *you* get that nervous feeling, you ought to recognize it as the great opportunity it is and say to yourself, "Here's the nervous feeling, that hope-and-fear quality that makes playing sports such a special opportunity. I'm not going to hide from it. I'm not going to worry that my palms are sweaty or my stomach is in knots. I'm nervous. Great. Just what I wanted."

Then go out and do your thing. You may make the game-winning shot or miss a one-and-one that loses the game. There is no assurance, regardless of what you do, that you will be a hero. Even Babe Ruth lost games by striking out with the bases loaded. Even Kobe Bryant shot an air ball that lost the playoffs. The final outcome will often be a matter of luck and inches. You can't always control that. But you can control your feelings along the way. You can really enjoy your nervousness, or you can be crippled and scared by it. It is up to you. It is a choice *you* have to make.

But think of it. Why not walk up to that free throw line in the final seconds and enjoy those knots in your stomach? You may win the game. You may lose it. Of course you are nervous. But why not walk up there and enjoy the whole thing?

Why not?

93
ALWAYS KNOW THE NEXT MAN

Many basketball players recognize the situation they are facing. But a good player knows the next man; that is, he knows not only what the situation is but what it is about to become as a result of *the next man.*

For example, you are dribbling downcourt in what appears to be a 2-on-1. But what is it about to become? Is the next man who is hustling to enter the play on your team making it a 3-on-1, or is he on the other team, meaning if you don't hurry it will be a 2-on-2? In the first instance, you can take your time and even have the confidence of a trailing rebounder on the way; whereas in the second instance, you need to be sure you hurry so that a final bounce pass is not intercepted.

A good player learns to anticipate the next man all the time. Why hurry to score a 3-on-3 when a trailer is just about to come to the free throw line for a wide open shot from fifteen? You might never realize, especially after you score a 1-on-1 fast break with a great move, that you looked stupid because it was possible to simply drift off and pull the defender away from the basket and then slip the ball to your teammate coming down next.

Remember that good players recognize not only the situation they are facing, but also the situation that will arise as a result of the entry into the play of the next man.

When you beat your man to the basket and get picked up by someone else, *is* there a teammate wide open for the "dish off," or is the next man a little guard sneaking back to pick off your pass?

When you are being defended by a man you know you can beat to the basket, can you get all the way in for the layup? Or is there someone on the defense who can get in your way? When you get in there, are you going to be surprised that someone is in your way? Or do you already notice him or anticipate his arrival and therefore are prepared to pass off?

You should always assume the arrival of a next man and know whether it is going to be your teammate or opponent. Will the next man make the situation you face easier or harder? Sure, you can lob the ball over the defender's head, but is there some other player who might figure in the play? You have to know who is coming next.

94
NOD TO THE COACH

When your coach tells you how he wants you to do something, if you understand what he is telling you, nod to him.

This seems like an obvious thing, and hardly a tip for a good basketball player yet very often players fail to do this. Nodding to the coach tells him you understand his instruction, and more importantly it gives the coach a good feeling about telling you.

You may think a small thing like nodding is not necessary, that it is enough to look your coach in the eye while he is talking and just take in the information. But it is not enough. Nodding to your coach will give him that little bit of extra satisfaction that will urge him to do his best—he's only human, too—and to keep helping and working with you.

This should apply not only to the times that the coach is talking directly to you, but also to the times when he is talking to the team in general or when he is specifically correcting another player. Get in the habit of listening whenever your coach is talking and nodding when you understand. Your nod does not have to be some grand gesture. Just a slight tilt of recognition and eye contact that says, "I've got it, Coach."

It makes sense to make it enjoyable for your coach to work with you. Your success is intricately tied to his opinion of you and the confidence he has in you. A little nod when he speaks goes a long way toward establishing the kind of player-coach relationship that leads to winning basketball.

95
NOISY SCREENS

Many basketball players exchange or slide-on-by when they are supposed to set a tough screen that forces the defender to go around them. This is especially true with screens away from the ball. It is easier to slide on by, so *that* is what most players do most of the time. But, to be a good player, one who sets screens that result in teammates getting wide open, you should concentrate on making your screens emphatic so they are real obstacles for the defense.

The best way to make an emphatic screen is to make it noisy. Run to the defender you are going to screen and land (but don't actually jump first) solidly and loudly on two feet. It is very easy to make a loud noise with two sneakers on a gym floor, and the effort to do that is usually all that is needed to remind you to really set an obstacle in the path of the defender.

There is another benefit to making an emphatic, noisy screen. The main reason most screens away from the ball don't cause the defense much difficulty is that the cutter leaves too early; therefore, the screener is encouraged to slide-on-by just to keep from fouling. The two-foot noisy screen teaches the cutter when to go. "Don't go until you hear the noise." In fact, your coach may tell you, "Don't go *unless* you hear the noise."

If your team uses a lot of screens, especially screens away from the ball, your effort to screen emphatically can really help your teammates get free. Noise is the key. Making noise on your screens forces you to set the screen emphatically, and it helps the cutters to leave at the right time.

96
NOSTRIL TIME

Nostril time is any time you have the ball near the basket. Take the ball straight up into the nostrils of the player guarding you, even if he is a lot taller than you. It is much easier for a shot blocker to get to a fade-away in most cases than to defend a shot put up past his nose.

A shot taken right up through the nostrils forces the defender to defend himself and keep his hands near his face, instead of outstretched and waiting to swat the ball. In addition, foul trouble is a constant worry of good shot blockers (or any player), and a ball put up near the nostrils will often be awarded two free throws if there is contact.

Remember, any time you have the ball near the basket, it is nostril time. It is time to get tough and go for the basket, *straight* for the basket, right up past the defender's nostrils.

THE LITTLE LAYUP SHOOTER

Would you call him a failure? He was a little kid, and he couldn't quite raise the ball to the basket. He put the ball way down by his hip and pushed with everything he had. But the ball just wouldn't get over the rim. Still, he stayed there all alone, flinging that ball upward again and again. He never did make one that day. But he stayed there a long, long time.

O

97–Nothing **OFF**–balance counts

98–**ONE**–on–**ONE**

99–Going for **ONE** shot

100–Defending a team that is playing for **ONE** shot

101–Be **OPPORTUNISTIC** on offense...and defense

102–**OUT**-of-bounds stuff

103–**OVERPLAYING** on defense

97
NOTHING OFF-BALANCE COUNTS

Imagine your reaction if, before a big game, the referees got all the players together from both teams and announced that, in addition to the usual rules of the game, they were going to call every player for a violation any time he got off-balance. An off-balance shot, a pivot against a double-team, a pass not thrown with authority, a lunge on defense....

Only mediocre players would have to object to this new set of rules. Good players don't do off-balance things. They don't want fadeaways; they don't want to throw a pass when they are leaning backwards or the wrong way; they don't like the feeling of lunging and getting off-balance on defense and having to recover. Good players are constantly on balance—*not* because they have better balance, but because they don't do things that throw them off-balance.

Think about the "new rules" the next time you play. Think that "nothing off-balance counts." When you learn to play a whole game and play hard and not do things off-balance, *you can play.*

98
ONE-ON-ONE

Most players enjoy playing one-on-one and especially like the challenge of showing they can beat someone else. Certainly, there is value in proving to yourself that you can beat others. This gives you confidence when you get in a game that you can score when you get the ball.

However, one problem comes along with playing one-on-one. That is the tendency to hold the ball too much, look around too much and jockey back and forth too much. In the driveway or on a playground, with no clock, no defensive help and no coach, it is fine to back into the basket and use three or five reverse dribbles to get yourself in closer. And it is effective sometimes to "rock" back and forth until you get the advantage you want. But in a game, using up time like this usually brings not a better opportunity but more defenders. It is likely as well to bring a coach's voice saying, "Get rid of the ball," or "Pass it," or "Run the offense."

Therefore, if you enjoy playing one-on-one and if you want it to help your game as well, you need to play one-on-one in a way that you can use the same moves in games as you use in the driveway or on the playground. This means you cannot rely on backing in and using a lot of reverse dribbles.

Play one-on-one by facing the basket and making a quick move to score. Plan on scoring with one or two dribbles rather than scoring by lazily dribbling around and looking leisurely for a good opportunity. These kinds of rules are especially important if a big man is playing a smaller man; otherwise, the bigger man can back in every time and protect the ball until he gets a layup—a great one-on-one move but not of much value in a five-on-five game.

There are other ways to get good practice from one-on-one. Play "five seconds to score" from midcourt. This game will require a good dribbling fake and burst of speed if you hope to get yourself a good shot. By playing "ten seconds to score" in a full-court situation, you have to learn how to slow up a dribbler on defense and know how to advance the ball upcourt quickly when you are on offense.

You may also try a staggered start situation, where one player gets the ball at the top of the circle and the defender has to begin a step behind. The play starts as soon as the guy with the ball moves, and you may add a rule such as "no stopping." That means once you go, you have to go all the way. A good player should learn, even against a taller player, how to get off a good shot once he has a one-step lead.

If you have someone to throw you the ball, you can play with the thrower standing out of bounds. Then you have five seconds to receive the ball, and on defense, you can stop your man by keeping him from getting the ball for five seconds, just the way it is in a game. The thrower can also stand at the top of the circle and you can start on the side in a very typical game situation with the opportunity to go backdoor or get a direct pass.

It makes sense to put tags on the game like "ten seconds to score," or "five seconds to get it in and three seconds to score." These situations are much more game-like. They prepare you for doing the kinds of things you need to be able to do in games.

The world is filled with superstar playground "one-on-oners" who can't play in a real game because they are so used to dribbling with their heads down or wandering around with six or seven dribbles before they make up their minds what to do.

There is an old coaching adage that makes sense for one-on-one just as it does for the rest of the game: **The way you practice is the way you'll play in the game.** No use playing one-on-one in a way that keeps you from getting better. Put the pressure on yourself. Score with a dribble or two, score facing the basket and learn to do whatever you do immediately, a moment after you get the ball from the defender.

99
GOING FOR ONE SHOT

It is common to see a team with the ball near the end of a quarter or half play for one shot by holding the ball. They spread out, use up time until the clock winds down to fifteen seconds, and then try to score. Their purpose is to gain two points or maintain the same score, while being sure that the opponent gets no more chances to score in that period. One problem with this tactic, or perhaps players' execution of this tactic, is that very often the ball is held too long, till the eight second mark or so, and the shot finally taken is a very poor-percentage shot that amounts to a waste of a possession.

If you are holding the ball for a last shot, be sure you start an offense with 15 seconds left and that you get into it in a hurry. It is better to get yourself a good shot and let the other team worry about having time for a rebound and a desperation shot before the buzzer. It is ideal to take that final shot with five seconds left. This gives you time for a rebound and allows little time for the other team to get the ball upcourt into good scoring position should they get the rebound.

If waiting for the ideal situation means passing up a good shot with ten seconds left for a wild throw with two seconds left, it's a poor exchange and doesn't make much sense. Start your offense in plenty of time, at 15, and take the first good shot that comes unless you feel sure you can get the ball inside at any time. Then you might wait a few seconds longer. But only a few.

100
DEFENDING A TEAM THAT IS PLAYING FOR ONE SHOT

An intelligent team that wants to hold the ball for one shot at the end of a period doesn't usually tell you by holding up one finger and yelling "one shot, one shot," though many good teams do. When you are going for one shot, it is smart to stay in your regular offense and alter the rules to something like, "Absolutely no shooting unless you get a ridiculously easy layup."

However, if you are on defense and you are playing one of those teams that spread out and yell, "One shot, one shot," use your head. They have given you some valuable information. They have told you that if you gamble for a steal and miss, most likely they are only going to dribble back around and kill time because they are not looking for a shot. **If they start playing for one shot with a minute left, that gives you about 45 seconds of free time or gamble time**, which is license to steal.

If your coach tells you to stay back passively in a zone, do that. If he says nothing, it makes sense to get out on your man and give him a chance to make a mistake. Especially if your team has a tall center, you can send four men to swarm the ball and usually, with just one man back protecting the basket, the other team will stay in a keep-away and not even try to score.

Use the time to put pressure on them and make them suffer for giving away their plan not to try to score for a while. If the clock winds down to 15 seconds, you can get back in a good solid defense to stop the shot.

101
BE OPPORTUNISTIC ON OFFENSE...
AND DEFENSE

In every game, lots of baskets are scored that require no cleverness, no particular ability, and neither a difficult pass nor a difficult shot. They simply require a player or two who are looking for opportunities to get easy baskets—perhaps by sprinting downcourt when the defense is loafing, cutting to the basket when a defender turns his head, or taking the ball toward the basket any time the defense allows that to be done easily.

Watching many players play, you get the impression someone is making them run downcourt with their heads down or making them run slowly. What excuse do you have for not at least starting down quickly just to see what may happen? If you are a point guard, why not dribble down quickly just to see if you can pass someone and give a teammate an easy basket?

The same goes for defense. Good players get seven or eight steals a season—not a huge number, but seven or eight more than most players—just by occasionally doubling back after a basket to see if they can catch the inbounds passer tossing a ball carelessly into the point guard. This is something you don't need to do every time, but why not get in the habit of trying it once or twice in every game? Why not guard the player taking the ball out of bounds and, once or twice per game, dart out suddenly to try to intercept the toss he has gotten into the habit of making from a side-out-of-bounds situation? Why not try to cut in front of the logical receiver in a jump ball situation when you know your team will not control the tap?

There are so many times, on offense and defense, when a good player *seems* to be resting away from the ball, but his mind is constantly asking questions. "What if I darted out there? What if the ball is suddenly passed inside? What if I make a big fake at the ball? What if I stand here as though I'm not paying attention?" A good player is always looking for an opportunity, some way to draw a charge, a chance to put on a one-man press when the others have trotted away, heads down, or maybe a chance to cut into the basket behind the defense. A good player doesn't necessarily move more than a mediocre player, but his *mind* works harder. He is always looking for a way to do something else, something more usually right at the time the mediocre player is congratulating himself for having done his job.

102
OUT-OF-BOUNDS STUFF

It is appalling how many balls are thrown away on in-bounds passes, especially at the end of a game against pressure when there is a fool-proof method of getting the ball in play.

Regardless of whether you are taking the ball out under your own basket or against a full court press or at the side of the court, you can always get the ball by having the man close to the ball go away and set a screen and then come straight back for the ball. If the screen is set properly, the cutter cannot be guarded except by a switch. If a switch occurs, the screener will have a defender on his back and, therefore, be able to run to the ball, free for the pass.

Set a good screen and come to the ball. The play works so well, it is difficult to understand why so many players jockey back and forth and stick a hand in the air and often end up reaching for a pass thrown six inches from their defender's fingertips. It is also difficult to understand why so many players (who don't even plan to go away and screen) line up just a few feet from the out-of-bounds line. Where can you run to when you line up just a few feet from the out-of-bounds line? You have no choice but to run away from the ball, making a pass to you a bad risk, or play midget league ball and ask for the ball while standing there with your arms reaching over the out-of-bounds line.

When you want to get the ball from out of bounds, make sure you stand 15, or at least ten, feet from the ball and then set a screen. If you haven't worked it out with a teammate so that he knows you are setting a screen (and so that the player making the throw-in knows), stand 15 feet from the ball and simply run hard.

Too often you see a player, who is overplayed by only one man, standing in the corner and calling upcourt for help. Doesn't he know that one man, even one faster man, can't possibly guard one man and keep him from receiving an in-bounds pass? If you will run hard one way, then run hard the other way, you will get free. The problem in getting free comes with jockeying, that terrible habit players have of moving one step back and forth but going nowhere.

In playing defense against a team taking the ball out of bounds, there are many situations, but usually your coach will determine how you should play. If, for example, you are full-court pressing, your coach will usually tell you whether to allow the in-bounds pass or whether to front your man to make him throw the ball over your head.

In playing defense under the other team's basket where a slight mistake could result in a quick layup, the tendency of defenders is to play too far out on their men and consequently let themselves be beaten into the basket. So, whether you are zoning underneath or playing man-to-man, you should remember to play about half-way between the ball and the man you are guarding (or the man in your area). Do not play forearm-against-man all the way out to the free throw line and have to worry about a fake and a cut to the basket. **Playing "half-way between" gives you plenty of room to react to cuts, it makes it impossible to screen you effectively and it encourages the throw-in to be a lob** over your head. And a lob is a pass you have plenty of time to react to and a good chance to steal for a layup, if you are alert.

103
OVERPLAYING ON DEFENSE

Overplaying a man and trying to keep him from touching the ball is very difficult work, but the players who can do it will win games for their team even if they aren't good dribblers or shooters. No player can score without the ball. So if you can keep a player from touching the ball, your value to your team on defense is obvious.

The biggest problem players have in trying to overplay a man is the tendency to line up *even* with the guys they are guarding. You cannot line up even with an offensive player and hope to beat him to the ball after he breaks for it. To overplay effectively, you have to *cheat,* the way you would try to win a race against a faster runner. You get a head start—you start out in front of the man.

This head-start concept makes perfect sense to anyone when talking about races to finish lines. There probably is not a little kid in the world who hasn't yelled, "Last one to the tree is a rotten egg!" or some such thing and taken off first and arrived before the others. Yet, players fail to put the same concept to work in overplaying. Somehow, they fail to realize that overplaying a man is nothing more than *racing him to the ball*. The one difference is that there is no exact finish line, but there *is* a finish line, and it is a race.

Once you realize that overplaying is simply a race to the ball, it should be easier for you to understand the common sense in the following rule that is crucial to successful overplaying: **The closer you are to the ball, the closer you are to your man.**

Conversely, the farther away you are from the ball, the farther away you are from your man. Or you might say, *the longer the race, the larger your headstart.* Put this way, it makes sense, and yet, game after game you see players—even gutty, determined players—trying to stop a guy by staying right on him when he is forty feet from the ball.

OVERPLAY OFF THE BALL

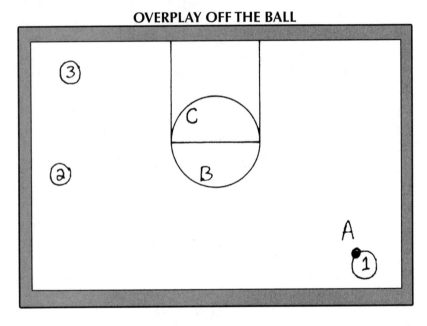

Even in an overplay defense, you play off your man when he is away from the ball.

Playing far away from your man when he is far away from the ball has other added benefits beyond making it easier to race him. When you are away from him, it is nearly impossible to set an effective screen on you since you can easily go to either side of the screen and still stay between your guy and the ball. However, the same screen is very effective if you are standing next to your man when it is set. In addition to being able to avoid screens, your position off your man tends to discourage penetration by other offensive players.

When you are playing a man who is in prime receiving position, 6-15 feet from the ball, you have to guard him closely because any slight opening he gets is enough room to get the ball to him. The way you play this man depends on your objective. If your objective is to keep him from touching the ball, you have to be sure that your front foot is farther out than either of his feet. In other words, your body is closer to the ball than his *and* it is closer to the line (either the ten-second line or the sideline) than his.

OVERPLAY NEAR THE BALL

The X's on defense are both closer to the ball (and closer to the nearest line) than their men are. The only possible pass is a backdoor bounce or lob.

In this type of overplay, you are knowingly risking giving up the backdoor cut for the basket because you don't want to let him receive a perimeter pass.

You overplay him on the outside, and you are ready to sprint toward the basket. If you play him even, you have to try to be ready to sprint in both directions at once, and then every tiny fake will draw you off-balance.

To get a clearer picture of this, you might think of a base stealer in baseball. Good base stealers often take a longer lead off first base when they want to bother the pitcher than when they want to run to second base. In the first instance, they can get very far off the base, but they are leaning back and are very ready to get back the moment a motion is made toward them. When they want to steal second though, they are more likely to take one step less off first so that they can lean toward second and be ready to spring for second base the moment the ball begins to be pitched.

Remember, these rules apply to overplay defense, when you are faced with a situation (like the clock running out) that forces you to take risks and prevent passes. Your feet are only farther out (from the basket) than your man's feet in a total don't-let-'im-touch the-ball situation. In this overplay prevent situation, if your man goes backdoor, *turn with your eyes on him* and sprint with your arm outstretched. You just might touch a ball the moment you look back toward it. Given the choice, remember, when your man cuts, take your eye off the ball, not off your man, for a split second. Then look to the ball as soon as you can.

P

104
PASSES THAT SHOULD'VE BEEN CAUGHT

This tip should be obvious, but often it is not. Many players fail to realize that every pass is a transaction between two players. The passer throws a pass that he believes the receiver can catch, and the receiver tries to catch it. If the pass goes out of bounds or off a leg or is mishandled for a travel, it is the passer's fault as much as the receiver's, even if the receiver should've caught it—because the passer made an error in judgment by throwing a pass that "should've" been caught instead of one that was caught.

When you first hear it, a "he should've had it" can sound reasonable enough, especially when everyone can see that the ball went right through the receiver's hands. However, in the course of seasons, the excuses seem to hold less and less weight. Somehow, good players seem to consistently throw passes that manage to be caught while complainers and guys with unfulfilled potential seem to be throwing passes equally well, but many of theirs sail off legs and out of bounds and should've been caught. In winning and losing, in points and assists, there is a huge difference between the ones that should've and the ones that are.

Perhaps the good player understands just a bit more about the transaction idea, and he gives it that little bit of extra effort to make sure the ball is caught. On the other hand, the "should've passer" is probably just a little more concerned with throwing the ball well than with the end result. Maybe it is merely luck that season after season some players' passes get caught while others' seem like they should've been. But don't bet on it.

105
PATIENCE

Patience is a word coaches yell all the time, but very few players have it.

Most players grow up playing against older, better players, and they learn to take every opportunity they get because opportunities don't come very often. Or they get good enough that every time they get the ball, they sincerely feel they have a good chance to score or a chance to make something good happen, so they try. It is understandable how players learn to be impatient, but impatience does not win games. Unless you are playing an obviously weaker team, the players on the other team will have about the same ability as the players on your team, so winning will depend on which team takes the better chances and the fewer risks, that is, which team has more patience.

A good player can get himself a shot every time downcourt, but a shot doesn't win games. *Making* the shots you decide to take is what wins for you. But are you willing to wait just a little longer to get a shot you can make? Are you willing to throw one more pass?

Patience applies to defense as well. A quick player with good hands is always a threat to steal the ball, and very often he can create a turnover by leaving his man and "jumping" a dribbler or double-teaming the ball. However, is he willing to wait for a good opportunity? Or will he run out at the ball too soon and leave a man wide open for an easy basket?

There are no hard and fast rules governing patience, which is why so few players are able to develop a good balance between patience and initiative. You can improve your patience and make your initiatives more effective by constantly asking yourself: "Should I have tried that? Should I have taken that shot? Should I have hoped to slip that ball in there by a few inches?"

Some of the most spectacular plays in a game should not even have been attempted. This is another reason why a player has difficulty learning what is patient and what is impatient or forced. The quick pass for a backdoor layup is a good example. It may miss the defender's hand by an inch, then bring the house down with a slam dunk. Can the coach say, "Don't throw that pass. It's too dangerous?" He probably won't say anything at all, and then later in the game, with the thrill of that slam dunk assist imprinted on your brain, you are likely to make the pass again, though this time it may be intercepted.

So...what is patience? Never trying anything? Never going fast? Never flying into the basket? No. Patience is learning what you can do and what you cannot do, knowing your limitations and playing accordingly. Be patient enough to wait to do something until you get a chance to do something you know you are good at. You won't score even those every time. But over the course of a game, and especially of a season, the players with patience will be the big winners.

106
P-DRIBBLE

The name "P-dribble" came from a pro player who yelled at a little kid who was dribbling too much in a camp game. "Don't stand there peeing with the ball," the pro said, "go someplace."

So many players P-dribble, stand around bouncing the ball on the floor, going nowhere. But few are probably aware of how devastating the results are of go-nowhere dribbles. The more go-nowhere dribbles that are taken, the fewer passes that are thrown. Especially, there are fewer split-second, perfectly-timed passes because the ball is usually coming off the floor at the moment a cutter is free. The result is that fewer cuts are attempted and, therefore, fewer people get open.

Many coaches talk of the importance of moving without the ball, yet few players learn to move without the ball if they play with P-dribblers. It is discouraging to cut free while your teammate is dribbling, going nowhere and not ready to pass. Few players are likely to sustain their effort when they aren't being rewarded with quick passes and teammates looking for their movements.

One of the best ways to be sure that *you* are not one of those players who discourage teammates from moving without the ball is to promise yourself not to P-dribble and not to dribble at all unless you are going forward. Does this requirement seem as though it is going to hamper your game? Probably only if you don't play very well.

What good are sideways dribbles and backward dribbles? Why do you need them? For every excuse: "But I had to take it back out and set it up," "But I was off-balance," "But I wasn't sure what I was going to do yet." There are a dozen other possible moves a good player can make.

You can slow it down and set it up with a pass. You can get on balance without dribbling. You can think better when you *Don't* have the ball and put more pressure on the defense, too.

The point is, you do not have to P-dribble at all. **You can play an entire season without taking any backwards or sideways dribbles.** You can play a whole season committed to either going forward or passing off. When you get a whole team that is willing to do that, willing to pick the ball up and look for teammates, and willing to condition each other to move without the ball because no one is interested in needless dribbles, you will have a team that moves and plays to win.

The next time you play, count your P-dribbles, and count all your excuses. Count all the reasons why, in your particular situations, you *had* to dribble at your feet or to the side or backwards. Then realize that a good coach wouldn't want to hear your garbage reasons. He would want to see you learn to pick the ball up and pass it off and learn to play the game without those needless dribbles or those needless excuses. You could play the rest of your career without taking another P-dribble. And you should.

107
PICKING UP A DRIBBLER IN THE MIDCOURT AREA

In a full-court press or against a fast break, you may often be faced with a situation where an unguarded dribbler is coming at you. Many players make the mistake of trying to move toward the dribbler to stop him. This is fine if you have a teammate hustling alongside the dribbler, but if you don't, running toward him will enable him to pass you easily.

Anytime you have to stop a dribbler, try to influence his direction and then move along with him. Try to cut him off 15 feet down the court, *not* where you are.

RETREAT!

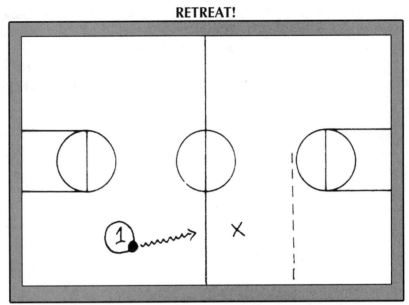

This dribbler must be cutoff or at least challenged near the dotted line, not at midcourt. You cannot cut off a good dribbler where you are or by running at him.

108
PICKUP GAMES

Every basketball player knows of the problems with pickup games. Make a big steal near the end of the game, and you can forget about going down to the other end for a layup. The guy you picked clean will be walking out of bounds, not saying a word, showing everyone that it was absolutely obvious you took off his arm to get to that ball.

Call it face-saving or call it a lie, whatever you like, but no one gets a clean steal near the end of a pickup game. No one loses face in a pickup game. No use arguing over that call, throw him the ball and start again. Get another clean steal if you can. It's great practice. So what if he walks straight out of bounds again? You don't need to win pickup games that no one will ever remember. But you do need to get good practice.

Good practice is what it is all about. Almost every player who ever became a star learned his shakes, his moves, his stuff in pickup games. Pickup games are where you try new things. No one cares if the ball goes out of bounds, just so the move looks good and the ball doesn't roll down the hill or under a car.

One big problem is that a lot of players spend so much time legislating and refereeing that they don't get very good practice. *That* doesn't make sense at all. When you play in pickup games, if you really are trying to improve your game, forget about the refereeing and forget about all the guys who shoot and dribble too much. Chances are they think you are one of them. Go there to get better.

If there is a guy who shoots too much at your playground or gym, wonderful. Guard him and don't let him touch the ball. **If you spend a lot of time getting disgusted because everyone loafs on defense, you're crazy. Everyone loafs on defense all over the world. Big deal.**

Get practice defending a four-on-two or a three-on-one. There is too much to learn to waste your time complaining. Push yourself to get down the court first on offense. So what if they don't give you the ball? Fight for offensive rebounds while counting how many times during the game you got *so* open that even the rat league ball hog *had* to pass to you.

If you are an especially good organizer, try to shorten the games. You would be better off playing shorter, harder games, than long, drawn-out loafers' games. In almost all pickup games around the country, the games are long enough that everyone plans on loafing the first seven or ten baskets and then plays hard when the score is 9-8 or 17-15. Yet, what excuses do *you* have for loafing even if the other *nine* are? See how many balls you can touch on defense, see how many rebounds you can get, see how often you get open for what would have been easy layups *had* you been playing with guys who were willing to pass. Just because the others want to play at the offensive end doesn't mean you have to give in to complaining.

You are a competitor and you don't like to lose, not even in a pickup game. But use your head. Your ultimate objective is to get better, not to become a better complainer. Get back on defense and stop them yourself, or at least come close and do your best.

Your time is never wasted if *you* are doing your best. If you lapse into complaining, as is so common in many pickup games, *you* are wasting your own time.

One final word…If you are lucky enough that you don't recognize the circumstances described here as "the universal pickup game syndrome," consider yourself lucky. You are one in a million.

109
POINT

Since defensive players are supposed to see both their man and the ball at all times, and since there are no pockets in most basketball pants, a good place to put your hands is out to the sides, one hand pointing to your man and the other hand to the ball.

Not that you have to have your index finger on each hand pointing like Uncle Sam on an Army poster, but why not have one hand keeping track of the ball while the other keeps track of your man? Why not have your hands up at the shoulders where they are ready to touch a ball if it comes? With hands up and open fingers pointing to the two things you are wanting to keep in your view, you are constantly reminded of your objective: to keep both in view at all times.

Though most coaches do not demand that you point to both the ball and your man, there is not much excuse for doing anything else with your hands. Keep those hands out and up and point. The effort at pointing constantly will almost certainly tune your concentration more finely and help you to play better defense.

110
POOP

POOP means **P**ivot **O**ut **O**f **P**ressure. Often a player with the ball, especially one who has used his dribble, gets a defender moving into his face, pressuring. And the reaction of the player with the ball is to lean backward, off-balance, and force himself to throw a weak pass to the side. (Once you lean backward, you hardly have any other option.) This tendency to lean backward is a bad habit and not something you must do. Even if the ball is over your head when the defender moves into position with his arms up in your face, there is a move that can quickly put you back on the attack. The move takes no talent, just the thought to do it.

To pivot out of pressure, or POOP, you need to twist your upper body a quarter turn to the side and then bring the ball down to your waist alongside your body (on your side, not straight down the front). By giving that small quarter twist, **you put your body between the defender and the ball, and you put your elbow in his face as you lower yourself into a crouch** where you have strength and mobility with the ball. The elbow in his face is not meant to hurt him, but its presence certainly keeps him from sticking his nose too close in case he is getting any ideas about going for a steal.

Crouched over the ball, no one can take it from you, and that elbow allows you some room to move a bit to find on open teammate.

The habit of pivoting out of pressure takes about a minute to learn. (You don't even need a ball to practice it.) It will be very helpful the first time a player steps into your face, and you instinctively make a quarter turn away from him, crouch and stick an elbow near his nose. It is not that you wish to hurt anyone, but you do want to be on balance and *you* want to be the aggressor, not the guy leaning awkwardly backward.

111
POSITIVE THINKING GARBAGE

You guys gonna win tonight?"
"I don't know."
"What d'ya mean you don't know? You gotta think positive."

That's a rather familiar exchange between fans and players, and as a result, there has developed a certain misunderstanding through the years about what positive thinking really is. Most people confuse positive *thinking* with positive *talking,* which is what the fan above was concerned with.

You don't win games or better your performance with positive talking. Saying you are going to win isn't going to make you win. It may be better than walking around saying you are going to lose, but *saying* anything isn't the answer. Games are won and lost on the court by performers, not by talkers.

There probably has never been a losing team that didn't fill dozens of pre-game locker rooms with words like, "We're gonna take these guys. We can do it. Yeah, we'll beat 'em." But they still had no trouble going down to defeat after defeat even though not one of them ever spoke of the possibility of losing.

Good players often think about the possibility of losing. In fact, many of them think more about the possibility of losing than they think about the joy of winning, and there is a very good reason for this. Good players are usually accustomed to winning, so for them winning carries with it no great joy. A certain measure of satisfaction, yes. But not jumping-up-and-down joy. What motivates a good player is not so much any thrill involved with winning, but instead the wrenching disappointment, the agony of losing. You think about losing, about that feeling of walking into the locker room, taking a shower, staying awake that night going over every play and sitting in class the next day, still unable to get it from your mind. It hangs on you like a sickness and makes you feel like you are suddenly less of a person. Maybe it shouldn't. But it does—to winners.

So, don't think about losing? Don't talk about it? Maybe not to fans who won't understand, but to yourself or to your teammates, you know how you feel and you know what motivates you. Winning is not going to depend on you telling some fan, "Yeah, we're goin' to give 'em hell!" It depends on preparation and concentration and a deep-down desire not to be beaten. It takes not a *wish* to win—everybody has that—but a gut-wrenching hatred of defeat. "Gut-wrenching hatred" may not sound pretty, but that seems to be something that good players have, even more than a will to win.

In any case, feel free to *think* whatever you like, and don't be afraid to think hard about losing. Tell the well-meaning fan whatever you find best, and **remember what you will feel like playing out those last few minutes, behind by ten, having to foul and hope they miss, feeling the gloating joy of their fans and walking home a loser.** Think about losing all you like, because *that* kind of negative thinking just may be the best motivator you have.

In fact, if more players would spend more time thinking of defeat, they probably would loaf less and do more when the game is still within reach. Down ten with a minute left should *not* be the first time it enters your mind that you may lose. The opening tap might be a better time, so extra effort gets *you* the first basket of the game, not them.

112
PREP

PREP stands for **P**rime **RE**ceiving **P**osition, a place you should never be unless you are wide open for a pass. One of the biggest faults of players that results often in turnovers for teammates is standing in prime receiving position, 10-15 feet from the ball, but not moving and too closely guarded to throw a pass to.

Just one player standing close to the ball but not free forces the player with the ball to go the other way and limits his options. Anytime two players stand in prime receiving position but are not open, a turnover is very likely to result, either from a risky pass, a double-team, a five-second call, or any other number of bad-risk possibilities. These may look like the dribbler's fault but are actually the fault of his teammates who clogged the area around him and prevented him from doing something good with the ball.

PREP should stand out to you like a slam dunk in a midget league. When you get within that critical distance from the ball, you have to feel it immediately—are you open for an easy pass or aren't you? If it is not easy to get you the ball, you should leave that area more quickly than you came, and clear it out for someone else to come running for the ball.

If the player with the ball has to wonder whether or not you are open, *you are not open. Leave. Get out fast.* Let your teammate throw to a man who is running to the ball. Don't make him throw you a ball that he has to wonder if you can catch.

PREP. **P**rime **RE**ceiving **P**osition. It's a place you are when the player with the ball is looking for someone to pass to. It's a place you are *not* when the player with the ball is on the move, easily able to beat his man. It's a place you are *not* when you are being well-guarded, but a place where you *are* when you are doing the guarding in an overplay defense.

PREP is not any particular spot or distance from the ball, but you know it when you watch any game. You know the distance at which players like to throw safe passes—not so close as to allow a double-team and not so far as to permit an interception.

Think of the importance of PREP, of being there when the ball needs an outlet, of leaving there quickly when you're not open, of clogging that area when you are on defense. Control PREP, and you control the game.

113
APPLYING PRESSURE

Effective pressure is continuous, not on-again off-again. But being continuously on your man (in man pressure) or being able to get someone quickly on the ball (and people quickly in the prime receiving areas in zone pressure) takes a lot of effort *and* intelligence. A quick dart-out to steal should not be confused with pressure. *That* is a quick dart-out to steal. That's all. If you get it, fine. If you don't get it, though, you let the other team off the hook and enable them to relax and get their confidence. Pressure, to be effective, must be continuous action. It must not be *attempts* to steal but constant *threats* to steal.

Almost all players will make a mistake if you give them the opportunity. Very few players for example are comfortable dribbling in a crowd with their weak, usually left, hand. A dribble now and then with the weak hand they will accomplish nicely. But being forced to keep the ball there is another story. If you can keep the ball in your man's weak hand, he will very likely make a mistake, providing his teammates are not wide open for passes.

The reason continuous pressure is effective is that basketball players are very instinctive. They will throw passes they should not throw or dribble places they should not dribble, **if they can be forced to do several things in a series rather than one thing at a time** in exactly the way their coach went over it in practice. If they get a chance to sprint out to the ball, then make a good pass after a dribble or two, they are likely to be able to do just what their coach has taught. However, if they come out for the ball and they aren't free, they have to think about options and movements they are less accustomed to. **The more things you make them do, the more tired they get, and the more their concentration slips.**

To apply effective pressure, you have to have the energy to make it continuously difficult for the offense. By doing this, your weaknesses, which every pressure defense has, will not be exploited. In zone pressure, there are always offensive players open, but if you hustle, get to the ball, distract the passer and force him to turn his back to one side, the open men are no longer able to get the ball.

Like so much of basketball, this is common sense, but it is a sense that players often fail to employ during a tight game. For example, players needing the ball at the end of a game, five points behind with several minutes left, often *let* their man get the ball and then get up in the man's face. If you let your man get the ball with ease, that means he will be collected and ready to burst ahead when he needs to pass you on a dribble. He is only likely to dribble carelessly or throw a pass poorly if he has had to work to get the ball. If he has to work for the ball, he has no time to collect himself, he is tired, he is irritated by you and his teammates are not precisely where the coach told them to be (and where they were) yesterday in practice.

Although sometimes you may feel as though your effort is in vain, continuous pressure pays big dividends. Teams *will* throw the ball away if defenders stay close. If you make every pass difficult, every dribble worrisome, you won't have to go for a steal. The other team will make a mistake for you; your concern need not be with when or how. Just apply the pressure and wait.

If you need a steal *now*, pressure defense is not what you are talking about. That is risky, steal-now defense. Pressure is "slapping some heat on 'em" and keeping it there. Off again on again is not pressure. Many poor players can handle that kind of situation with ease. Do it, rest, do it, rest...is just the kind of rhythm a poor player needs. To apply pressure, you make every phase of the game difficult and you wait. A mistake will occur soon.

114
BEATING PRESSURE

Beating the pressure of three blitzing linebackers in football takes strength, quickness, guts and ability. If you don't have those things, despite your good intentions and great attitude, you could get knocked to the turf all night long. But in basketball, no one is allowed to knock anyone down, and no one is even allowed to bump you.

In other words, basketball pressure is mostly hype, a bluff. It's false advertising, a sort of "Hurry! Act Now! Supply Limited!" with the warehouse full and no one buying. Basketball pressure is a ruse, a fraud to get you nervous and disorient you *so that you make a mistake.*

Do you understand that fully? They run around and wave their arms, and sometimes they even run at you with two or three guys, leaving people wide open everywhere **just to get you to think you are in a**

game with blitzing linebackers. They have to make you think you can get knocked to the turf when they know that even their own coach told them, "Don't touch them. Don't foul."

To get a team to apply good pressure, a coach has to do a selling job. "If you guys do this (overplay, get close, wave your arms)," he promises, "they will make a mistake. Just watch and see."

But players aren't easily sold. **Every day in practice, their second team scores layups against that same pressure.** Everyday in drills, their second team gets the ball upcourt many times. So why should they believe the coach? How can he be sure a group of first-teamers won't do what the second team does—and even better?

Isn't it true that almost anyone can bring the ball upcourt on another man, one-on-one? Even a center with the aid of a few reverse dribbles will get the ball upcourt on the quickest defensive guard almost every time in practice. And nearly everyone can get away from another man to receive a pass or go backdoor after a few seconds. One man just can't stop one man at anything. Players know that. So, why is pressure supposed to work?

It isn't. And it won't. Unless you let it. Unless you get nervous and start treating waving arms like blitzing linebackers. The answer to beating pressure is to **remain calm and strong.** Keep your objectives firmly in mind: make decisive moves; come to crisp, sharp stops; throw short, snappy passes; run quickly wherever you go.

Pressure doesn't begin being effective until you start thinking about stringing moves together, taking two more dribbles, throwing lob passes and getting short rests. As long as you are thinking strong, you should play strong. You may throw a pass away now and then, just as you can anytime. But pressure will not bother you if you realize that (1) they are waiting for you to make a mistake, and (2) a mistake will usually come at the end of a tentative, strung-out play, not at the end of a brisk fake, two strong dribbles, a quick stop and a short, snappy pass.

115
PULLING OUT A DEFENSE

Many times when you are ahead, your coach may decide to pull the other team out of a packed-in zone and make them come out and play you man-to-man all over the court. When this happens, it is important that you be ready to run an offense immediately after the other team does come out.

Too often the team on offense stands around and continues to throw "hairy" passes, ones that are nearly intercepted. And why? You know you are pulling them out, so you have plenty of time to decide what you are going to do when they get out there. Call the offense you want to run *before* they make your perimeter passes difficult, not after you have almost lost the ball two or three times. A good rule of thumb: **The first time it becomes difficult to throw a perimeter pass by just standing there, run your offense.**

In some cases, only one or maybe two defenders may come out to put token pressure on the offense while the other three stay back and the defense remains a zone. If they want to stay in a zone, fine, let them; but don't try to control the ball with two little guards just barely sneaking the ball past a defender who is between them.

A TENTATIVE KEEP-AWAY

Note that no one on the court is wide open. The offensive players are still playing as though their objective is to attack the basket, not (as it should be) to get the ball.

The whole offensive team needs to spread out and move the ball to the open man dynamically. Dynamically means with a sense of enjoyment, a taunting sense of "Run your butts off, you fools." It is not passing the ball tentatively in a sort of scared keep-away, but spreading out, sliding into the open spots, moving toward the ball and making sharp, quick passes to players ten feet in the open. This can be done easily if only the attitude of the team with the ball is right. You don't think, "Keep it away." You "zing" that ball and make them run.

A DYNAMIC SPREAD OFFENSE

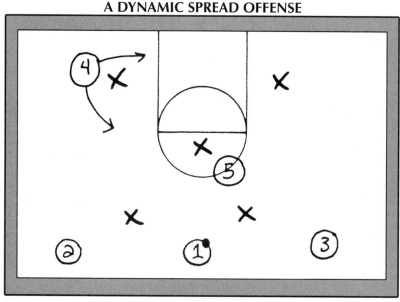

Here, the offense is spread, and four players are out past the free throw line. All of them are seeking the ball and are ready to come to get it to make passes easier to throw.

116
PUTTING THE BALL INTO PLAY

A point guard must be especially attentive to how to put the ball into play, but this tip applies to any player who is trying to get the ball to a certain teammate.

When the point guard brings the ball down the court, his job often is to get the ball to the wing. When a wing man gets the ball, he may have to get it to the corner or back to the other side. When you are required to get the ball to a certain man, it makes utter common sense to get closer to the man you want to throw to. Yet, game after game, players force the ball to other players and give the defense time to intercept because they try to pass from too far away.

It should be clear that a six-foot pass is easier to complete than a 15-foot pass, but players often throw difficult 15-foot passes (or even longer ones) that barely get there or get stolen because they do not think to dribble a bit closer and then throw the pass.

STARTING THE OFFENSE

A guard, or any player, should not stop in the middle of the court but instead should choose a side (at about midcourt) and dribble toward a teammate to shorten the pass.

Shortening a pass is not necessary, of course, if the defense is allowing you the pass you want to throw. But if the defense is overplaying your passes, it is foolish to pass from far away. Use a dribble to get close so you can force the defenders to guard against both the straight pass and the backdoor.

Q

117
QUESTION YOURSELF

Don't just go out there and play your same old way. You aren't as good as you could be. The only way to be as good as you can be is to question yourself constantly.

"Am I ready to help, to stop a layup, to touch a pass, to hit a dribble in the three-second lane? Am I often the first player down the court on offense? The first back on defense? Have I really tried for each offensive rebound, or am I often bailing out too soon? Am I blocking out for defensive rebounds? Am I on my way to the ball on each defensive rebound, or am I often standing and watching my teammates get it? Am I aware of the clock? Should I tell a teammate it is time to go for the backdoor? Can I draw a charge against one of their awkward big men who has to push himself to get back to cover our break? Should I tell the referee first, instead of getting knocked over for nothing?"

There is no end to the questions you should be asking yourself as you play. There is so much a player can do that never gets done. You can't afford to just go out there and play if you really want to improve.

118
LOOKING QUICK

Looking quick, like a guy with lightning speed, is often more a matter of using the defender's quickness against him rather than having lightning-quick feet of your own.

You can have great quickness, but if your habit is to fake out your man and, instead of taking advantage of him, fake again and let him recover, then even though you *are* quick, you don't particularly look quick because you don't get anything done. It is better to dribble downcourt and give your defender the impression that you are about to switch hands and direction. Then, when he thinks he is cleverly anticipating your move and darts out to get the steal, you fly on by him to the basket leaving him leaning the wrong way.

A lot of players use too many fakes, or they make their fakes from too far away from the defender. These fakes are not effective. You want to learn to move up near the man guarding you and to control the ball well enough that he can't take it from you. **If you can let a defender stay close to you without fear of losing the ball, every slight nod and lean of yours will force a quick reaction on his part that you can take advantage of,** if you are ready.

Of course, it is not easy to learn to control a ball so well that a quick player cannot get to it, but if you practice, and if you are conscious of the fact that it *is* possible, you can use the man's quickness against him. **You can control the shifting of his weight** and keep dictating the action so that you, not he, looks quick.

You will always look quicker than a man you maneuver into leaning the wrong way at just the moment you decide to go the other way. It is easier said than done, but there are good players who do it. So can *you*.

119
IMPROVING YOUR QUICKNESS

Quickness is probably the number one requisite of a good basketball player, so nearly everyone feels a need to be quicker. People will tell you that you cannot improve your quickness, but that's not true. It may be true that you will never be an Allen Iverson or Steve Nash by working on quickness drills, but you definitely can improve your quickness.

You can devise your own drills, and a couple are suggested below. But regardless of what drill you use, it is your thinking that counts. Quickness is the ability to get from one spot to another nearby spot very quickly. To do that, you have to *want* to get there quickly and you have to *feel impatient* on the way no matter how quick you are.

For example:

Quickness Drill #1:

Stand on the free throw line, both feet touching the line. On your own internal "Go!" rush to the top of the circle, touch that circle line with both feet and get back. On your way there and on your way back, be thinking, "Gawd, this is taking a year!" Hurry! Get there, get back. No, no, no. You're a *turtle*. Try again.

Impatience is the key. You have to want to get there faster, and you have to hate yourself for taking so long even though it will take a real turtle just a few seconds. Get there, get back, push yourself, make those legs move.

Quickness Drill #2:

Pick a few objects 7-15 feet apart, and touch them all as fast as you can. Don't run around in a circle touching them in order; go back and forth. Your objects could be the free throw line and the marks on the lane. Touch the first mark, get back to the line, touch the first mark on the other side of the lane, get back to the line and so on.

Touch them with your feet , next time touch them with one hand, with two hands. Touch the side of your house, a leaf, the edge of a sidewalk, anything, back and forth *just so you are impatient* and really trying to make each step go faster.

One caution: Don't make your quickness drills into difficult conditioners that you dread doing. And don't make them so long that you get tired during them. Conditioning is one thing; quickness is another. If your mind is on the difficulty of the effort, on your fatigue, you aren't going to be using your mind to develop the kind of impatience and concentration you need to get your legs going faster. If you really want to improve your quickness, you don't want to be battling fatigue at the same time. "Get there, get back, get there, get back." It is not a marathon that is going to make you quicker, it is moving 7-14-21-28 feet faster than you could before. Naturally, in a game, to be able to *use* your quickness, you need to have the energy, the conditioning to be ready and willing. But to practice your quickness, do it rested, so that all your concentration is kept on the impatient effort of putting one foot in front of the other sooner.

Two more suggestions.

1) "Fight" with your dog. Fake and feint, go forward and backward, tap the dog on the snout and try again. Most dogs will readily get involved

in a game of quick transition. Run at a dog, it runs; back off, it comes. A young dog will be willing to play all day, and *you* can get excellent practice dodging and darting and faking and moving.

2) Try putting four guys around the foul circle, and you stand in the middle. Their objective is to slap your butt without getting their outstretched hand slapped by you. You'll get dizzy spinning around, but they'll keep your feet moving fast if they've got any kind of competitive urge and sense of humor at all.

Whatever drills you use, move your feet and hate the passage of time. A few minutes a day will certainly improve your quickness.

120
QUICK-RELEASE GROOVE SHOTS

Golfers especially talk about "grooving" their swing, and in almost every sport a player strives for that feeling of "getting in the groove," the feeling that everything is going just right. In basketball there is one quick, specific way to practice shooting that is very effective for putting your shot-off-the-dribble in the groove.

Stand at the free throw line. (From "head on" the ball comes back to you faster, you don't have to chase it from side to side. If you have a "feeder," stand anywhere you like, about 15 feet out.) You want to be at a distance where you can shoot well, and you want to get a lot of shots in a short period of time. Tune your concentration onto just the thing you are doing. You want to practice getting off your shot with a *quicker-* than-normal release, not so fast that you throw it at the basket and fail to follow through but definitely faster than you normally shoot.

Stand there and put one hard dribble at your feet, move both feet slightly (a few inches each), and be impatient to get that ball off the floor, out of your hands and into the basket. It might seem as though this hard-dribble-not-going-anywhere is unrealistic, since you will never take tiny steps like this in a game. But what it does is groove your shot off the dribble so that **wherever you dribble to,** no matter how many dribbles you have taken to get there or how big your steps, **your last dribble and steps begin to feel like the grooved dribble-steps that you practice all the time,** that one quick move and shot that you learn to make "in your sleep."

That's what "the groove" is all about. You practice that hard-dribble quick-release shot from a place where you are good, and you develop confidence. You feel you can hit that shot anytime. Then you get in the game, and **every shot from every place at the end of every dribble "kicks" you into rhythm,** the same rhythm you develop confidence in by doing that one thing over and over in a situation that is easy.

It might be even better to practice 462 shots a day where you drive full speed from the midcourt line to the free throw line, stop abruptly, go straight up and shoot. But who is going to do that? Who has the energy? Or the time? There are too many things to learn, pickup games to play in, ball handling drills, one-on-one moves. No one is going to shoot 462 hard moving, abrupt stopping shots per day. But you can shoot 100 quick-release groove shots a day and not be at all tired or even use up much time. When you get a hard-driving chance from midcourt to the free throw line in a game, it won't feel like a new experience. It will seem as though you've practiced it thousands of times.

You definitely need to work on a quicker release. Most players take more time to shoot in practice than they will get in a game. It is fine to practice shooting slowly, concentrating on correct form, so that you get confidence that you can shoot well. However, some of your practice must overdo it so that the shots you get in a game seem easier, not harder, than the ones you get in practice.

It is very easy to slow down a shot in a game when you have time to do that, but almost any shot speeded up to get it off misses. Therefore, once you've practiced a quick release, there will be no such thing as speeding up your shot in a game. Either you get the groove shot that you work on all the time, or you get an easier shot, but certainly nothing faster.

One final note. If you can't hit 8 or 9 of ten from the free throw line almost every time, you aren't ready to practice quick-release-groove shots. First, you need to learn to shoot. *Then,* learn to shoot faster. It is difficult to imagine any coach wanting a mediocre shooter to learn to get off more shots!

It is the very good shooter who needs work on the quick-release-groove shot so that his game percentage is at least comparable with his practice percentage. Being good at "H-O-R-S-E" does *not* assure you that you will be a good game shooter. But once the quick-releasers pop in from all over in practice, they will pop in from all over in games, too. A groove knows no distinctions!

121
"NEVER QUIT"

Sometimes people overdo the idea of quitting and how awful it is. "A winner never quits, a quitter never wins." That's a catchy line, but catchy lines are not to be taken 100% literally all the time.

If you are fourteenth man on your team, never getting in the games, and you have a chance to get on another team where you will get to play, quit. If you don't like the sound of the word, tell the coach politely that you are "dropping off" or "changing" teams. **There is nothing wrong with quitting when you are merely making an intelligent choice for a better use of your time.**

However, when quitting involves not a better use of your time but merely a poorer use, then quitting *is* bad. A poorer use of your time is when your team gets behind, and you are still playing, but it is obvious that you have quit trying to win, you have quit hustling, you have quit playing with enthusiasm, and you have quit giving your best effort. There is no excuse for giving less than your best in practice, in games, in any circumstance. Learn to give your best *routinely,* and don't quit doing your best regardless of what those around you are doing.

Quitting when there is a better alternative (like going home to work on ball handling drills instead of remaining in a pickup game where no one is trying hard) is intelligent and should not be confused with quitting-but-still-going-through-the-motions.

R

122
THE RACE TRACK

The "race track" is a name for the area between the two three-point arcs. It is the area where nothing good ever happens on offense. Baskets are scored most of the time inside the arcs, assists are usually thrown inside the arcs, and rebounds are grabbed inside the arcs. Even most defensive steals are made inside the arcs, and most charges are drawn there. If neither team is full-court pressing, almost nothing ever happens between the arcs. Does that tell you anything?

If someone were giving away money in two stores across the street from each other, what would you do? Hang around in the street? To get the money, you'd make sure you're in the stores. To do good things in basketball, you have to be where the action is. That means spending as little time as possible in the midcourt area. Players tend to trot through that area and rest there and watch the game from there, which is exactly why it is named the race track. If you want to be a good player, you need to race through there. By getting in good enough condition that you can sprint each time up and down the court, you can put tremendous pressure on the other team, prevent numerous baskets every game, and create many opportunities to score for your own team. But how many players are conscientious enough to turn the midcourt area, as a matter of habit, into a race track? It is a very simple way to become a good player. It just takes a very large commitment of physical effort.

ON YOUR MARK, GET SET...

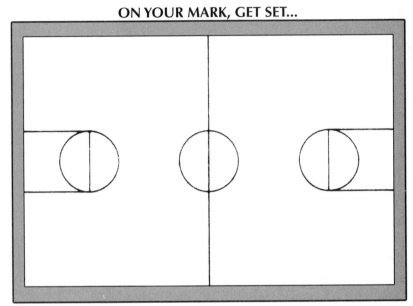

Gooooooooooooo!!!

123
REACHING

Reaching for the ball is a foul. Do you understand that? Not "reaching for the ball and hitting someone's arm." Just "reaching." Period. The end.

If you reach for a ball to steal a dribble, or to hit it out of a player's hand, it is a foul. It does not matter in the least whether or not you touch the man. Touching has nothing to do with it. Referees call fouls for reaching because when you reach, it *looks like* you are fouling.

If you really do understand this, you will never reach again, or at least if you do and you get called for a foul, you won't walk around the court mumbling that you never touched the man.

Remember, touching the man has *nothing* to do with it. If you reach for the ball, *expect* a whistle. Nine out of ten times a whistle will blow, and the referee will not even bother looking to see if you made contact or not. Referees understand the game of basketball well enough to know that coaches teach players not to reach. If you reach, the referee knows he can call a foul without even worrying about the coach getting on him because all he has to say in retort is, "Sit down, Coach, your player reached." He won't even say that you *hit* him or you *slapped* him or *killed* him or *took his arm off.* He doesn't have to. Coaches and referees understand that reaching is going to be called. So players may as well realize it and just consider reaching a violation all by itself.

Remember, whether you touch the man or not, reaching is a violation.

Reaching is a violation.
REACHING IS A VIOLATION.

124
READ THE DEFENSE

To play good, high-percentage basketball you have to know what the defense is trying to do to you. It is not simply a question of whether they are playing a man-for-man or a zone, or changing defenses, but *how* they are playing whatever defense they are playing.

If you pass the ball and cut through, and no one follows you, then regardless of how sure you are that they are in a man-for-man, you had better not keep on going. If no one goes with you, find out immediately why not. If he fell, you can go on to the basket and get an easy layup. But if he went to double-team, you are of no value moving away from the ball. You should curl back toward the ball the moment you realize that no one has gone with you. You need to be an immediate outlet for the man with the ball. And there is no way you can do that unless you are constantly aware of what the defense is doing.

Reading the defense also applies to getting the ball to a cutter or to a big man posting low. You have to be sure you throw the ball away from the defense. This seems like common sense, but many good players just toss the ball without ever making an effort to throw it to a particular side, *away* from the defense.

125
STRIPPING A REBOUND

One of the most satisfying, impressive and easy-to-do plays in basketball, especially for a guard or a small forward, is to strip the ball from a rebounder. The play is satisfying because it can enable a little man to get the ball cleanly from a big, strong center who perhaps went a foot over the rim to get it first. It is impressive because few people do it, and you seem to have extremely fast hands when you do. Finally, it is very easy to do.

You simply hang around where rebounds are being grabbed, and when the rebounder comes down with the ball, you put your hand, palm up, at his chest. That is all there is to it. A hand, palm up, at the rebounder's chest.

The tougher the rebounder, the easier the strip in many cases. Very often the rebounder will bring the ball down hard out of the air and pull it straight into his mid-section where he feels most powerful and in control of the ball. His problem is, however, that on the way to his mid-section there is a hand at his chest that he is not aware of. That hand will *automatically* poke the ball out of his grasp and leave it lying softly in the palm of your hand.

This works so well that it will be a big surprise to you the first time you do it. If you have never done it, you would imagine that a muscular center pulling down the ball would simply shove away the weak little arm of a 5'8" guard. But it doesn't happen.

The little guard needs no strength to poke out the ball, nor does he need quick hands or any concern at all for timing. You put your hand at the player's chest, and the ball just stays there on your hand. It doesn't bounce up in the air, it doesn't look like a foul to the referee—the ball stays there in your hand.

For the big guy who just awed the crowd with a dynamic leap and a powerful grasp of the ball, it is a "Now-you-see-it-now-you-don't" kind of magic. He grabs the ball away from two or three other powerful, leaping players, and somewhere on the way down, when he has no idea he is even in any danger, the ball suddenly leaves his hands and there isn't even a struggle.

This is not to say that the attempt works every time. If a rebounder twists his body in the air on the way down, it will be impossible to keep a hand at his chest. Or if he concentrates on bringing the ball to his chin, not to his waist, he will prevent you from stripping it. But, there will be times, even against clever rebounders, that they forget you may be there or they concentrate particularly hard on pulling the ball away from others. The tougher the rebound, the more likely they are to bring the ball instinctively to the waist area.

It is impossible to overemphasize the thrill of getting a strip like this the first time you do it, or when you really need it in a big game. It really does work like magic, in that it requires so little effort or ability, yet it makes you look so good.

126
"HANDLING" REFEREES

Although guys in striped shirts often seem as though they must be from some other planet because they call things on you that you don't even come vaguely close to doing, referees are actually human beings subject to the same motivations and inclinations as players and coaches. Referees attempt to "call 'em as they see 'em." They make the easy calls correctly because even a referee intent on cheating wouldn't want to demonstrate that openly, and they have difficulty with the hard calls.

When the game is close near the end, they get nervous just like players, and they are likely to blow their whistles quickly at anything that doesn't look quite right. When they are getting a lot of criticism, they are likely to get angry and want to get back at those who are criticizing them, and they may also question themselves. "Was he right or was I?" If they make a call that they realize is probably wrong, they will have a tendency to want to make up for it by watching the other team a bit more closely—not to cheat, but to make sure they don't let anything slide on that side.

Above all, and despite the fact that coaches, players and particularly fans use referees as scapegoats and blame them for everything, 95% of the referees do their very best to be fair, maybe even more than that. Not very often does a referee come to a game with the purpose of cheating for a particular team. Most players finish their whole careers without ever having had a referee with that intention. Some may be a bit more swayed by fans and circumstances than others, but they don't come to cheat. They would all like to leave knowing that no one hates them and that everyone feels the game was refereed fairly.

In view of all this, it is appalling that players go through game after game, season after season, complaining to referees. Don't you understand that **the more you complain, the greater is the referee's tendency to notice the violations you commit?** That should be clear. The more you play with matches, the better your chance of getting burned. The more you come to the referee's attention, the better your chance of hearing the whistle blow.

If you are in the habit of questioning the referee's calls, he is certainly going to want to show you that he knows what he is doing.

The result will be that every time you even begin to shuffle your feet or begin to make contact with someone, he is going to blow that whistle. On the other hand, if you are a gentleman, if you are in the habit of saying nothing and giving the impression that you are a hard worker, all business and a good solid basketball player, he will not be looking to call anything on you, and he may avoid calling something if he can. Because of human nature, intelligence should tell you that it will pay to act like a good sport, to give the referee a good impression of you and to run and get the ball for the referee if it rolls away and so on. Call them "brownie points" if you like, but why not?

Some day in a big game—when there is a play where it isn't quite clear "Is it a foot shuffle or isn't it? Is it a charge or a block?"—you will get the break if you have acted as an athlete should. And the call will go against you if you have been a complainer or a hot head. You can call that cheating if you like, but that is simply human nature. You would be wise to take advantage of it.

127
RELEASING EARLY FOR AN UNMOLESTED LAYUP

Any time a player gets away with releasing when a shot goes up, and his team gets the rebound and throws him a long pass for an easy layup, it looks terrific. It picks up the whole team and demoralizes the opponent. (It also drives the opposing coach bananas.) However, any time a player releases and the ball rebounds to the spot he vacated, and the *other* team gets the offensive rebound and scores an easy basket, it looks awful, it picks up the other team, and it demoralizes your team. (And *your* coach goes bananas.)

That leaves a few choices.

1. You can never release, and no one will ever get an easy basket (or go bananas).
2. You can release occasionally and hope for luck (so their coach goes bananas, not yours).
3. You can release at certain times when it is not likely to hurt you but possibly could get you an easy basket.

In other words, you want to release once or twice in a game when the percentages are very much in your favor.

When do the percentages favor releasing? Many guards do it when their man penetrates since they think they have no one to block out. However, a guard should look for a big man to block out if his man has beaten him because usually one of the big men on his team will have to pick up his man, leaving a man free. So, while the guard penetration may seem like a good time to leave because the guard isn't back, it is not a good risk. If your man beats you, you should be thinking to make up for it by intercepting his pass to the man left open or at least by blocking out that open man.

The best percentage time to release is when you find yourself going for a rebound and suddenly bumping into one of your own teammates who is bigger than you. If you bump a teammate, it might be possible that you could quickly alter your position and get the ball in some other spot, but it doesn't happen very often. Usually, you don't have time to get to the spot where the ball is going to come down. Someone will likely already be there. What normally happens when you bump a teammate is that you stand there and watch the game. Maybe occasionally you wait there on your toes and the ball does go to him, and it is deflected off his hands and then you get it. But not very often.

The next time you bump into a teammate in the process of going toward the basket, turn around and take off. You will not be leaving a spot where the ball is going to fall and make you look bad by resulting in an easy basket for the other team, *and* you will even have time to tip off your teammate about what you are doing. "I'm going!" you can blurt out the moment you bump him. Then if he does get the rebound, there is a good chance he will be aware of you if you do get free.

There may be other good situations, as when two guards work it out in advance, so that one is particularly ready to cover a large area and pick off any loose ball that may come. But the "bump-and-run" is one of the best because it involves a reflex you can develop and respond to immediately, and there is no way the other team can prepare for it. No one knows, including you, when you may suddenly be seeking a rebound and bump into a taller teammate. But when you do, then shout, "I'm going!" and be gone.

128
RELEASING TO GUARD A STRONG, LOW POST MAN

Normally, when you are guarding a low post man, you try to overplay on one side and force a pass to be thrown toward a helping teammate or toward the baseline under the basket where the low post man will not be effective if he gets the ball. However, if you are playing someone who spreads out well, holds you out with his strength, and presents a good target to the passers, you might try releasing in order to steal the pass.

If you play a stronger player tightly, keeping your body right up against his, you may actually help him. This lets him know exactly where you are. When the ball is thrown, *he* is likely to get it because he can hold you out. You can try to wave your arms and look tougher and more menacing than you really are (to discourage the pass from being thrown), and another strategy is to take a risk now and then to intercept, especially if the man is very good at scoring once he gets the ball.

If you are in this situation and a gamble seems worthwhile, probably your best chance is to release. Take your body off the man, move behind him or away from him or wherever you can or must in order not to let him feel where you are. If he cannot feel where you are, there are two benefits: (1) He cannot hold you out, and (2) if he does get the ball, he will be more tentative with it because he will be concerned about locating you.

Of course, your job is not easy. By backing off the man, you force yourself to come from farther away to get to the pass. But, if you feel he is very likely to get the ball anyway, the risk is worth it, because often you can scoot around in front of him and intercept the ball while he waits for it to come.

Low post men rarely go to meet the ball. They hold their ground and wait for the ball to come to them so that they can be in good scoring position. Therefore, there is that chance of darting in front of the ball at the last instant. In addition, it is much easier to scoot past an outstretched arm, and it will look more like a foul if he tries to hold you out, than if you are trying to get by a firm forearm that keeps contact with you the whole time.

You cannot expect to guard a good post man the whole game and keep him from getting the ball by staying off him and darting out when the ball is passed. But in combination with fronting and hand-waving at the side, you may very well find a time when releasing will get you a steal and make the guards very wary of trying any more passes into the man you are guarding.

Releasing is something to try when you are guarding the low post man, and you can feel that the pass is going to be able to get to him and you are not going to be able to do anything to stop it. As long as you don't use it as a frequent tactic, you have a good chance of getting good results when you need it.

129
RUN THROUGH THE BALL

Certainly against a press or pressure, and anytime you are not wide open, you should receive a pass by running through the ball. Don't wait for the ball to come to you. Go and get the ball. Tackle it if necessary.

Many passes are intercepted because the receivers wait for the ball. Get in the habit of going to the ball *with your body,* not just leaning or reaching toward the ball with your arms.

You may never get much credit for preventing an interception by running through the ball, but you will help your team win games.

READY, AIM...

Don't listen to people who try to keep you from getting your hopes up. Get them way up. You can take disappointment later if things don't work out. (By then you'll have new hopes and plans to think about.) But for right now, aim for the stars. Go for it.

S

130
SAVING THE BALL

When a ball is going out of bounds, and you see that one of your team members hit it last, and you know you can't get it and stay in-bounds, naturally you are going to try to bat it or push it in-bounds so your team at least has a chance for it.

The only time you should not do this is under the other team's basket when pushing it back into play could very well result in a quick layup for them. In this case, if you cannot get control of the ball enough to tap it directly to a teammate or hurl it all the way downcourt toward your basket, it is better to let the ball go out of bounds.

In all other cases, when a ball is going out off your team, if you do not know where a teammate is, throw the ball toward your own basket. And throw it high, if you can, to give someone a chance to get to it before it goes out of bounds. Maybe your team will pick it up for a score. At the worst, the other team will get it, and your team will have plenty of time to set up on defense.

More important than this business about how to save the ball, however, is how to react when you see a ball going out of bounds and you are not the saver. It doesn't matter which team is saving the ball; develop the reaction of going immediately at the ball. If your own teammate is going after it, you can yell to him to flip it to you. If the other team is going for it, maybe you can intercept the flip pass going to one of their players, or you may get it because the saver flips it back weakly, hoping that his team gets it.

Certainly, you will get no ball being saved if you are in the habit of watching when that happens. Watching is what 90% of the players do. But an alert player can steal or save 10-15 possessions a season just by running toward any ball that is going out of bounds.

131
SCOT

SCOT is a combination word taken from the beginning and end of two other words, "**SC**oring" and "sp**OT**." A scoring spot is any place you can score from, a distance from the basket within your effective shooting range. It is a useful term to yell to a teammate when you get open and are ready for a shot, and it is a useful concept for explaining how good players play the game.

Go to any midget league game, and usually you will see nearly everyone far away from SCOT position. Occasionally, someone will cut to the basket or into SCOT position. But watch a pro game, and it looks very different. All five players spend practically the whole game in SCOT position.

No one wants the ball outside SCOT because everyone wants to score, and everyone wants to get the ball where he can shoot from, so that he has the options of faking, shooting or making any move he wants. Getting the ball outside of SCOT means that you can only score on a dribbling move because you will have to dribble to get to the area you can score from.

In a nutshell, good offensive players play in SCOT nearly always and only occasionally (when help is needed) do they cut out, whereas mediocre players like to play out of SCOT and occasionally cut in.

The question you need to answer is, how much effort do *you* put into getting the ball in SCOT so that you have all your options to score? Are you working constantly to get the ball in scoring position? Or are you content to hang around outside in midget style and do nothing most of the time? Being a good player without the ball is nothing more than constantly striving to get free for a pass in your SCOT position. In SCOT, you're a threat. Out of SCOT, the defense can relax.

132
SECRET PLANS

This title sounds significant, and it is, but it is very simple. Good players plan with each other. In football, the wide receiver comes back to the huddle and tells the quarterback he can get free going long. In basketball, players have to communicate with each other, too. A fist might tell a point guard you are going backdoor. But when? You need to do it in practice. Time it just right. Run up, stop and go. Bang. Layup.

Take time to work on things before or after practice. How is the defense making it tough for you? Find a way to counter with a quick clear-out, or a pre-planned give-and-go, or a screen, or a cut.

Much of what looks spontaneous and unrehearsed to the fan has been carefully planned and practiced many times. Why hope that your point guard will spot you open when you have the opportunity to tell him what you are going to do before you do it? Talk to each other. Know what your teammates are going to do.

You can do more than simply know your team's offense and defense. Within those frameworks, there is still a lot of room for individual initiative, creativity and planning if you care enough to take the time to do it.

133
SEEING THE BALL...31:52

In a 32-minute game, you should **see the ball about 31 minutes and 52 seconds.** That means you should always see the ball except for about two seconds out of every eight minutes—times when you need to turn your head very quickly toward your man for an instant on a backdoor cut (before picking the ball up again as soon as you turn), or when you need to sprint downcourt because you know no one is back and they have a guy open who could get an easy layup, or for a split second when you screen away from the ball.

You may be able to come up with a few more times when it is okay to take your eye off the ball for a second, so you might want to decrease the seeing-ball-time to 31:44, giving yourself four seconds a quarter instead of two.

However, there is no excuse for ever getting hit in the back of the head, no excuse for being turned the wrong way when an opponent is driving in for a layup and no excuse for not knowing exactly where the ball is at all times. You do not trot downcourt with your head down on offense, you cannot just guard your man and watch only him on defense and you should not spend your time thinking about when it is okay to turn your head.

Turn your head away from the ball only when it is absolutely necessary and even then with great reluctance. Know where the ball is at all times. A good player knows where it is all 32 minutes, and his eyes are on it for all but a few seconds of that time.

134
SEEK-HIDE-N-GO

This is a play on words for hide-n-go-seek, which is what players do too often—they hide and occasionally they seek the ball. But a player's movement without the ball should not be arbitrary.

If the player with the ball has used his dribble, or looks like he is in trouble, or has two or more men on him, you should *seek hide* (cowhide, leather, the ball). If the player with the ball is not in trouble, if he has a dribble left or is on his way to the basket, you should *go* to the basket or clear out and be ready for a shot).

Don't just stand around. Anytime you don't have the ball, follow one of two simple rules.

1. If the ball is in trouble or potential trouble, seek it by running straight at it. (If you get right next to the ball and you don't get it, then *go* again.)
2. If the ball is not in trouble, but on its way or about to be on its way to the basket, you need to go, get out of the way and be ready to get a pass in an open spot.

Fans like to talk about a great leaper's "hang time," but coaches are more concerned with players' "hanging-around time." How much time do you just hang around without either decisively going to the basket to try to get open or decisively running to get the ball?

You should be doing one or the other all the time. Either seek hide, or go. Don't hang around.

135
SETTING SCREENS

When you are setting a screen for the man with the ball, you try to help him get a path to the basket. If you set the screen on the defender's side, it is too easy for him to slide through and get by you. If you set the screen directly behind the defender, it is too easy for him to get over-the-top. Your position should be between those two positions, straddling the defender's back pocket, **your belt buckle against his back pocket.** Stay low, wide and firm; and as soon as the player with the ball uses the screen (goes by you), roll to the basket keeping the defender you screened on your back.

If you remember to **roll without ever taking your eyes off the ball,** your footwork will be perfect and will enable you to keep that man on your back. If you roll and fail to keep your eyes on the ball, you may sometimes get hit in the head or at least "handcuffed" by a quick pass that your teammate is forced to throw early because he is picked up on the switch.

When you are setting a screen away from the ball, put yourself directly between the man you are screening and the ball, and be ready to turn (keeping him on your back) and ask for the ball.

Always screen wide, low and firm, but don't worry about stepping to the side or sticking out a leg to make the screen a little better. Let the player using the screen make a fake in one direction and run his man into you. *He* has to do the work once you set a good solid screen for him.

There *is* a way, however, to give a teammate a bit of help on a screen away from the ball. After you set the screen and as soon as you see which way the defender is going to get by you, you can pivot directly in his path—and get away with it!—simply by turning your back to that defender as you pivot and raising your arms up calling for the ball. By raising your hands and calling for the ball, it will look like a routine screen-and-turn-to-the-ball situation, and only you will know that you "just happened" to turn into the path the defender chose. If you keep your eyes on the defender as you do this and pivot into him, you almost certainly will be called for a foul. But by turning your back on the pivot, most likely you will never be called.

Although these finer points may help you occasionally, by far the most important thing is simply that you *want to be an obstacle.* You must want to make it difficult for the other team to get by you. Most players set screens only with a sense of duty because their coach makes them, and they have the tendency to "bail out" or set the screen weakly.

If you are willing to set good strong screens, you can help your team win games. Try to remember what it is like playing *against* someone who sets good strong screens. That player makes it miserable for you, and that is exactly what you want to do to other defenses.

136
SETTING SOMEONE UP (WITH SPACE)

Many guards think they are great ball handlers because they can dribble well and because occasionally they penetrate into the lane and pitch to the big man for an easy layup. But good dribbling and an occasional assist do not make a good ball handler.

There is a more subtle skill that the average fan never notices, but which is really the mark of a great ball handler. It has to do with how you use your dribble. Most players dribble for the purpose of scoring. If they score, it's great. If they don't, they flip the ball back out to someone else, and something has to start over. Their flip-outs, though they never even think about it, are almost always outward, away from the basket, to a man who has to move out, away from the basket.

A good ball handler who uses his dribble to set someone up almost always **attracts the attention of a second defender before he gives the ball up,** so that he can toss the ball to a teammate with some space to operate in and with that teammate's defender having to scramble toward him to make up that space. This may seem like a tiny point, but it is very important. **Players who get the ball with space, and with a defender having to recover toward them, are much more effective** than players who have to get the ball going away from the basket and then have to fake to try to generate their space or get their defender off-balance.

A good ball handler, even on a routine pass to the wing, may often threaten a slash to the basket before passing, just enough to get the wing man's defender leaning toward the ball handler for a moment and not quite in position to play perfect defense on the wing.

With one good point guard and one good scoring forward, often very little offense is necessary other than getting the scorer the ball in a place where he can shoot it...with a little space, or maybe just a "bad lean."

137
SHOOTING PRACTICE

Competition helps you get better, but not if the competition is too much better than you or too much weaker. Fortunately, for shooting practice, everyone has the ideal competitor available at all times. That competitor, about as good as you, with about the same temperament, the same spirit, drive, hustle and perseverance is You-Yesterday.

Every day that you go out to practice shooting, you should try to beat You-Yesterday. Once you take 20 or so "form shots," you should be ready to compete. Form shots are shots taken two feet from the basket, not banked in but each one swished without touching the rim, while concentrating on the proper form—elbow directly under the ball, ball rolled off the finger tips to give it backspin, the follow-through complete so that the arm is fully extended and the fingers point to the ground after the shot, not to the sky.

Shoot and count 100 free throws, 100 jump shots off a right hand dribble, 100 off a left-hand dribble, 100 "zone" shots, 100 shots about three feet beyond your comfortable shooting range and 100 quick-release groove shots. By counting and striving to beat You-Yesterday, you keep your mind off fatigue and heat and swimming pools and other distractions, and you get better faster. You cannot expect to make rapid improvement by "shooting around." Every day you need to strive to beat You-Yesterday.

Keep a chart or put a star on a calendar for every time you beat You-Yesterday. Often, it helps your motivation to see your progress in stars. Or you can make a paper chain, adding a link for each day you win. No player is too old to be stimulated by these kinds of visual rewards.

A paper chain may not look like much to anyone who enters your room, but it will mean a lot to you, and it will show you exactly where you are in your practicing. You cannot fool your own paper chain. Did you improve in the past two weeks, or didn't you? Did you even take the time to shoot 600 shots during that time—and count them?

Get a strip of paper and fasten the edges together with a staple, forming a small ring, and write the number of shots you made on it (out of 600). Every day you make more than You-Yesterday, make that strip of paper a different color. One glance at your chain before you go to bed at night tells you what you've been doing.

At the end of a summer, you should have a long chain, and a lot of colored strips. But will you? Will you make the effort? Or would you rather just shoot around?

SHOOTING CHART

600 — SHOTS PER DAY — 600							
D A T E	ONE HUNDRED OF EACH TYPE OF SHOT (100)						
	FREE THROWS	DRIBBLE STOPS (RIGHT)	DRIBBLE STOPS (LEFT)	ZONE SHOTS	BEYOND RANGE SHOTS	GROOVE SHOTS	600 SHOT TOTAL
1							
2							
3							
4							
5							
6							
7							

*There is no secret to good shooting. Shoot 600 shots a day for the next three summers, using the proper form, and **you** will be a good shooter.*

138
SNORT

Snort is what a grizzly bear does when it walks around the woods challenging the world. Snort is a tough word, and it is also a made-up word for **SN**appy and sh**ORT**, the kind of passes you want to throw against pressure. That's all there is to this one.

Whenever you meet a full-court press or any sort of pressure, don't think, *Oh no, a press.* SNORT. Feel tough. And throw snappy, short passes.

No pressure defense can bother tough players who throw snappy short passes. SNORT.

139
SPIRIT

Spirit is not something that appears only when your team has just come from behind to win a big game and everyone is hugging at mid-court. Everyone has spirit then. You need spirit when your team is behind, or especially in practice when you have been on the court for two hours and nothing is going right. Your legs are aching, you're out of breath, your blisters are gnawing at your shoes, the coach is disgusted and has nothing to say but negatives and it appears that he plans to keep you there two hours more.

Now you're talking spirit. *Now* you find out what you're made of. If you can recognize this kind of situation and commit yourself to *filling the air with positives,* this effort may be more important than any play you ever make in a game.

You cannot always expect a coach to be positive. Sometimes, even if he believes in positive reinforcement, the team will be playing poorly, and for him to speak positively would be lying and glossing over the mistakes.

But **players can always be positive.** They can fill the air with encouragement for each other, and they can alter the negative atmosphere through their own efforts if they have the energy and willingness to do it.

140
STALLING AND THE "SOONER" CONCEPT

There are many different kinds of stalls, but all of them end up having two key ingredients. Players need to be conscious of doing both of these things sooner.

The first ingredient is passing. Any stall requires passing the ball. Too often players hold it when a teammate is open, or take a few extra dribbles, and then the pass is difficult to throw. Against a pressure defense, when you are stalling, throw the ball to the open man as soon as you see he is wide open. Don't wait. If you are the primary ball handler, then give it to him and be prepared to get it back, but don't wait until he is almost covered. *Pass sooner.*

The second ingredient is receiving. When you get to prime receiving position, if you don't get the ball immediately, you should leave sooner. Players hang around too long in the prime spots, making passes to them difficult to throw and giving the defense a chance to get back into the game. If you get open, fine. But if you don't get the ball, don't stand there mumbling. If you don't get the ball, you don't get it. Clear out quickly so the next man can come running. Any time you are standing for a few seconds, a pass is very dangerous if the defense cares about winning and applying pressure at all. You need to remember, GO-GO. Get Open or Get Out *sooner.*

141
STATUE CHARGES

Even though this idea has already been covered under "Taking a Charge," it seems worthwhile to name this idea and fix it firmly in your mind. Many defensive players get good defensive position and suddenly lose it just before taking a charge. They are with their man, in position perfectly, and at that last instant when they should draw the contact and get rewarded with the referee's whistle, they suddenly quit moving their feet, they straighten up and brace for the contact (they become a statue). The player with the ball makes a quick change of course and goes right on by, by ten feet.

Don't let this happen to you. If you have worked hard to get good defensive position, keep it. Don't become a statue. Keep your feet moving, stay low and be prepared to alter your position slightly as the player with the ball tries to slightly alter his.

It is a fallacy that you are not allowed to be moving and still draw a charge. As long as you get to the spot first (without cutting in front of the offensive player at the last instant), you are allowed to have your feet moving, and you should. By keeping your feet moving—to the side and back a little so you can't be called for blocking—you are prepared for that slight change of position that will enable you to be fully in front of the offensive player. And, in case he makes a great move to evade you, you will be able to go with him instead of just standing there and letting him go on by.

Take charges with your body low and your feet moving. Not like a statue.

142
STEALING... FROM THE AIR

Lose the idea of stealing a ball from a man. You can only get a ball from a man if he makes a mistake. Trying to take the ball from a man is likely only to get you a foul or throw you off balance so that he can take advantage of you. Naturally, you can fake and try to force a dribbler to make a mistake, and you should. Your thinking is to *force a mistake,* not get a steal.

When you think of stealing a ball, you should think of stealing it from the air. In other words, think of stealing a pass, not a dribble or a ball being held. Stolen passes often result in easy layups and not in fouls. Being alert to steal a pass is good, solid defense. It is being ready to dart out when the offense is careless or underestimates your quickness. Stealing a ball can be a great benefit to your team that can pick up everyone and change a negative momentum. So, go for steals when you get a good chance, but remember, you steal passes—balls that are in the air, not balls that are in a player's hands.

Occasionally, you can slap *upward* at a ball and knock it out of a player's hands, but again, your thought is to knock it loose, then steal it from the air. Any thought of directly taking the ball from a player has few positive results unless the player is very poor.

Force a mistake and *then* go for the steal—from the air, not the player.

143
STOP ON TWO FEET

Some great plays are made when a player penetrates, jumps off one foot and glides to the basket, and then slam dunks the ball or puts in a little scoop shot or "dumps off" to a teammate for the score. The crowd loves it, and the penetrator gets a great feeling gliding through the air, yet he has probably doomed himself to several upcoming turnovers as a result.

There is nothing wrong with gliding through the air for a layup. But the problem is, once you have been successful off one foot, you are not likely to be able to concentrate well enough to stop on two feet when that is necessary. Since the one-foot jump-and- glide takes less effort and looks more impressive (when it works), a lot of players jump-and-glide all the time and must consequently trade a lot of walking calls, poor passes or charges in exchange for their occasional successes.

You will score (or enable a teammate to score) a higher percentage of your penetrations if you concentrate on crossing the free throw line and coming to a quick stop. Naturally, you have to be prepared to protect the ball because you will draw a crowd, but from inside the lane you can get yourself a very easy shot or you can throw the right pass at the right time. If you jump in the air, you force yourself to make the play before you come down; so, often you have to throw a pass you would rather not throw.

A further advantage of the two-foot stop is that it is usually possible to make a quick decision at the last instant not to stop if the lane opens and you see there is room to take it in for the layup. But if your concentration is on the one-foot jump-and-glide, it is extremely unlikely that you will be able to stop yourself if the opportunity is not there. In other words, by concentrating on the two-foot stop, there is a very real chance that you will still score all the plays off one foot that you would have, but you will reduce the turnovers and forced passes that you would have had by going in off one foot each time.

Two-foot stopping gives you control and enables you to concentrate on getting inside without worry of how you are going to make the shot. That means you should get inside more often once you realize that being there is an objective all by itself. If you can use your dribble and fakes and slashes to penetrate into the lane, you are a good player—*if* you stop on two feet and make the play. If your habit is to penetrate and glide, then even though you are getting there, you may not be a good player at all. More likely, you are losing a lot of games for your team by doing well against the weak teams and poorly against the good ones.

Remember, this is not to say that you should never go in off one foot. Sometimes you should. But usually your concentration should be on being in control, on two feet, after your penetration. Think:

Slash and stop.

144
DRIBBLE-STOP SHOTS

Most good players know they should pivot on their inside foot when stopping for a jump shot off a quick dribble-move (you pivot and stop on your left foot if you are dribbling down the right side with your right hand.) What many good players do not realize, though, is how important it is to **roll the inside shoulder** during that quick dribble so that it looks as though you are going for a layup, not preparing to stop and shoot a jump shot. "Rolling" your shoulder means bringing your shoulder down toward your belt buckle, bringing it across your body. This simple movement of lowering your shoulder puts the defender back on his heels and gives you a lot more time to shoot.

This is one of those subtle tips that seems almost insignificant, but it's very helpful once you learn to do it. You will truly be surprised at how much more open you are at the end of the "roll." Most players have the habit of practicing a dribble-stop jumper by taking one or two dribbles very obviously to the side while keeping their shoulders square to the basket during the two dribbles. The result is, they do it the same way in games, and the **high, squared shoulders tell a defender immediately,** **"Jump shot,"** which allows him to get in your face with his hand.

By concentrating on rolling your inside shoulder down across your body and by making that last dribble look *and feel* like a dribble on the way to the basket, not to the side, you will get defenders off you and give yourself plenty of time to take the shot.

145
STREAK!

S treaking is the name given to crazy college kids who take off their clothes and sprint across the field in a crowded stadium. It is not called merely sprinting, because the action is excited, wild and probably exhilarating. Streakers are never apprehended by just one policeman. It takes five or six at least. That is how this term has become associated with offensive rebounding. A shot goes up—streak for it.

When you consider the idea of streaking for the ball, you realize that a block out attempt is incidental. It is an obstacle, of course, but not something that is going to stop your movement. A good block out may stop you from getting the ball, but it should not even come close to stopping your motion, your piston-like feet, or your windmill arms.

Streak for the ball. It does not mean drift toward it. It does not mean even run for it or go for it. It means streak, the way you would move if *you* suddenly had all your clothes off and 50,000 people were watching *you* fly across a stadium. Do you think one policeman could get in *your* way?

Do you think you go for offensive rebounds like that?

146
STUFFS YOU MAKE AND MISS

T here is only one thing worse than getting beaten or getting behind-for-the-first-time by a slam dunk. It is having a chance to win or get-ahead-for-the-first-time and missing a dunk.

A player should think carefully about that before he tries to stuff at every possible opportunity. A stuff can be a great play that ignites the crowd and changes the momentum of a game—if you make it. But that same thing can happen in reverse if you miss.

If you are good at slam dunking, slam it in the game when you get an opportunity. Why not? But if you aren't good, and you realize as you go up that there is a significant risk involved, you would be wiser to hold your slams for next year.

147
SUPERSTITIONS

Get superstitions working for you.

A lot of athletes have superstitions and rituals they go through before a game. Not too many would expect to lose if a black cat crossed their path on the way to the gym, but a lot of athletes do concern themselves with what they wear, or the order in which they put on their clothes, or whether they make their first warm-up shot or their last one, and so on. Probably most of this is merely to fine-tune concentration (though the player himself may not be aware of it) or to reduce nervousness.

In these situations, your particular ritual, if you have one, is fine. You are free to enjoy it and go ahead with it.

But some players carry this way of thinking too far, and they begin to believe and let their game performance be affected by statements like, "I can never hit in games if I'm hitting in warm-ups" or "I never play well in a game if I've done well in practice the day before." The statements can even become things like, "I just can't play well on that court," and "I just never play well on Saturdays."

When your harmless superstitions and rituals get you to the point that you are trying to have a bad day in practice (so you will play well in the game the next day) or trying to miss in warm-ups (so your game shooting will be on), you must realize that you have gotten carried away in your thinking. You have become not merely a bit superstitious, but just plain stupid. A mind does seem to have the tendency to bring about the things it believes in; therefore, you need to realize that *you* are causing your own poor performances by a faulty way of thinking.

Whatever your superstitions, you can alter them to work for you instead of against you. For example, take the matter of warm-up and game shooting. If you are hitting in warm-ups, think, *Wow, I'm hot tonight.*

There is no logical reason why your hitting should stop once the clock starts. If you're hitting now, there is every reason to believe that this will be one of those nights you can put in everything. If you are missing in warm-ups, think, *I am almost certain to hit well in the game. I'm too good a shooter to keep missing like this.* Either way, you should be able to think when the game starts that you are likely to shoot well. You have every right to think that provided you have practiced diligently and have become a good shooter.

If on any summer day you can walk to a court and pop in nine or ten out of ten free throws, superstition should play no role in how you shoot during the season. One game you may go only eight for ten, and the next game ten for ten. But every game you are going to shoot well, because good shooters shoot well. That's all there is to it, and that is how you should think about it.

Don't talk yourself into some negative situation under the guise of superstition. Under the guise of intelligence (if you don't really have it!) use your mind to work for you, not against you. Black cats notwithstanding, good players will outplay mediocre players a huge majority of the time regardless of how anyone dresses, what day it is, what court it is, or who hits or misses in warm-ups. Let the other guy wear the same lucky jock strap every game if he thinks it will help him win. Because it won't do him a bit of good after *you* fake it off him.

STUPID

A stupid player is one who spends a great deal of time and concentration on questioning the coach's judgment instead of doing his best to make the coach's decision work.

T

148
TAKING ANOTHER TEAM LIGHTLY

Fans and news commentators like to talk about this, and coaches worry about it, but taking another team lightly is something that should *never* happen to a good player. In fact, taking another team *any* way should never happen.

What should happen, regardless of who the other team is, regardless of whether you are in a game or just practicing, is that your attention should be focused on your personal execution. Get a good shot each time downcourt, go after every rebound aggressively, make short, snappy passes, get wide open to receive the ball, and play tough, proud defense. When you do these things, it won't matter if you are playing the Boston Celtics or the Bad News Bears—your execution will be the same.

Some games naturally get you more "up," more nervous before the game and more likely to yell in the locker room as you dress. But none of these feelings should influence your *habit of play.* You play tough, alert, in control and with pride...no matter who you are playing, where you are playing or how many points ahead or behind you are.

Once you realize what habit of play means, and once you commit yourself to doing your best at all times, you are free to take a team lightly or heavily or to the Senior Prom. *How* you take them won't matter any more.

149
TALKING

Talking to teammates, helping each other verbally, is one of the most obvious differences (if you are on the court) between good players and mediocre ones. "I've got that man." "Take 'im!" "Get through." "Help here." "Bring 'im here." "Go through." "Watch behind." There are dozens of comments that get repeated over and over in games, and they do help a team perform better.

Just getting in the habit of calling out your man each time on defense, and getting your teammates to call out theirs, will end up saving baskets over the course of a game and season. Talking your teammates through screens, telling them when you are in good help-position ready to pick up their men, motioning for them to clear out or cut through the lane, alerting them to cutters or players trying to sneak behind your defense—all of these and many more situations happen often in games. If you are not now in the habit of constantly talking during the action of the game, you may be surprised at how often your mere words can help your teammates make a play.

Less-experienced players tend to think that many of these situations are obvious. ("It was clear there was a screen there. Why should I bother to tell him?" Or "It was clear I had that man and he had the other man, so how could it help just saying what was already obviously going to happen?") They don't bother to say anything.

But these situations are *not* always obvious. Talking is very often what makes them obvious. Talking ends any possible confusion that may arise. And talking prevents the short hesitations (Is he thinking what I'm thinking? Should I take that man, or shouldn't I?) that frequently are all that a team needs to get the slight advantage necessary to score.

Talking helps a team coordinate its activities, assures that everyone is working together and encourages players to do decisively what they otherwise may do haphazardly or a second too late. Talking, even saying the obvious, helps you win games.

150
THANKING YOUR TEAMMATES

The value of expressing gratitude for services rendered was widely known and demonstrated long before Mr. Naismith or even peach baskets were around. That value is immediately obvious on a basketball court because of the very special social nature of the game.

Score a layup and strut back on defense as though you are a one-man team, and you may very well find that, the next time you get free under the basket, the most you will get is the opportunity to rebound. On the other hand, by saying "Good play," "Good pass," or "Good help"—anything where you acknowledge the successful efforts of a teammate, you are likely to find that your teammates are more aware of you, enjoy playing with you, and that they make a bigger effort to get you the ball when you get free.

Thanking your teammates, then, is not much more than simple intelligence, **even if you are a selfish player who just wants the ball more often.** Acknowledging others' efforts builds teamwork and team spirit. Whether you point at a good passer or give a "high five" or merely nod in a way that the crowd doesn't even notice, your gesture will get through to your teammate, and both of you will benefit from the exchange.

151
THE THREE-ON-TWO FAST BREAK

There isn't much difference between players who can adapt quickly to various situations and players who take stupid risks for no reason. Certainly, if you are coming down the court on a three-on-two break and you see an opportunity to drive by one of the two defenders for a layup or a dish-off assist, you should do it, and it will look like a great play.

The problem with relying on your ability to adapt is that you are likely to be less consistent. And the result may be that you will get layups and make great plays against weak teams (who you would have beaten anyway), and you will charge or get your shot blocked against the good teams when you need to score the most. For this reason, it may be better to forget about quick adaptations on three-on-two breaks and simply learn how to score them using the same method every time.

Bring the ball down the middle. If no one takes you, get across the free throw line and hit the short jumper (if you are smaller than the two defenders) or take it in for a layup (if you are taller than either defender).

Most defenses will stop the ball, playing in tandem (one defender behind the other). In that case you should get the ball to the side. Some coaches want wide cuts and expect their players to time the pass and cut just right in order to score layups. If your coach wants that, learn to do it the best you can. It *can* be done by a good ball handler and by sharp cutters who can hit those fast-moving shots off a quick pass. But for most players, even good players, a higher-percentage situation is to get the ball to scoring position on the side, so the ball must be guarded. If the side man is not picked up by a defender, he shoots, and all three go for the rebound. If the side man is guarded, that leaves a two-on-one situation that can be exploited easily if the middle man moves toward the ball.

SCORING THE 3-ON-2 FAST BREAK

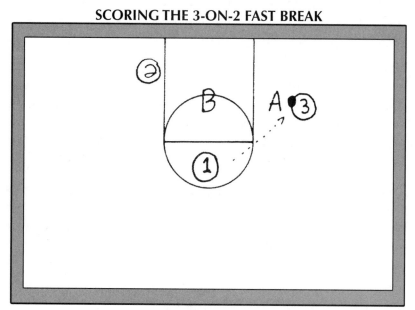

It is a mistake for 1 to pass and stand in the middle, allowing "B" to stop the pass to "2" and still get out to "1" to make the shot difficult.

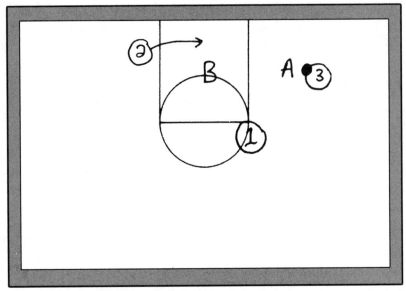

The middle man (1) goes to the corner of the free throw lane on the ball side while the other cutter (2) stays near the basket. In these positions, there is no way that defender "B" can guard both 1 and 2.

The middle man should give the ball to the better-shooting wing man, in case the defense backs off, and be sure to give him the ball at least one full dribble away from scoring position or after he has already gathered himself and is standing there. Be careful not to give it to him in that in-between area where you will force him to make a quick decision on the move and maybe charge or have to throw a jump pass or shoot a difficult shot.

Once the wing man has the ball in scoring position, it should take only one pass to score (assuming he does not shoot himself). By looking at his teammate on the baseline, the side man will force the defense to guard that pass and give the outside shot.

152
TIGHT-ROPE WALKING

This balancing act has already been covered under "Imaginary Lines," but it seems worth repeating for emphasis. In almost every game, even in games featuring star players or pros, someone who dribbles to the basket and scores, or is about to, is called for stepping on the baseline. Or the whistle blows for a line violation on the sideline against a full court press. The player called for the infraction usually looks astonished or mumbles that he was pushed, but none of that should ever happen.

Don't dribble anywhere with the hope of missing the line by an inch. Don't take the ball some place that demands a high wire act to get there. Don't get your body in a position where a slight push can put you out of bounds. Play strong, expect a push, and be sure your body is prepared to get moved a bit on your way to the basket. If there is only an inch or two to spare, there isn't room to go at all. Leave tightrope walking to the Flying Wallendas.

153
KNOW THE TIME

This is not a tip—it is a warning. If you are trying to become a good basketball player, don't ever find yourself dribbling casually upcourt when suddenly the buzzer goes off ending the quarter or first half. Nothing tips off your lack of awareness any more than the buzzer or horn surprising you.

You should know the time and the score at all times. Look up every time the clock is stopped and make sure it sinks in. What is the time? What is the score? Both of these questions should pop to your attention every time the whistle blows. Before you wonder who traveled or who the foul was called on and before you frown (if the call is on you), check the score and time. Need that point be made more emphatically?

The moment you hear a whistle, check the score and time. If you plan to mumble or stomp or shrug or smile, *wait* until you have checked the score and time.

It only takes one player—*you*—to make sure that your team isn't setting up a play when it should be hurrying up a shot. And it only takes you to alert your teammates to defend the sudden long pass a team may throw when they realize there are only seconds left.

154
TOUCH BALLS

A lot of players think they play good defense if their man doesn't score very many points. But maybe they get a lot of help from their teammates and maybe they don't give much help. These are important considerations in determining good defense, and so is the idea of touching balls. Good players get their hands on the ball on defense. They deflect some passes going inside, they hit a dribble in the lane and they touch one or two of their man's passes.

There aren't any foolproof schemes as to how to get this touching done. Mainly, you have to want to, and you have to be in position. When your man is about to throw a pass, you need to be near him, trying to put your hands where the ball is, so that anytime he throws carelessly or without faking first, you will touch the ball. You won't get it every time. No one will. But **you will get one or two a game if you are trying to touch each one.** You won't touch every dribble in the lane either, but you have to want to, try to, and lean that way, constantly expecting that the big guy inside is going to put a ball on the floor that you can get to. The same goes for any passes thrown when you are not guarding the ball. You have to think that a ball may be passed at any second in the area near you, and you have to be ready to dart out and touch it when it is.

In the next pickup game you play in, keep a count of how many balls you touch—not on offense, not on rebounds, but just on defense by being alert. You don't have to count steals only. Perhaps the ball will be passed successfully from one player to another despite your touch. Don't worry about that. Get in the habit of touching balls, and the steals will come along naturally.

When you get to the point that you can guard your man and help on defense *and* get four or five ball-touches a game, *you* can play defense.

155
TOUGH KID

Make sure you know which kid on your team is the most aggressive at getting loose balls and being ready to go after the ball unexpectedly. If you have a guy like this on your team, and you let him know that you will look for him and throw the ball in his direction any time you are in trouble, you will mobilize him even more and save a lot of turnovers. Nothing inspires a player more than knowing you are counting on him, and you are going to throw him the ball, especially when the player is one who likes going after balls anyway.

This concept and the value of praising effectively and motivating, is covered under double-teams, but the idea is not confined to double-team situations. On the jump ball circle, or especially against any pressure or in a dribble-used situation, you need to have an outlet that you have confidence in—a guy you can throw to who you know will be coming hard to the ball and will be very reluctant to let anyone get to it before him.

Fans won't notice all the turnovers that a tough kid can prevent, but you will. And your team will. Make sure you know who your tough kid is, and make sure *he* knows what you are thinking. There isn't a tough kid in the world who won't take pride in being recognized; and he'll give you even more effort as a result of that recognition. In fact , even if your team doesn't have one of these aggressive, rowdy types, designate someone. You may be surprised at how well someone responds to that role if given the assignment and that trust.

Wouldn't you go all out to get those passes against pressure if you knew your teammates were counting on *you?*

What do you do now when you're taking the ball out of bounds, the time is ticking to four seconds and you need to throw the ball in somewhere? You probably find the most-open man you can, and throw the ball and hope. Try instead finding your tough kid.

156
TRANSITION DEFENSE

Transition defense is more than getting back to the other end, though certainly hustling back is the first prerequisite. If you aren't back, you can't expect to stop anyone. You have to be willing to sprint back on defense, and you have to be willing to **sprint with your eyes on the ball and with an awareness of where the offensive players are.**

It is not enough to scramble back to the lane and raise your hands and look menacing. If the ball is coming down one side and you can prevent a pass from going to a cutter breaking down that side, often you can stop a fast break from even developing. By running straight back to the lane, the ball can advance with a quick pass down the side, and you may find yourself scrambling to defend a two-on-two with a lot of space to make up between you and the ball.

A TYPICAL ERROR IN TRANSITION DEFENSE

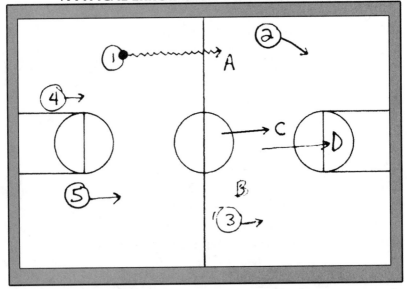

The defender "C" could have prevented a good scoring opportunity by running at "2." But by running straight back to the lane, failing to recognize that "2" is the most dangerous man, he allows "2" to get the pass and break for the basket in a position where he will be very difficult to defend.

Your first consideration is getting back and making sure someone is a there to defend the basket and stop the ball. Secondly, you have to sort out men quickly and **take the most dangerous man.**

No one can say in advance who is the most dangerous man. Sometimes, you may have to split two men and guard them both until more help arrives. Other times, you may have to run out to the corner to guard a very good shooter man-to-man even though your team is playing a zone. You cannot simply run back to your zone position (if you are playing a zone) or run back with your man (if you are in a man defense).

Transition defense is a different defense entirely. You get back, protect the basket, take the ball, take the most dangerous man or men and hold everyone off until your whole team can get back and get into your set defense. Many times in a game, a 3-on-4 becomes a 1-on-1 because players in transition defense run back to the lane (even sprinting) rather than finding and taking (and perhaps only needing to trot over to) the most dangerous man.

157
TRANSITION FROM WALL TO BALL

The transition from help-defense (far away or two passes away from the ball) to overplay defense (near or one pass away from the ball) is one of the most difficult plays that a good player must master on defense. To make the transition smoothly and quickly, you must maintain awareness of both your man and the ball at all times. You cannot hope to concentrate on one and then the other and constantly be rushing to compensate for your momentary lapses.

Your position on defense must continuously reflect your awareness of the man and the ball. As the ball approaches your man, *you* approach your man. It does not matter whether the ball moves toward your man or the man moves toward the ball, your job is the same. The closer your man is to the ball, the closer you are to your man.

You know in advance that the ball's objective is to get to your man—or into the basket—before you can. Your objective is to beat the ball to your man while being in position to beat any dribble to the basket.

Probably the play which results in the most baskets being scored in a tough, well-played game is when a defender in help-position is beaten to a pass into the lane. The defender's eyes get interested in the ball while his man sneaks behind him or rests behind him and suddenly darts across the lane for the ball.

THE OFF-SIDE CUT IS A COMMONLY SCORED BASKET

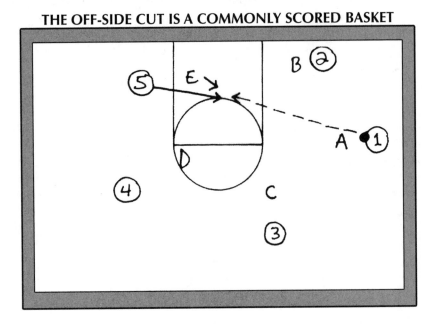

The defender's bad habit is to wait too long to move. If you wait until the cutter is beside you, he certainly will beat you to a spot six feet in front of you.

You must recognize a cut *before* your man gets to you, so that you can get in front of him. Usually, if you can change the course of his initial cut, you will force him to an area where he cannot get the ball since other players (perhaps even his own teammates) will be in the way.

You cannot allow help-position to mean "pause and rest position" for you as it does with so many players. That short pause and rest, that momentary lapse, results in many baskets each game at every level. Any time you are "off the ball," (on the wall) two passes away, when your man is not dangerous, you must expect that very soon you will have to make a quick transition to beat him to the ball. Offensive players far away from the ball who are momentarily catching their breath and standing are just those who have the energy and willingness to burst out for the ball. Anytime you get to that "wall" or helping position where you are inclined to rest a moment because your man is resting, catch yourself and be ready to move abruptly because most likely you will have to.

As coaches frequently say, the time to rest is on offense, not on defense. Catching your breath when your man does is dangerous. You know how often the off-side men cut to the ball and score. Don't let an initial burst of speed beat you. Be ready for it, and alter its path.

THE VALUE OF ALTERING THE INITIAL CUT

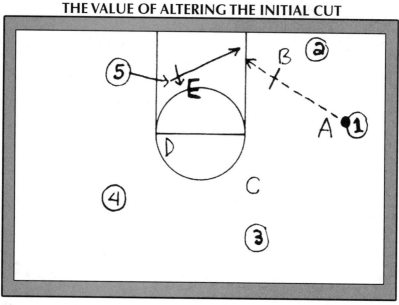

The pass to 5 is blocked by "B" even though 5 is open. (Naturally, you cannot always expect help from a teammate, though often you will get it.)

158
DON'T DRIBBLE INTO A TRAP UNLESS...

...Unless your receivers are in positions where it is clear to you that you will have an easy pass to make, immediately, as you begin to be trapped.

This is especially obvious against a half-court trap where you will often see a good player stop and look just before crossing the middle line. You do not want to cross that middle line, be double-teamed and have nowhere to throw the ball. Instead, you want to call your teammates into position—one nearby to your right, one nearby to your left and a third nearby in the middle.

Whether you meet a potential double-team on a full-court press or a half-court trap makes no difference. Bring three teammates near you (do it verbally if you have to). Then you can dribble into the double-team with confidence and be ready to throw the ball past it at the moment (or just before) you meet it.

A defense cannot possibly double-team you and cover all three nearby receivers. If they do that, they are committing all five defenders and leaving your fifth player wide open by the basket. If they are keeping one defender back, they will be trying to guard your three nearby receivers with two defenders. This can be very effective if one of your receivers is not actively seeking the ball, spread away from the other two. If you make sure all three *are* in position before dribbling into the double-team, you will have no difficulty beating it.

159
TRY HARD

This seems like a superfluous tip. "Everyone knows that." But actually few players do. When a coach goes to a camp or a game to watch people play basketball, **it is almost always obvious that one guy plays harder than the rest.** Not necessarily better because it is not always true that the harder a player plays, the better he plays. Some players go too wild and get out of control and make foolish turnovers or unnecessary fouls. But certainly, every player must strive to play harder while continuing to play with the control and savvy that are equally important to playing well.

Many players get so involved in the motions of the game that they forget that they could sprint faster, they could get to more loose balls, they could fight for more rebounds and they could help more often on defense. At the end of each game, many players are not really tired, and there is no excuse for that. If you find yourself completing games and feeling quite capable of doing it all again, you may think that suggests good conditioning. But it is more likely that you simply don't try hard enough. Of course, the converse must be looked at skeptically as well—just because you are tired after a game does *not* mean you tried hard. It may mean that you were out of condition or that you used your energy poorly.

While there are many possibilities, ask yourself one question. When coaches or fans come to watch a game you are playing in, is it obvious to them that *you* are the guy playing harder than everyone else? Admittedly, some players have a smoother exterior than others. But anyone who ever watches you play for just one minute ought to already have the impression, "Whew, he plays hard."

160
TURNOVER DISCRIMINATION

Despite the way they look in the post-game statistics, all turnovers are *not* created equal. A pass to the side that goes out of bounds is a turnover that should happen about once per career. It is doing nothing. It is going nowhere. If the ball is caught, you aren't any further ahead than had it not been thrown at all. So a pass out of bounds to start an offense is inexcusable.

On the other hand, a pass to a cutter breaking backdoor to the basket is worth a mistake now and then. If he gets it, you have an almost certain two points. If you don't throw it at all or only throw it when you are absolutely sure you can get it there, you may find your cutters don't feel like cutting very often.

If you are a guard, especially, you must show your teammates that you are looking for them and that you want to hit them when they get free. If you do not want to throw a pass because you aren't sure you can get it there, you need to at least grimace as you fake the ball, showing that you wanted to throw the ball but couldn't.

The time remaining in the game is a factor that also influences the inexcusability of a turnover. If you are five points ahead in the final minutes, any pass which isn't absolutely sure is inexcusable. The risk is not worthwhile. Also, at that point in the game, your teammates can expect to waste a few cuts to the basket, and they can expect not to receive the ball every time they get partially open. You don't bring down team morale by carefully holding onto the ball at the end.

In the beginning of a game, to reward a teammate's cut or to take a chance on a return pass to a teammate who has pulled down a rebound and given it to you and hustled to the other end, the risk is often worth it. But passes to nowhere for nothing, risks at the end of a game, attempts at spectacular plays—these will hurt your team a lot more than a forced pass on a two-on-one back to the guy who stole the ball in the first place or a risky pass inside to a man prepared to move against a good opponent with four fouls.

All turnovers are not created equal. You have to be smart just to know how to mess up correctly!

161
THE TWO-ON-ONE FAST BREAK

Passing back and forth is the best way to score the two-on-one break because it never allows the defender to *act*. The defender can only *react* to each pass.

If you are defending the two-on-one, you want to stay away from the ball, preventing a pass, and force the ball to be dribbled into the basket while you fake and try to get the dribbler to pick up his dribble or make a pass that you are prepared to intercept. At the last minute (last split-second really), you can try to distract the shot or get in the dribbler's way to take a charge since many offensive players will continue their momentum after shooting or throwing a pass.

The important thing is to stay near one player and keep the ball in the other player's hands, preferably the guy on the left side who most likely is right-handed and, therefore, more prone to miss the eventual shot or throw a bad pass from that side. With the ball on the left side, you fake and threaten until the last instant, and then you try to get over to distract the shot, take the charge or block the right-handed pass. Do whichever seems best at the time. It usually depends on the size and speed of the dribbler. If you are taller, wait and try to bother the shot. If you are smaller but quicker, get over to the ball sooner and look to draw the charge.

On offense, how do you play against someone who moves to cut off the right side and prevents you from passing back and forth? Look at the situation. What may seem like a two-on-one may actually be a one-on-nobody. If your pass is still being prevented by the time you get to the free throw line, take the ball decisively to the basket and score. Forget about cute stutter steps and last instant jump passes and behind-the-back whirls. Take the ball in and score.

Most defenders do not think fast enough to get to the right side. They come back in the middle of the court hoping to guard both men. This is the defender that should be left there spinning in his tracks as the ball flies back and forth by him.

The whole battle of wits and moves and countermoves comes down to one simple concept, as it so often does in basketball. Who is dictating the action? On offense, you try to make the defender react to your passes; when you get to that point where you know you can't be stopped, you take the ball in for the layup. On defense, you try to make the player with the ball worry about you; your best chance of doing that is by keeping the ball on the left side of the court as you fake and feint at the ball.

Once you have the basic objective in mind—to dictate the action—there is only one thing left to do: practice. It doesn't matter how aware you are of what you would like to do, the first time you bring the ball down the court for a two-on-one and a quick, smart player makes the most dynamic fake at you that you have ever seen, you will pass the ball and he will be waiting for it. You have no choice. You think he really is coming, but he is not.

Or perhaps you try to play intelligent defense by moving to the right side, and a fast player simply takes the ball in for an easy layup on the left that you didn't distract at all. (And your coach may yell, "At least you can *try* to make it difficult, can't you?")

Practice dictating the action, whether you are on offense or defense. The practice will pay off and not only enable you to score the two-on-one about every time (and recognize the difference between fakes and real lunges), but also stop some two-on-ones on defense.

One final point. If the guy on defense happens to be a shot-blocking center (as he may be if you have beaten a zone press) and you are a small guard, you should consider pulling up and taking the 12-foot jumper. Although a lot of coaches say, "Only a layup on a two-on-one," a small guard will hit a much higher percentage of 12-footers than he will hard-driving layups against shot-blocking centers. So, if you are a little guard and you recognize this situation, unless your coach tells you, "Positively layups only," you ought to think about pulling up for the easy jumper inside the free throw line.

UV

162
DRIBBLE-USED SITUATION

A good team should react to a used dribble like a flock of hungry vultures to a carcass in the desert. A used-up dribble changes all the rules of defense. Suddenly, no one needs to help, the ball cannot penetrate to the basket and a pass must be thrown in five seconds. That means it is time to climb all over your man. Overplay him so he cannot get to the ball. If you're guarding the man with the ball, get in his face with your forearm an eighth of an inch from his nose and try to deflect the pass.

Don't double-team a man who has already used his dribble. Stay on your own man and prevent the pass. Remember, the man with the ball has only five seconds to get a pass away, and in this case (different from an out of bounds situation) you do not have to give him three feet of space (nor is the other team likely to be set for quick screens and cuts to the ball.).

A dribble-used situation is an excellent opportunity to force a turnover, *if* your team reacts like vultures and plays tough immediately. Don't be content to let your man use his dribble and then just stand there, off him, as though you still respect his speed and dribbling ability. When a man has used his dribble, get on him—all over him. And when you are not guarding the ball, "zip" to overplay position and don't allow your man to get it. The dribble-used situation has "turnover" written all over it. Play accordingly.

Note: Your response on offense should be obvious. With the ball, try to make sure you have someone to pass to before picking up your dribble. Without the ball, if you see a used-up dribble, run to the ball immediately and get it before the defense has time to attack.

163
THE V-CUT

The V-cut is an offensive move you need against teams that like to run-and-jump and make quick switches or double-team.

THE V-CUT

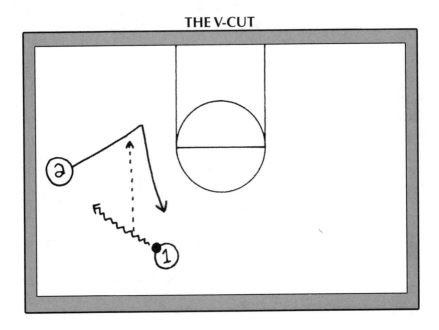

As "1" dribbles toward "2," number 2 begins a cut to the basket so that he can receive an immediate pass from "1." But if the immediate pass is not possible, "2" does not continue to the basket. He makes a sharp "V" back, so that he cannot be kept from receiving the ball by a double-team or a run-and-jump switch.

You make the V-cut when a teammate dribbles toward you, so that you are free for a pass if your man leaves you to take the dribbler and so that you are free on the other side if the defender originally guarding the dribbler hopes to pick you up or intercept a pass to you. The V-cut also leaves you free for a quick pass if the defense has put a double-team on the dribbler and has left you unguarded.

The V-cut is something you have to think about and use discriminatingly. The normal reaction when a teammate dribbles toward you is to go for the basket. However, you do not want to be on your way to the basket (and continue all the way to the basket) if the player with the ball is double-teamed by *your* defensive man.

The V-cut enables you to make an initial cut toward the basket in case the ball can be thrown to you immediately, but it still allows you to be free for an easy pass if the ball cannot be thrown to you immediately.

164
VIOLENCE

While violence may not be valuable on children's TV or in society, it certainly is necessary to be a good basketball player. This does not mean getting in fights and throwing elbows on rebounds; it means doing things forcefully and quickly and abruptly—things like faking, cutting, darting out on defense, streaking for rebounds, sprinting downcourt on a fast break. People don't normally talk of the necessity for violence with regard to these types of activities, and the too-frequent result is a casual basketball player who looks great going through the motions in his backyard against his little brother, but who doesn't know how to do anything when he gets in a game against tough competition.

To get your thing done anywhere, you have to learn to do the things you do violently. Fake like you really are going, move like you really are in a hurry, sprint the way you would if a hive of bees were suddenly on your tail and dart the way you would if you were just about to step on a large, hungry snake. Do you get the picture?

Chances are, you don't play that way now. Think about it. If you don't play violently, your career is very likely nearing its end. You have to play in a way that you mess up your hair and ruffle your shirt and dirty your hands.

Check your elbows and knees. Many coaches say you are not a basketball player if you don't have two or three abrasions. You can't play basketball the way you throw a frisbee at a family picnic. You just cannot play good basketball gently.

165
VISUALIZING

In his great book called *Psycho-Cybernetics,* Dr. Maxwell Maltz cites again and again the value of visualizing a task before you try to perform it. Apparently, the process of "seeing" it in your mind's eye aids the brain in giving the body the commands necessary to make the thing happen during the time of the performance.

For a basketball player, this type of visualizing has all sorts of applications. As you lie in bed the night before a game, you may actually affect your performance the next day positively by "programming" your mind with visions of activities you will need that next day. Picture yourself blocking out and grabbing rebounds, recognizing and making quick switches on defense, helping and recovering, getting free in scoring position and going up for a perfect shot with the right form.

Not only the night before the game does this work, but *during* the game, such as when you are walking to the free throw line about to shoot. See yourself standing there putting up a perfect shot and watching it fall cleanly through the net.

There is actual scientific data indicating that by programming pictures of success, you are more likely to succeed. Use this process in your own behalf. Get in the habit of putting pictures of you performing successfully in your mind. It may help you to imagine a whole set of gestures—like going to a card catalog, taking out a card with a particular title on it, putting that card in a slot in your head the way you would place a slide in a projector and then seeing yourself in the act of performing the task correctly.

You can make up any game with yourself which helps you "see" more clearly. The beauty of it is that it is very likely to work, whatever you do. Naturally, you are not suddenly going to stuff the ball if you have never before touched the rim, but you might very well hit a pressure one-and-one that you otherwise would have missed. Visualizing tasks in advance definitely aids you in the later performance of those tasks.

W

166
THE GREAT WALL

Every time the ball is at the sideline, there is a wall from basket to basket."

What? A wall?

There might not really be one, but you would be wise on defense to imagine a wall running right up the middle of the court, separating the court into two distinct areas: (1) the ball-side, where folks are playing basketball (and where all five defenders are playing defense), and (2) China.

PLAYING THE WALL

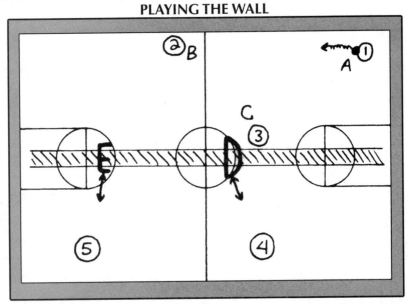

When the ball is at the sideline, all defenders play on the ball side of the court. Defenders (E and D) guarding players in "China" (4 and 5) play on the wall.

Let the offense put as many players in China as they wish. Would you follow your man to the water fountain if he left the court for a drink?

If not, then don't follow him to China either. On defense, when the ball is at the sideline or near the sideline (distinctly on one side of the court), make sure you too are on that side of the court, ready to help against a penetration or a pass to the basket.

If they try to throw a lob pass to a man on the Chinese side of the court, there is plenty of time to get there, provided you are alert and ready to go as soon as the pass is thrown. You may not intercept every pass to China, but you should be able to get there in time to play good defense when the ball comes down.

ON THE WALL

"Wall" position applies equally well to half court defense. Stay on the ball side of the court.

If this concept makes perfect sense to you, you are probably already in the habit of playing good help defense, and you need merely concentrate on getting to the wall quickly each time the ball is passed away from you to the side. If this concept, however, does not make sense, if you feel that playing good defense requires you to stay a lot closer to the men in China, you are unwittingly costing your team many baskets that *you* could have prevented.

Any time the ball goes to the sideline, whether you are in a man defense or a zone, you should get to the wall in defensive help-position. Let the offense put all the players they want in China. Nothing against the Chinese, but China is far away. *you* stay where the action is.

167
WASTING MOVES

When you see a player use nine terrific moves to get the ball up-court, don't be impressed by his dribbling. He doesn't know how to play. You can't afford to use nine or even three or four moves to get the ball up the court. You are making yourself more vulnerable to a mistake the more times you reverse or go behind your back or through your legs, and most likely you do not have a sufficient awareness of the court during all that activity.

Watch any good player with the ball and usually all you will ever see is one move, one burst of speed or one change of direction. One. Not nine. You don't want to give the defense time to double-team or recover position, and you don't want to use any more energy or any more moves than are necessary. Many players throw a great fake and then, instead of taking advantage of it and beating their man, they throw another fake, obviously because they are not aware of the effects of their moves.

Ideally, if you know you have a move that will throw your defender off-balance, you should get up the court with a protected dribble and save that move until you get all the way to scoring position. There, your quick move to get open will result in an immediate scoring opportunity and give the defense no chance to prepare to stop you. If you get open 80 feet from the basket, you will likely get the ball upcourt, but your chances of creating an easy scoring opportunity are not nearly as good, especially if the guy you beat is a hustler who is scurrying to catch up.

You can get yourself open immediately and get the ball upcourt, or you can protect your dribble and beat the man when you get nearer to the basket. Doing some of both makes sense. But switch-dribbling and reversing and reversing back and going through the legs and behind the back—all that just to get the ball into the frontcourt is a waste of ability and a lack of savvy.

Good players make easy things look easy, and even a lot of hard things look easy. Taking the ball upcourt on one man is not hard, so don't make it look hard with nine clever moves. Learn to accomplish things simply. The habit will pay off in tough games.

DRIBBLING UPCOURT

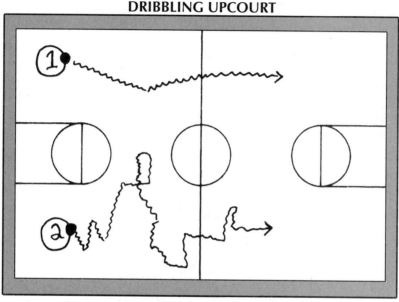

Number "1" is a ball handler. His path is direct and economical. He uses one move most of the time to advance the ball upcourt.
Number "2" is a dribbler. He uses nine great moves to get the ball upcourt, a waste of time and energy and ultimately risky.

168
WHERE AND WHEN TO GIVE THE BALL

A good player is not content merely to see the open man and pass the ball to him. Just as important is where and when you give the ball. On a fast break especially, a big forward or center (and very possibly any player) who is running hard to fill a lane is likely to walk with the ball or charge if he is given the ball just behind the free throw line in that "in-between" area. Should he put the ball on the floor once? Or should he take a long step and score without the dribble? A good ball handler will not require that his cutters make those kinds of decisions. He will give the ball at just the right time, just where the cutter can handle it easily and put it in the basket.

It is difficult to say precisely where and when you give a man the ball because each situation is different. But you do have to be aware of this whole concept, of making it easy for the man you pass to, so that when the situations arise, you can begin to feel the difference between an easy-to-handle pass and a hard-to-handle pass. You don't throw a hard pass if you can throw it softly. You lead him, but not too far.

Finally, you will have to use your own judgment on what is too hard, or too far ahead, or too soon, or too late. The more you watch games and the more you play, the more you will notice the difference in ball handlers. Some are making it difficult for their teammates, while others are almost putting the ball in for them.

169
WHOSE MAN WAS THAT?

One of the most ridiculous questions asked on a basketball court is, "Whose man was that?" after someone drives in and scores a layup. Don't *you* ever ask that question, and make sure you know the answer if you ever hear it—because a man driving in for a layup is *your* man. He is the man of everyone on the team. Good defensive position requires that you be as close to your man as possible *and* still be in a position to keep the ball from penetrating for a layup.

There are some instances when this may not apply, such as when you are guarding a super outside shooter whose 20-footer may be a better percentage shot than many of his teammates' layups. But in most defenses, zone or man-to-man, you should be able to cut off a penetration to the basket from whatever position you are playing. That means every drive-in layup must have beaten not one man, but *five*.

So, whose man scored that layup? Yours. And everyone else's, too. If there is no other choice, leave your man and stop the layup. At least by forcing one more pass, the ball has a better chance of being mishandled—thrown poorly or bobbled or walked with—or being intercepted by one of your hustling teammates. If you force that one more pass, *then* you can ask a more appropriate question: "Whose man threw that pass?"

170
USE THE WIDE SIDE OF THE COURT

Unless you get the ball in the middle of the court, there is a wide side and a narrow side to go to. Of course, any side is fine if you can go that way and score a layup or a shot. But when you cannot score, it is a good idea to take the ball to the wide side of the court so you have more options, more people to pass to, than you would on the narrow side where help-defense is possible.

If you are forced down the sideline, you can often fake that way and then bring the ball back to the wide side as the defender goes for your fake. If you cannot fake your defender, you either should not go or you should know what you are planning to do with the ball before you do go. Don't just put a few lazy dribbles on the floor and suddenly find yourself in the corner with no place to go.

Little guards especially have the tendency to drive the baseline and get stopped before having a chance to shoot, and their chances of turnovers are great. If you are not tall and strong, the baseline is the worst place you can have the ball. Do not go baseline unless you feel certain you can score or draw a defender on you and "dish off" to a teammate.

THE WIDE SIDE AND NARROW SIDE OF THE COURT

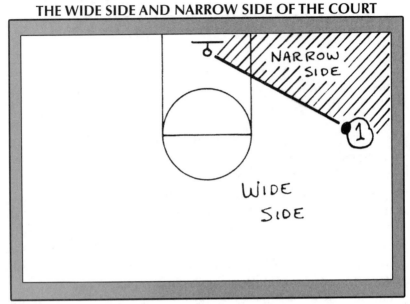

Unless you can score or set up a teammate immediately, you do not want to even start a dribble down the narrow side of the court. Help-defense is effective on the narrow side of the court, but impossible on the wide side.

Do *not* mosey down the narrow side of the court just hoping something good will happen. Nothing good will happen on the narrow side of the court unless you see a definite opening and take it quickly and decisively.

When no opening is there, make an effort to bring the ball to the wide side of the court, especially when your team is stalling. Refuse to take the ball to an area where your options are limited. Take the ball to the wide side where potential helpers must guard their men, not to the narrow side where the defense can "pack" that side of the court and overplay the passing lanes.

171
MOVING WITHOUT THE BALL

This aspect of the game is often treated like a wondrous mystery. Everyone knows that a player who can move without the ball is very valuable to a team, but seldom are the specifics of doing it explained. A few concepts are all you need to be excellent without the ball. You do not have to be fast, you do not have to run until you are out of breath and you do not need some special knack.

First, you need to drift constantly, not run hard and sprint everywhere, but keep moving all the time. Even when you are basically standing or staying in one place, you will be drifting a bit to one side and the other (for a reason to be explained below).

Second, you need to make short bursts of speed to the ball or to the basket from time to time.

That is simple enough and describes your movement—**drift and burst, drift and burst,** hardly ever coming to a flat-footed stop.

Where and how to move are dictated by one simple concept: **Stay behind the head of the guy guarding you,** and be prepared to burst out for the ball any time you see the opportunity (especially whenever he turns his head to find you, in which case you burst the other way). Whether you go to the ball or to the basket or out away from the basket depends on the way your man plays you and how he turns to find you.

If he refuses to turn to find you, then you can stay on his back all night and burst past him whenever you get the attention of the player with the ball. A defender cannot be ready to beat you to the ball if he cannot see when you start. On the other hand, if he turns back and looks at you often, you are taking him out of good help-position and making it easy for your teammates.

One final point you ought to remember, **any time the ball penetrates,** whether with a dribble or a pass, **expect to move a couple of quick steps.** Where to take those steps will be dictated by where the ball and your defender are. Most of the time, two steps to wherever seems best to you at the time will free you for an easy pass in scoring position. When a ball penetrates, your defender and all defenders are forced to make quick adjustments and decide on how much help to give. If you stand in one place, defenders have an easy help-and-recover situation. But by moving a couple of steps (they don't even have to be exceptionally quick steps), you can put yourself in a position where a help-and-recover reflex doesn't work.

X

172–186—XYLOPHONES

XYLOPHONES

There aren't many words or basketball terms beginning with "X," nor do many pre-game warm-up pep bands have xylophones. But a xylophone is an instrument with a graduated series of wooden bars that makes music when struck by small wooden hammers. All of which seems like sufficient reason in this game of X's and O's to give you or hammer into you a final series of thoughts pertaining to a wide range of subjects.

172. When dribbling the ball in the midcourt area, go fast. Defenders are looking to swat a dribble from behind, and you cannot expect it will not happen to you. Go fast in the midcourt area.

173. When you throw a long pass, lead the man and lay it out there so it stays, rather than skims out of bounds. A ball thrown to "stay" out ahead can be taken on the dead run, on the fly, low on the first bounce, or high on a bounce. If you throw a skimmer, it must be perfectly thrown or it will result in a turnover. So put some arch on a long pass, don't throw the ball like a line drive.

174. Against a press, if you and a teammate are screening for each other, make sure the screen is made by the man coming from the ball side, so that both the screener (after he "rolls") and the cutter are moving *to* the ball. If the other player sets the screen, both players will be moving away from the ball.

175. If you cut by a player with the ball and get a hand-off from him, get in the habit of "skipping" past him without dribbling (unless, of course, you see a path wide open to the basket). By skipping past the screen and retaining your dribble, you can force the defense to commit and still have all your options. If you dribble immediately and get stopped by a good jump-switch, a help-and-recover or a double-team can be very effective.

176. Practice shooting difficult layups. Most players practice only easy, unmolested ones where there is plenty of time to get the steps and the timing done perfectly. The problem is that most game layups are not like this. Many times you must go off the wrong foot, or you have to change your course or your shot suddenly. If you haven't spent time practicing these, how can you expect to make them in games?

177. Don't fall into the bad habit of "circling out" after grabbing a defensive rebound. Either throw a quick outlet pass or take the ball straight out on a power, protected dribble.

178. If you often find yourself in games pivoting around looking for someone to throw to, you don't play well. Good players get rid of the ball before they get in a jam. They are careful not to dribble into jams and not to pick up their dribble unless they have first found someone to pass to.

179. When you recover a loose ball running away from your basket, don't recover it with a dribble. That gives any man behind you a moment longer to get to the ball, even though you arrived there first. Better to grab it, let the man sail on past you, pivot and put a dribble out in front of you to take advantage of the five-on-four. (Always assume there is a man coming. Don't be careless.)

180. If you are fronting a low post man, often you can confuse him if you face him. That makes it difficult for him to hold you out without fouling, and it puts you in a good position to run forward to leap for a lob they might try to throw over your head.

181. When a strong player is holding you off the boards or trying to keep you away so he can receive a pass inside, often you can confuse him by taking your body off him and brushing his side with your hand. That may make him think you are on that side while actually you attempt to get around him on the other.

182. Try to take advantage of the "even up" factor after a technical foul on your team. At this time, to show he is being fair to both sides, the referee watches the other team more closely than usual. Therefore, after a technical (or after any very questionable) call, it is no time to throw up a quick jumper. A ball taken aggressively to the basket will almost certainly be rewarded with a couple of free throws.

183. On many rebounds or in loose ball situations when both you and an opponent grab the ball at the same time, your best chance of coming away with the ball is to turn your body into your opponent.

While this will not work every time, often the referee will call a foul on the other guy because it will look as if he is reaching around you or is draped over your back.

184. When getting back on defense, get in the habit of running with one eye looking back over your shoulder at the ball. When you get to midcourt, turn your body around and face the ball and back-pedal the rest of the way. Don't make it depend on where the ball is or how fast it is coming. Back-pedaling from midcourt is a good habit that will save you many baskets over the course of a season, often just by discouraging the offense from making an effort to fast break.

185. If your shot is often falling short or if it seems like an effort all of a sudden to get the ball to the basket, you may have begun shooting on the way down. Many players lapse unknowingly into this error. Let your body weight help throw the ball upward instead of working against the motion of your arm. If necessary, to correct the problem, shoot on the way up and don't try to jump so high until your shot begins to feel good again.

186. What excuse do you have for not following through completely (elbow fully extended, fingers pointing to the floor) every, every, every time you shoot? Why would you let anything so important be a "sometimes situation?" You should follow through fully on every shot you ever take, from now until the end of time. (Almost every player in the world will nod to this advice, but very few will heed it.)

SOMEDAY...

You may hit it big in the stock market or graduate from med school or take a round-the-world cruise, but you'll probably never find anything that matches the thrill of beating someone to a loose ball in a big game and feeling the instant approval of 10,000 screaming fans.

YZ

187
YOU ARE RESPONSIBLE

One characteristic of nearly every good player is the habit of looking inward, of taking the blame, of feeling sincerely responsible for losses and failures. A teammate may have missed a last second shot, the coach may have used the wrong defense or the referee may have blown a big call. But what could *you* have done differently in spite of all that ? What could *you* have done to win?

Taking responsibility does *not* mean making some noble gesture like telling the press it was your fault when you know you are going to get credit for scoring 25 and making a valiant effort. Anyone can do that just to hear his words refuted. But really taking responsibility means actually *feeling* responsible deep inside, actually looking inward for the fault. It means having the type of mind that expects a teammate to miss a tough shot at the end, expects the coach to use a questionable defense, expects the referees to miss some big calls and yet still expects to play in such a way that those obstacles will be overcome.

When you walk away from a court having scored 30 points in a losing effort and you can feel sincerely responsible for the loss (not pretending as though you are responsible), you are a player, you are a winner and you are the kind of athlete everyone wants to play with and coach. You may be able to fool a lot of people with whatever attitude you try to project, but you will not be truly "there" until you can convince yourself. When you finally develop the attitude that *you* are responsible, that it is up to *you*, then you are there. *you* can play.

188
ZONE ATTACK RULES

The following five rules are useful against any kind of zone: full-court press, half-court trap or match-up. The rules are number-coded so you can easily remember them.

 1. "Lead" passes are especially effective against zones when the ball has come from one side and is faked to the other side, "leading" the defense to the other side before returning the ball to the man who first passed it. Since zones are geared to moving quickly with the ball, the lead pass can get the zone off-balance and make the defenders tentative.

 2. Engage two. Get two players on you before passing the ball, thus always passing to a 4-on-3 advantage. It is useful to think of "engaging" two defenders rather than getting "married" by them. When you engage two, you are still able to get the ball to all four of your teammates. In a "marriage," your options are cut off by the defensive pressure, and you cannot exploit the 4-on-3 advantage. You want to take the ball *to* the defenders but be prepared to make the pass before they have a chance to control you.

 3. Form triangles. When you are next to the ball, get a position ready to receive a pass by forming a perfect triangle with the two nearest defenders. This puts you in a position of maximum danger to them, since both will have to take you when you receive the ball, thus forcing the zone to scramble to guard each pass (and commit two defenders to the ball whether it wants to or not).

 4. Two plus two. There are always four players who do not have the ball: two who are next to the ball in triangle receiving position, and two others who hide or relax behind the defense, always looking for the opportunity to seek the ball by running directly toward it. Most zone offenses that fail do so because players away from the ball do not actively seek the ball; they stand and watch.

5. All five players should try to stay in scoring position so they remain dangerous and must be guarded by the zone. A pass outside scoring position gives the zone a chance to rest. If only three players are dangerous, the zone can guard all three with the three remaining defenders.

By engaging two defenders and having all four other players always in position to threaten the zone, the defense must scramble to cover each pass. Quick ball movement, then, is not so important as movement of the ball to the most dangerous spots. (There are several other points about zones which have been covered in this book. See "Equiangular triangles" #44, "First-pass shots" #51, "Fling" #53 and "Zone shots" #190.)

189
ZONE DEFENSE

There are many different kinds of zone defenses: match-ups, passing-lane defenses, aggressive traps, and packed-in versions that give outside shots. But they all have one common characteristic. Despite players' thinking that zone defenses are for resting, all zones require a player to **be ready to move quickly in two opposite directions.** For that reason, even though you may have to move less while playing a zone, you should get more tired because, if you play it correctly, you must always be ready to move. You must always be between two positions or two men, both of which you want to be able to get to, either before the ball or at the same time.

Another common thought associated with zone defenses is, "Get your hands up!"—a good thought since outstretched hands make it more difficult for passers to get the ball to the open areas that all zones inevitably have. However, raised hands mean little if players are not ready to move. A just-standing-there zone may work in a midget league or against a very poor team, but to beat a good team with a zone, you must be very active, almost able to be in two places at once. Never get off-balance, be ready to move in two directions and keep your hands ready to deflect passes.

Finally, you need intense concentration on blocking out for rebounds when playing a zone defense because it is often not obvious who you should block out. You have to find the nearest or most dangerous rebounder quickly and keep him off the board. This may involve the difficult effort of leaving the ball side to get to the other side (where a missed shot is more likely to fall) to block out a player who is already on his way in for the rebound.

In many cases, this "weak side streaker" may actually have a better chance to get the ball than you do, but you will have a hard time explaining that to any coach. Zones are supposed to be good defenses for rebounding, and no coach will want to hear that a certain player in a certain situation had a better chance to get the ball than you. You have to concentrate and make an extraordinary effort to get to the weak side and put your body against that player with the better chance.

Be ready to move in two directions—hands up!—and always look to block out.

190
ZONE SHOTS

Zone shots are the kind of shots you get normally against a zone, shots where you are standing in position to shoot, the ball swings to you and you shoot without taking a dribble. These shots do occur on semi-fast breaks and against man defenses as well when a team has to help on a penetration and therefore leaves a man open in shooting position.

Because this type of shot opportunity comes up often, be sure you specifically practice these shots. If you are practicing with another player, you can throw to each other. If you are practicing alone, you should throw the ball to yourself by tossing it out with some backspin so that you can set yourself and receive the ball just as you would against a zone. Many players are in the habit of holding the ball before they shoot or taking a dribble first, simply because that is the way they always do it when practicing shooting. Simulating game conditions in practice is important to scoring the percentage your ability merits in the games.

The major point to remember with zone shots is to have the same foot as your shooting hand (your right foot if you shoot with your right hand) always a bit in front of the other foot when you go up for the shot (since that is the most comfortable, balanced shot you can take). As you receive the ball, you should be moving your back foot forward, so that you get some body movement and momentum going into the shot rather than trying to go straight up for the shot off two planted feet.

Assuming you are a right-handed shooter, if you are receiving a pass from the left, your back foot is your left foot, and it comes almost up to but not quite even with your right foot for the shot. If you are facing the right for the pass, your right foot is the back foot, and it moves up past the other foot as you receive the ball and prepare to take the shot.

Usually, it isn't too hard for a player to get the footwork right on this because players want to shoot with their right foot forward. What you must be careful about is the tendency to hop into the shot as you receive the ball, moving both feet, a habit of many players which takes longer, is less firm and balanced and may get you called for traveling if you bobble the ball at all or get a bit too anxious. Keep one foot firmly planted as you wait, receive the ball and go up for the shot. Only one foot moves.

POST-GAME STUFF

GLOSSARY OF MADE-UP WORDS AND IDEAS

ALTERNATING CURRENT...concerning passing and ball movement; holding the ball one time, then getting rid of it quickly the next; the player's decision to hold the ball and look, or to pass the ball immediately, is based on what the player did who gave him the ball

BENT-ELBOW PASS...pass made by cocking the ball at the side at waist level with the elbow bent and then throwing the ball over the opponent's ear with a quick roll of the wrist

B-U-B...stands for **B**all-*you*-**B**asket, the position a player must be in at all times on defense (except on an out-of-bounds play or a dribble-used situation); *"You,"* the player, must always be between the ball and the basket, able to stop a dribbling penetration

BUBBLE...the private area of a player with the ball; the area in which a defender must be in order to worry the player with the ball and make dribbles or passes or shots difficult

BUMP-N-RUN...a common football term that in basketball refers to the idea of releasing for a possible fast break layup any time a player bumps into a bigger teammate on his way for a rebound when playing defense

CHINA...the side of the court away from the ball; the side where there should be no defenders when the ball is at or near the sideline of the other side

CLICK...the act of passing the ball just one-eighth of a second after receiving the ball; a player must know where he is going to throw the ball before he gets it in order to make a click pass

DANCE...the "4-step" that should be used on every defensive rebound;

(1) Hands up, yell *hey!* (2) Turn your body to block out. (3) Move toward the ball. (4) Sprint to the other end for offense.

EQUIANGULAR TRIANGLES...refers to where to stand to receive the ball against zone defenses. A player gets in position with relation always to *two* defensive players, letting his body and their bodies be the three points of a triangle with equal angles and equal sides.

FAT DEFENSE...**F**ake **A**nd **T**hreaten; the effort and gestures a player makes to try to get the man with the ball to commit, whether playing ball-defense or off-the-ball defense

FLEET...comes from two words, **FL**oored f**EET**; players on defense jump too much, need to keep their feet on the floor at all times outside the three-second lane; reminds players not to jump to block passes or shots outside the lane

FLING...against zone defenses, a two-pass play that takes the ball from one side to the high post to the other side for an easy shot; the high post keeps his back to the basket and "flings" the ball to the other side as soon as he gets it

GNAW-POCKET...the defensive effort a player makes when the ball is dribbled by him; the act of keeping the head down and chasing the dribbler with the mouth right near the player's side pocket, where the pocket could be gnawed or bitten; reminds consistent effort to catch the ball once beaten

GOGO...comes from "**G**et **O**pen or **G**et **O**ut;" the way of thinking when trying to receive passes against a pressure defense; a player must get open immediately for a pass or get out of the way for another receiver

HIDING...what too many players do on semi-fast breaks or against pressure when they need to get open to get a pass; refers to any passive playing when aggressive ball-seeking would be useful

HOOK-STEP...a move to get the ball, usually on the low post, by wheeling around behind an overplaying defender and hooking him with an arm and leg on the other side

HUSTLE-CAT...the response to a mistake, "Hustle and **C**all **A** **T**eammate" into action as a result of the sudden, new situation; this takes attention off the mistake and puts it immediately on the new situation

IMAGINARY LINES...the lines a player draws on the court mentally a step in from the actual lines, so that inadvertent stepping on lines (violations) never happens

JOCKEYING...the act of trying to get open for a pass by moving back and forth basically in the same position; a common error

KUP...comes from "**K**eep **U**p **P**alms;" the palms of the hands should never face the floor on defense, not to block a shot, not to swat a ball, not to reach for a dribble or held ball

LONHOBIRS...shots that are well selected; the word comes from the first letter of each word of the phrase telling the kinds of shots that should be taken: **L**ayups **O**r (shots with) **N**o **H**and (in the shooter's face), **O**n **B**alance, **I**n **R**ange

NOSTRIL TIME...when a player gets the ball in low, near the basket, he must take the ball up through the player's nose, not away from the basket

P-DRIBBLE...standing and dribbling or dribbling lazily going nowhere; "peeing" or in position to pee, not to run; a player should not dribble unless he is moving with the ball, purposely going somewhere

POINT DEFENSE...refers to the necessity of seeing both the man and the ball at the same time and pointing to both to keep constant awareness

POOP...comes from "**P**ivot **O**ut **O**f **P**ressure;" rather than letting an aggressive defender hover over the ball while the player with the ball leans back off-balance; pivoting out of pressure can be accomplished with a simple quarter twist of the body before going into a crouch to get more strength and balance

PREP...comes from "**P**rime **RE**ceiving **P**osition," the area near the ball where a straight, crisp pass can be thrown; the crucial area to overplay in pressure defense and the crucial place to get open on offense when the ball is in trouble

QUICK-RELEASE GROOVE SHOTS...shots taken in practice with one quick dribble at the feet and an exaggerated, quick release in order to groove a particular rhythm on the last dribble of any move

RACE TRACK...the area between the two foul circles where nothing good ever happens therefore, an area that players should race through rather than trot

SCOT...comes from "**SC**oring sp**OT**," the offensive position that a player can effectively score from within his shooting range; a place where a player can get the ball and shoot immediately with confidence

SEEK-HIDE-N-GO...play on words that dictates purposeful movement without the ball; a player seeks hide (that is, leather) whenever the ball is in trouble, but he goes to the basket whenever the ball is moving forward or the player with it still has a dribble and is not double-teamed

SNORT...comes from "**SN**appy and sh**ORT**," a gesture of toughness and contempt; suggests the attitude an offense should have against pressure and also indicates the kinds of passes a team should try to throw against pressure

SOFO...comes from "**S**pin **O**ff the **F**irst **O**bstacle" when going aggressively for offensive rebounds

STATUE CHARGES...the bad habit of losing good defensive position by raising up and "going motionless" just before taking a charge, and then letting the offensive player dribble by

STREAK...the wild, excited, unstoppable sprinting effort of a nude guy running across a stadium OR of a player going for an offensive rebound, presumably with clothes on

TIGHT-ROPE WALKING...the bad habit of barely missing an out-of-bounds line, taking a course that permits very little margin for error and anticipates no slight bumps; a player dribbling the ball should avoid doing this

TOUGH KID...the idea of knowing in advance who you are going to throw to in case you get in trouble with the ball; the best outlet man against pressure or from out of bounds after three or four seconds have elapsed

THE (GREAT) WALL...the imaginary line that separates the ball-side of the court from the off-side when the ball is at or near a sideline; all five defensive players need to be straddling the wall, or within it on the ball side, to play good help-defense

Index

ABOUT THE AUTHOR

Dick DeVenzio gave his life to sports and to a set of beliefs, ideas and convictions mostly related to the intelligent pursuit of excellence in sports. The son of a very successful basketball coach, Dick grew up wanting to be a basketball star. That led to daily schedules and all-day practicing by the time he was in 7th grade. By 10th grade, he was a varsity starter, averaging 20 points a game—at 5'-6", and the next year he averaged 30—at 5'-9". In his senior year, he led Ambridge High School to an undefeated state championship, and his team is still considered the best ever to play in Pennsylvania. His name is in the Basketball Hall of Fame, on Parade Magazine's 1967 All-American First Five.

Two years later, at Duke University, Dick was an All-ACC selection, and in 1971, a First Team Academic All-American.

After graduating from Duke, Dick played and coached professional basketball in Europe and South America and founded the now nationally acclaimed Point Guard College.

Considered by many to be a basketball genius and a gifted writer, Dick's writings and basketball programs have inspired and influenced countless coaches and athletes. He died in 2001 at age 52.

OTHER BASKETBALL BOOKS BY PGC FOUNDER

RUNNIN' THE SHOW

Runnin' The Show spells out what it takes to be a real leader on a basketball court. How can a coach get the most out of his players? How can a player make everyone around her better and do the little things that lead to championship performance? Leaders have to sell their dreams, get players to work together, inspire teamwork, and understand people, attitudes and motivation. This is the last book Dick DeVenzio ever published and is a treasure for leaders in all walks of life.

THINK LIKE A CHAMPION

Think Like A Champion is a guide to championship performance for student-athletes. A treasury of practical advice broken down into 122 short sections on situations that athletes must face. Covers everything from choking under pressure, lack of confidence and playing with teammates you don't like, to shooting slumps, academics and how to increase your speed and agility.

THERE'S ONLY ONE WAY TO WIN

This is not a book of the exact science of basketball X's and O's, but rather a collection of insights into the methods and philosophies of how the game of basketball and life should be played. In every field there are exceptional people whose stories are both fascinating and instructive. This book relates insightful incidents from Coach DV's career and puts his guiding principles into words that can benefit coaches, players, fans, businesspeople, and anyone with a will to succeed.

Interested in transforming your game? Learn more about these 5-star books and explore all our course offerings by visiting https://pgcbasketball.com.